THE HOT LINE

The validity of ministry can be seen in its long-term effect on local church life. Peter Lawrence's book scores because it has found its origination and continuation within the weekly life of our small and sometimes struggling inner-city parish. The subsequent message to the reader is obvious:

1 what has happened amongst us at Christ Church can happen wherever a church leader is prepared to give God a chance to move in power;

2 taking this chance, ie 'risking it', will involve sometimes appearing to fail, but always allows the attention to rest upon a God 'without whom we can do nothing';

3 an attitude and approach built around the premise, 'Come Holy Spirit' will have impact upon all aspects of church life.

Reading other people's experiences may sometimes tempt us to try to 'carbon-copy' it. The honesty and 'earthiness' of *The Hot Line* will inspire the discovery that the supernatural life of the Spirit is ours for the church's asking!

Roger Jones — Director, Christian Music Ministries
Lay reader, Christ Church, Burney Lane

The Hot Line

PETER H LAWRENCE

KINGSWAY PUBLICATIONS
EASTBOURNE

Except where indicated otherwise
biblical quotations are from the
New International Version © International Bible Society
1973, 1978, 1984

Front cover photo: The Image Bank

British Library Cataloguing in Publication Data

Lawrence, Peter H
The hot line.
1. Christian life
I. Title
248.4

ISBN 0–86065–712–4

Printed in Great Britain for
KINGSWAY PUBLICATIONS LTD
1 St Anne's Road, Eastbourne, E Sussex BN21 3UN by
Courier International Ltd, Tiptree, Essex
Typeset by Watermark, Hampermill Cottage, Watford WD1 4PL

Contents

Acknowledgments

I am extremely grateful to the many people who have encouraged me and given me advice in the writing of this book. But before I thank anyone personally, I need to say, for their peace of mind, that I, only I am responsible and can be held accountable for everything which is written here. They have all helped me to say what I wanted to say.

I would like to thank David Pytches for commenting on the manuscript and helping me to sound more gracious than I am; I would like to thank John Wimber for challenging me to do some reading and thinking thirteen years after leaving college, and helping me to sound more up to date and intelligent than I am; I would like to thank Margaret Shaw for typing the manuscript, aided and abetted by Susan and Valerie, and using her expertise to make me sound more literate and educated than I am; I would like to thank all the many people who allowed their stories to appear in my book and checked all the facts for me, helping my memory to appear faultless; I would like to thank God who keeps turning up and doing special things which make me look good; finally, I would like to thank my wife Carol who knows what I'm really like and still loves me.

The author regrets that because of his commitments as vicar he is unable to undertake ministry outside his parish.

Preface

I knew Peter Lawrence as a student at St John's College, Nottingham. He was a brilliant golfer and cricketer: many is the century he made, and many the time he drove me crisply to the boundary. But there was about him that touch of cynicism to which he draws attention in the book. He is the last person I would have imagined becoming deeply involved in the charismatic renewal. And that is what, to me, makes this book such fascinating reading.

It is superbly written. It is humorous, self-deprecating, profoundly honest (especially about failure) and intensely readable. It has a strongly subjective strand, for it is the record of his own spiritual journey, but it is also theologically reflective and has patches of deep biblical study adding a new dimension to the text. Peter tells how he was unwillingly drawn into the close companionship of a God who speaks today, and learned to discern God's 'words' and pictures to deliver people from the dark grip of the demonic, to see at time the marvellous power of the Lord to heal, and to experience both the fellowship of Christ's cross and the reality of his Resurrection. The importance of obedience, trust and love come shining through this wonderful book. It will be such an encouragement to many. For it is not about somebody predisposed to signs and wonders ('signs and blunders' as he puts it of himself). It is about an ordinary man and an extraordinary God. It shows what Christ can do with someone who is willing to trust him fully and obey him implicitly. Not that Peter would claim to do that all the time: and therein lies some of the strand of pain which runs through the book. But how honest! For pain and glory are the warp and woof of all authentic Christian life, just as they were in the life of Jesus.

I have been enriched greatly by reading this book. I hope you will be too. Remember that the same God is your God and can do as much through you.

Michael Green
Vancouver

Foreword

Here is an easily readable account of how an ordinary Church of England clergyman, under the anointing of the Holy Spirit, has experienced God at work in a supernatural way in his own personal life and in his ministry to others. All along the writer shares both encouragements and his doubts, weaknesses and failures most disarmingly.

Clifford Longley, Religious Correspondent for the *Times*, has written recently (June 3rd 1989) of the 'barren years of the eighties' and has perceived that the church has come up with nothing new. The decade is almost ended and so far the eighties 'have not thrown up one interesting, original and powerful religious idea'. He believes that the recent Billy Graham Crusade was only a modernised version of an idea which worked in the fifties, and the Bishop of Durham's views were already old-fashioned at the time he gave them a new lease of life. While there is much to reflect upon in his article, Longley is apparently unaware of the significant influence of John Wimber on the English scene since 1981. There must be some fifty books in English which are a direct response to Wimber's impact on the Christian world. He has helped the church right across the denominations, from Roman Catholics to Pentecostals (including many Anglicans), to rediscover the power of the Holy Spirit for equipping the laity to do God's work here and now. Longley suggests that 'the revival of awe and mystery is what the nineties will be all about'. We respectfully suggest that awe and mystery are already being restored through signs and wonders in demonstration of the kingdom of God. I believe that some of this awe and mystery is reflected in Peter Lawrence's book.

Those clergy who have sensed hope for the church slowly ebbing from their souls and who are frustrated by their own pastoral impotence, could be greatly encouraged to read here of the experience of an ordinary parish clergyman who, while making no claims for himself, shares humbly and simply what he sincerely believes he has witnessed of the power of God in his own ministry and that of his laity today.

It is for this reason I am delighted to commend this frank and refreshing contribution by Peter Lawrence. He not only shares his experiences in ministering in the gifts and power of the Holy Spirit, but he shares his own assessment of what has happened at these times in the light of Scripture as his church has been stepping out in faith.

I would not necessarily commit myself to doing and saying everything exactly as Peter does or says it, but as more and more of us rediscover the reality of God's spiritual gifts for the body of Christ today, the contemporary church will need to sift out a corpus of wisdom, both in the area of encouragement and of caution, for handling such gifts. This book will provide a useful source of feed-back which will help towards that process. All too often such ministry has been mistakenly dismissed as in some way 'weird' because it is either so foreign to our materialist and rationalistic mind-set, too threatening to our traditional mode of practice, or too prone to pastoral mishandling by the inexperienced. Following, therefore, the dictates of both our pride and pre-judiced 'wisdom' we all too easily throw out the baby with the bath water. But should not a mature Christian want rather to be open to what God is doing by his Holy Spirit and seek to learn from it? It would be a pity if Christian people failed to see the potential here.

While keeping his readers racing along with him and maintaining a firm grip on the fundamentals of the faith, Peter Lawrence may at times appear to take liberties with language and seem to present a theology which is irrational. But without despising all systematic theology and God's gift of a sound mind, is it not true that any operation of the Spirit of God may be either rational or suprarational? God sovereignly chooses how. Do we not thank God that his thoughts and ways are so much higher than our thoughts and ways? Have we not too often sought to confine God to the limitations of our rationalism? Has not our God been far too boxed in for much too long? The Peter Lawrences of this world may blow our minds a bit, but that is no bad thing — in fact it could be a wonderful experience if it takes us back to a more realistic understanding of the gospel of Jesus Christ who is revealed to us in the Bible and continues manifesting his power in the world today through the work of the Holy Spirit. This is in line with Paul, who said, 'My preaching [was] not with wise and persuasive words, but with a demonstration of the Spirit's power, so that your faith might not rest on men's wisdom, but on God's power' (1 Cor 2:4–5). Peter Lawrence believes such manifestations are signs of the kingdom of God, which Paul clearly asserts is not a matter of talk, but of power (1 Cor 4:20). This kingdom has already come with Christ, but, the church believes, is yet to come in its fullness and glory when Christ will come again on the Last Day.

David Pytches
Formerly Bishop of the Anglican Diocese
of Chile, Bolivia and Peru

Introduction

This is a beginner's book written by a beginner for beginners. When it was suggested to me that I write a book after only two years of ministering in the power of the Holy Spirit at Christ Church, Burney Lane it seemed almost laughable. 'I'm only a beginner,' I complained to God. 'Why should I write a book?'

'That's why,' he seemed to say. 'If you wait until you've been doing it ten or twenty years, you'll have forgotten what it was like when you started.'

So here we are. Half a step ahead of some and miles behind the rest who've been ministering for years. When I began, it seemed to be doing what I thought God was telling me to do, both in his word – the Bible – and directly in my mind, which set the ball rolling. I believed Christians were called to follow the living Lord Jesus, and naturally to do this they needed to hear his voice and obey him. When I started trying to do this I made many mistakes but even so God appeared to honour the attempt and occasionally something would turn out right. For the first time in my life I found myself in small ways begin to do some of the things Jesus had done when he also ministered in the power of the Holy Spirit.

For me, getting started was undoubtedly the hardest part. Brought up in a cynical age with a natural tendency myself

towards defensive humour, there was always one voice ringing in my ears which held me back: 'Got a hot line to God,
have we?' it was for ever asking. I remembered Joan of Arc
claiming to have a hot line to God and ending up in the hot
seat, and I was never one with a burning ambition for mar-
tyrdom. But somehow, often at very low moments in my life,
God drew close to me and it happened.

So here is the story of a few modest beginnings, propped
up now and again with some biblical teaching. I've tried to
include all my first stories – good or bad – in an attempt to
encourage others to have a go. In these pages is my first
'word' from God which led to my first laying-on of hands
and my first healing service. You'll also find an account of
the first time I asked the Holy Spirit to come publicly and
privately, at home and away, and how striving to hear God
speak led me to witness my first healing and meet my first
demon. There is an account too of the first time I tried to
help someone else to hear God, the first time someone was
converted through ministry in the power of the Holy Spirit,
and several other personal 'firsts'.

It is a veritable collection of signs and blunders, with
laughter one minute and tears the next. It is a personal
account seen from my own viewpoint so that readers can
follow through one person's struggle to hear God and obey
him. I have tried to check the details of all the stories used
and obtained permission to include them from everyone
who is mentioned, wherever possible. I do apologise if anyone has been inadvertently overlooked. Unless stated, all the
names are the real names because we wanted the reader to
know the accounts are factual and authentic. Wherever
names are used the details have all been verified. We realise
this makes a number of us very vulnerable and may even be
ill-advised, but we have made the decision because we want
everyone to know this is what God has done with real people
in real situations.

Of necessity, I am learning to minister from a position of
weakness. If you knew me as my friends do you would be

amazed that God has been able to do anything with me, in me or through me. This being so, it is inevitably a book about God: his love, mercy, power and grace. If any story or teaching helps anyone else to recognise the voice of the Good Shepherd then to God be all the glory. God loves some decidedly odd people and has some very strange friends. This book is written by one of them.

1

Painful Beginnings

It was Christmas 1973 and the end of a very hectic term at theological college. I picked up my fiancée from Nottingham University and together we drove home to Virginia Water to celebrate the festivities with our respective families. 'I'm not sure,' she began cautiously, 'that I want to marry you any more. Could we become disengaged for six months and then see how we feel?'

Not marry? Disengaged? See how we feel? I knew how I felt. What had gone wrong? How would I tell my parents? What would my friends at college think? Was this it or could there still be some hope? I found myself grappling with the pain of bereavement while being denied the solace of grief, for she was still very much alive. Different kinds of thoughts thrashed around in my mind, but I managed to suppress them all beneath an external façade of quietude. 'I understand,' I said, 'no sweat. Take your time. I only want what's best for both of us.'

There are mercifully times in life when God allows us to see the limitations of our own efforts. For the next six months my inflated ego began to leak at the edges. Despite the pain and the loneliness God seemed very close, and although I had committed my life to Christ thirteen years before, it was only now that I heard the still, small voice of God for the very first time.

It all began when Ian, a friend at St John's College, invited me to a healing service at St Margaret's Aspley. Being temporarily bereaved and alone and therefore able to finish my essays ahead of time I was for once free to embark upon a spiritual adventure. Although I occasionally read a charismatic book I had never seen healing or even the laying-on of hands in action and I felt naively excited at the prospect. Would someone throw away their crutches, or leap out of a wheelchair, or would I perhaps receive healing for myself? The last thought bothered me a little as I felt fit and well at the time, but maybe I could ask God to improve my slight shortsightedness.

We arrived at a large traditional Anglican church which was virtually full, and only just managed to find seats about two-thirds of the way back. This was perfect because from there I could see the hymn board but not the numbers on it; if God chose to heal my eyes I would soon know about it. The service was decent and in order, with the robed vicar using a formal liturgy from the prayer book. At the appropriate moment everyone was invited to go up to the altar rail and kneel for the laying-on of hands, while three superstars went along doing the business. I took my turn with the rest, knelt and closed my eyes and in due course felt the warm hands resting lightly on my head.

'God says you must let go,' said one of the trio, and moved on. I looked up quickly.

'Hey, what about the eyes?' I thought, but kept it to myself as none of the others who had come forward had uttered anything. Disappointedly I made my way back to my seat and was not surprised to find I still couldn't read the numbers on the hymn board. Ian said the words spoken over us were an encouragement from God, but I wasn't certain what they meant and didn't feel greatly encouraged.

A month later the essays were still beating their deadlines and I was still alone, so we went again to St Margaret's Aspley for the monthly healing service. I sat in the same place and went forward at the same time, but received the laying-on of hands from a different person.

'God says you must let go,' the voice said, and I forgot to mention the eyes. 'That's funny,' I thought. 'Touch of the *déjà vues* here. I wonder if they say the same words over everyone? Perhaps it's part of the liturgy.'

'It's an encouragement from God,' said Ian.

'Oh, fine!' I mumbled, and went home to write another essay.

The term ended quietly and I drove home to Virginia Water for the Easter vacation alone. I met my disengaged fiancée briefly and we mutually agreed to continue as we were for the time being. After Easter I returned to college for the summer term and on arrival was asked to choose a parish in which to spend a month's placement. I asked to go to St Margaret's Aspley and was amazed to find my request readily granted.

I still remember meeting the Vicar, John Finney, for the first time. I was extremely nervous as I'd never before met a man who could hear God speak, and here I was in the same room, about to work with him for a whole month. He prayed for me: 'O Lord, confirm Peter's calling into the ordained ministry by effectively using him to minister to at least one person during his month with us.' I am not sure if I said 'Amen' or not. I was stunned and frightened. 'How on earth am I going to bluff this one out?' I wondered. Worse was to come: 'I think you might be just the person to lead Brian Hepworth to Christ,' said John. 'His wife has recently been converted and he's not sure what to make of it. Here's the address.'

'Right. I'll go this evening then,' I said nonchalantly, already wishing I'd chosen another parish. It's not easy to say 'no' to a man who has God on his side.

Brian Hepworth was worse than I feared: much worse. Ten years older than I, he had a senior post at Stanton Iron Works, voted Conservative and had a tough, no-nonsense, blunt Yorkshireman's character. I concluded very early on in the conversation that John Finney could only possibly have sent me because he'd tried everyone else. I listened, agreed with everything Brian said, contributed the occasional 'yes' or 'no' where appropriate and made my excuses as soon as possible. On leaving, his wife Jean handed me a note: 'Two people you might like to visit,' she explained. 'I can't remember who gave them to me.' I looked at the two names and addresses and agreed to call in.

The following morning I reflected on all that was beginning to take place and decided I'd better make sure I read my Bible and prayed every day if I was to have any chance of getting through the month. I read the Bible passage my daily notes had chosen for the day: 'Beloved, do not be surprised at the fiery ordeal which comes upon you to prove you, as though something strange were happening to you. But rejoice in so far as you share Christ's sufferings, that you may also rejoice and be glad when his glory is revealed' (1 Pet 4:12–13, RSV).

The passage didn't seem very appropriate so I spent the morning reading and praying, and made my way to Aspley for the afternoon. I visited the first name on the list and found myself listening to an old lady who would have sent a chronic insomniac to sleep. This is the nuts and bolts of ordained life in the Church of England and necessary preparation for all budding curates. As I tried eventually to make my escape by suggesting politely that maybe I should now visit someone else, she started telling me about her next-door neighbours. One was blind and the other deaf and both used to go to church until they'd become too frail and elderly to go any more. She was quick to add that no one from the church had visited them for years. 'Right,' I said with alacrity, 'I'd better make amends straight away,' and before she could start telling me about any more neighbours I left.

By now it was 3.55 pm and I was due to meet John in church for prayer at 4.15 pm. People who can hear God directly obviously pray in church every day without fail. 'Just time to pop in and see this elderly couple for a brief chat,' I thought, as I tried to open their gate. Normally I can manage

gates, but on this occasion I couldn't budge it: it was completely stuck. While I was standing there non-plussed, a
strange thought came into my head. 'Don't go here. Visit the
other address.' Inwardly I protested, 'This chap is blind, his
wife is deaf and no one's visited them for years.' The thought
remained: 'Not here, not now; visit the other address.' I
attacked the gate with new gusto, but to no avail, so in failed
desperation I went to the other address. (I went back the next
day and had no trouble opening the same gate!)

At the second address which Jean had given me a big,
middle-aged man came to the door. Bill Fox was the sort of
person from whom I would normally run a mile, particularly
if I met him in a dark alley at night, but he was crying and
when I said I'd come from the church he invited me in. As
soon as I stood in his lounge I became aware of his mother sitting in the corner of the room, crying too.

Bill's wife, Lucy, had been ill with cancer for two years and
more than one organ of her body had been removed in an
attempt to save her life; she was at present upstairs in bed. I
offered straight away to get in touch with John Finney, who I
felt sure would come and minister to her. Bill Fox refused my
offer politely, but asked me if we would pray for his wife by
name in the church services. Under no circumstances was
anyone going to be allowed to see Lucy or pray with her. That
was basically it – end of conversation. As a parting gesture I
scribbled down John's phone number in case he changed his
mind, and promised to pray for his wife in church. I was just
going when another strange thought intruded: 'Stay where
you are.' This was crazy, but for some reason I froze to the
spot. I looked at him and he looked at me. I couldn't think of
anything else to say to him and he couldn't think of anything
else to say to me: like a pair of lemons we just stood there.
Suddenly he grabbed my arm. 'She's heavily drugged,' he
said, 'won't wake for several hours. You can come up quietly
and say a quick prayer.'

'Me?' I thought. 'No, you don't understand. It's John Finney you want; I'm the one who just writes the essays.'

'Fine,' I said, 'lead on.'

When we entered the bedroom we were dismayed to see Lucy sitting up in bed, wide awake. Oh dear! He apologised most profusely to her, explaining that I was from the church and in a mad moment he'd given me permission to pray for her. At this point I took over and asked if she would like me to pray for her. She smiled and said, 'Yes.' I asked if she believed Christ could heal her. At first she was hesitant, but after a quick, loving glance at her husband she said, 'Yes, I do.' I laid one hand on her forehead and one on her hand and prayed a simple prayer. After I'd finished she said, 'I'll be all right now,' and I left – fast.

I drove to the church in time for our prayer meeting but John Finney failed to show up. Trembling inside I knelt at the altar rail and burst into tears. 'Beloved, do not be surprised at the fiery ordeal which comes upon you to prove you, as though something strange were happening to you. But rejoice in so far as you share Christ's sufferings, that you may also rejoice and be glad when his glory is revealed' (1 Pet 4:12–13, RSV).

Maybe the words were for me after all. Maybe these were not my tears but Christ's. I walked over to the vicarage and found John tucking into tea and cakes.

Two days later John was asked to do the funeral.

We went together to see Bill Fox and I made very sure the vicar reached the door first. Bill was, after all, a big man and he might well blame me for his wife's death. When we arrived, however, we found a completely changed person. He told us his wife had dramatically recovered following my prayer and had been able to get up and do the housework for the first time in months. Both of them believed she had been healed. Two and a half hours later she went to bed and in the morning woke up, hugged her husband, gave him a kiss and died. For several weeks Bill had asked the doctors to end Lucy's life and in his anger at their refusal had sworn at God repeatedly, pleading with Christ to come and take her. Christ had now come and he was at peace. Every night since she died he'd slept soundly, something he'd not done at all in the previous six months. At the gate of the house John said, 'What a lovely man,' and we went quietly home.

Jean was thrilled to hear how her note had been used, and maintained contact with Bill Fox afterwards. He went through some difficult times, but twelve years later accepted Christ for himself, was confirmed into the church and now goes to St Margaret's Aspley with his second wife, Janet.

As a result of this incident John asked me to minister at the next healing service. 'How do I do that?' I asked, hoping to be given the secret of success.

'You lay hands on their heads and tell them what God is giving you to say, or pray what God is giving you to pray,' said John. 'If you have any trouble starting,' he added, 'speak in tongues first. It tends to release the Spirit in you.'

'I'll just make it up,' I thought. 'No one will know. If I stick to generalities and pious platitudes I'll probably get away with it, and anyway I'm only here for one month.'

'We normally fast all day,' added John, as an afterthought.

I did as I was told: with a blinding headache from not having eaten since the day before, I laid my hands upon the first head. 'The Lord says he understands about your broken heart,' I mumbled. I hadn't meant to say that, it just came out that way. The lady burst into tears so I stayed with her in silence, leaving my hand gently on her head until she felt able to return to her seat.

An old man hobbled up with the help of a stick: 'Be healed in the name of Jesus,' I commanded, and an electric current shot down my arm and passed into the man. Next to him was another old man with a stick. 'Right, same again!' I thought. 'The Lord says you won't be healed until you put your relationships right,' I declared, and so it went on. Each time I laid on hands, waited, spoke in tongues silently and then gave the first thing that came into my head as sensitively as I could. There was at least one definite healing that night. My own headache finally went as I demolished a large plate of sausage and beans in the vicarage after the service.

To me it seemed I was making up the words which I was giving from the heart of a vivid imagination. Maybe there were some lucky flukes or the recipients simply read their own experiences into what was being said. It certainly didn't feel supernatural at the time. Like the time I was guided to Bill Fox and stayed to pray with his wife Lucy, it all happened very quickly and only afterwards did I see the awesome hand of God unmistakably at work. Then I merely worked things out the best I could as I went along, and did what I did because it seemed right at the time.

Perhaps the most unsatisfactory part of the healing service, and indeed many healing services, is the lack of feedback afterwards. To this day the two different people who spoke identical words to me ('God says you must let go') do not know the impact of their godly obedience nor the fruit which came from it. As for those I spoke over, we did hear later of a man who had been healed of an old war wound at the service, but no one knew who had laid hands on him. At the time I was not as sure as I am now that God had spoken to me, but, as Ian would say, it was a tremendous encouragement to go on and seek more.

On the last day of term my disengaged fiancée came to see me. She dithered uncertainly so I took the bull by the horns.

'You're not in love with me, are you?' I asked seriously.

'No,' she replied.

'Then we must finish,' I said.

'We'll still be friends,' she commented, but looked to me for confirmation.

'Of course,' I said, and we still are. As a parting comment she said, 'You ought to go out with Carol Hamilton; she'd be just right for you.' Carol was another girl from our church in Virginia Water and I just smiled: there was a fair amount of work to be done before I would be ready to look at someone else.

When she left I sat down in my room and cried for about an hour. At least I could allow my grief to surface now, and as I finally let go, God used my tears to heal the hurts and wash the wounds. While God was mending my yesterdays I was receiving strength to stand, new hope for the future and the freedom to risk being hurt again. I knew such vulnerability would be necessary if I were ever to love another, and I was grateful that I now knew something of receiving what God wanted to give me. Maybe tomorrow God might speak to me again?

Further up and further in

Fortunately there was no time to sit and mope as I left the next day for the Derbyshire Dales. I went to work in a hospice to observe and experience care of the dying patient and family in a practical way, spending my time as a member of the nursing team for three weeks. Our college was one of the more enlightened ones, insisting on giving us all practical experience and training that would benefit our parishes once we were ordained. I chose to be among the chronically sick and dying because Jesus spent a lot of his time with them, and I longed to be able to do what Jesus did.

'Please give me one, Lord,' I prayed, 'just one; one to walk out healed, to show the world you're still alive.'

The advantage of praying such a prayer was that I then began to expect and look for God's answer and guidance. This time it came not so much as a thought in the head or an automatic blurting out, but as a growing awareness and a 'knowing'. All kinds of factors added pieces to the puzzle as I struggled to learn this particular form of discernment.

Roy was an ordinary forty-year-old working-class mechanic who didn't have any contact with church and religion and found the Bible totally incomprehensible. He was strong and macho in appearance with a rugged, healthy look that seemed destined to deny the undertakers for many years, but looks can be cruelly deceptive. His body was riddled with cancer and the occasional grimace reminded those who knew him well of his constant courageous struggle with pain. Roy's wife had left him three times, but now visited him faithfully and there were encouraging signs that at last they were beginning to relate and share more deeply with one another.

There were sensible and logical reasons why I was drawn to Roy. The majority of people in the home were elderly and sick, and though they were just as much in need of Christ's love as any of us, humanly speaking it seemed to be a time for them to die. But my guts felt differently about Roy: life and health could mean a new start and a new marriage and if he found Christ his testimony would have far-reaching effects for years to come, but there were other reasons too. Frequent visitors to hospitals will know the difficulty and embarrassment of lengthy ministry to a patient in a busy ward, but Roy was in a room all by himself and very accessible. In his previous hospital a Christian nurse called Pat had been loving and caring towards him, far beyond the call of duty, so the soil was very much prepared. There was no logical reason why I should not share the gospel with Roy and pray for Christ to heal him.

The healing service at Aspley now seemed a long way off and the 'word' at the gate which had guided me to Lucy Fox so much easier to obey than this rather more down to earth guidance. The long build-up and daily search for direction created a tension which left me feeling far more uncomfortable than spouting on the spur of the moment had ever done, and at the centre of the tension was another voice: 'What if he isn't healed?' How do you recognise which voice is from God? The answer is, I knew. I 'knew' what God was saying and I 'knew' what I had to do.

'How would you react, Roy, if I said I thought God could heal you? Would you let me lay hands on you and pray?' I slipped this into the conversation casually in the course of the daily rounds, trying not to betray the practice I had put in beforehand.

'I'd feel very hopeful and rather frightened,' he said, so we made an appointment for nine o'clock that evening.

People in Aspley were praying that night as I began nervously by reading Luke 4:40 to Roy: 'Now when the sun was setting, all those who had any that were sick with various diseases brought them to him; and he laid his hands on every one of them and healed them' (RSV).

We talked for a while and then I laid hands on his head and prayed. I prayed for wholeness for himself and his wife, for a healing of relationships and memories, for the binding of Satan and for physical healing. He wept. 'I thought I'd feel silly,' he said, 'but I don't.' He told me he was feeling strange sensations, and I encouraged him to be honest with God and begin praying for himself, but he didn't think he could manage that, not yet. I don't think he believed me when I said praying was just talking to God, but we chatted a little about it before I left for the haven of my own room and a sleepless night.

'How's Roy?' I asked the Sister in the morning, somewhat breezily and matter-of-fact.

'He's worse,' she said, a little concerned. 'He's suffering a lot more pain and becoming very crotchety.'

I crawled away feeling very angry with God for letting Roy down and making me look a fool. Roy had struggled greatly to have anything to do with religion, had accepted my words in good faith and cried out to God for help like the blind beggar, but God failed to show up and I now had to go in his place. I made my way cautiously into Roy's room, fully expecting to be told where to go in mechanic's language. 'Will you come again,' he said, 'and do the same for me tonight?'

I returned at eleven o'clock that night and Roy was waiting. I laid on hands, prayed and again he wept. 'How about you saying a prayer?' I suggested, but he totally refused, and then it happened again. 'Stay where you are.' The same voice and feeling penetrated my soul as with Bill Fox. For one with the gift of the gab, waiting in silence while God did something without me was a new and strange phenomenon, but it worked again. Roy began to sweat and struggle with himself and finally a prayer came out. Without ever having read the Bible he summarised the gospel in one short prayer: 'Lord, I don't deserve your help, but I need it. Please help me, and give my wife and me another chance.' I realise theologically there was quite a lot missing, especially the cross, but this was at the very least the beginning of a salvation event as he turned to Christ for help. 'What will I do when you leave?' he asked, knowing I had only one more day left in the hospice.

Marjorie was the Assistant Matron, a personal friend of John Finney, and a former missionary. She was keen to know more about the healing ministry and laying hands on the sick, but until now the opportunity had never presented itself or seemed right for Marjorie to begin. We both laid hands on Roy the next day, but before either of us could pray he came in with another one himself. Marjorie later told me how she continued to lay hands on Roy after I left, and how he not only found Christ and peace before he died, but shared it with his wife.

So far I had prayed for two dying people who had not been physically healed.

During the summer vacation I adjusted to being on my own again, and concentrated mainly on cricket and golf before I returned to college in the autumn. Still being alone, I popped into Aspley from time to time and visited Jean and Brian. On one of my visits Brian told me of a vision he had received. In it he saw Christ with his arms outstretched and his wife Jean running away from him towards Jesus, and this frightened him. His grandmother had once told him he would marry in his thirties, be very happy, but not married long, and the first two parts had already been fulfilled. Jean suffered badly from asthma and a friend of theirs had already died of the same illness at the same age as Jean. Brian was frightened this vision would herald the fulfilment of the next part of Grandma's prophecy.

I responded to this sharing by speaking right off the top of my head. 'You have misunderstood the vision,' I said. 'Jean is already with Christ. The important factor in the vision is that you are not there. Jesus wants you to join him and Jean in their life. Grandma's prophecy is from Satan and Jesus has the victory over Satan.'

This reassured him and again the speaking out in the name of Christ seemed to come up trumps: some fourteen years later Jean is still very much alive and still happily married to Brian. But given the opportunity of speaking for Christ, I continued: 'With Christ you can't lose. If Jean had cancer, Christ is the only one who could heal her. If Jean died, Christ is the only one who could take her to heaven. If Jean died, Christ is the only one who could heal your bereavement. On the other hand, without Christ you can't win.' I could have gone on but it seemed right to leave Brian to add his own corollaries.

Later in the term a strange thing happened. Jean said she wanted me to come and spend a weekend with them when *Come Together* was on in their own church.[1] 'I've been praying very hard for Brian,' she said, 'and I think this weekend is going to be special.' This was a very odd request and one which threatened me as much as John Finney's original prayer. I was only fifteen minutes' drive from Aspley and I had college commitments every weekend so why should I stay there, and what would my tutor say? I found myself saying 'Yes', as did my tutor.

During the week there was a bad accident at Stanton Iron Works and Brian's friend lay critically ill in hospital. He was glad to see me that weekend. He readily agreed to attend *Come Together* and I said beforehand to Brian that I thought he was now standing on the diving board ready to take the plunge. In the middle of the evening opportunity was given for people to come forward and ask for prayer for the needy. Brian longed to ask for prayer for his friend, but courage failed him and we later learned his friend died at about the same time. Back home, at one in the morning I said to Brian, 'I think you've taken the plunge now, haven't you?' and he nodded. He had invited Jesus into his life when opportunity had been given during the musical. That, I realised afterwards, was God speaking but then it just seemed like one of those 'right at the time' comments.

We worshipped in church together the next day and Jean invited me for tea on Monday. Her enthusiasm led me to accept. Brian was late home that evening so Jean, their son Mark and I had tea together. Jean had a standing arrangement on Mondays and suddenly announced she was off. She asked if I would baby-sit until Brian got home, and she would come home before nine in case I could persuade Brian to come with me to the prayer meeting.

'Coming to the prayer meeting?' I asked Brian casually after he'd come home and eaten his tea.

'I'm afraid I can't,' he explained. 'Jean is always out on Mondays until at least ten o'clock and I'll have to baby-sit.' Brian was being led by his wife like a lamb to the slaughter. Suddenly I knew what 'being as wise as serpents' meant.

'If Jean is back before nine, will you come with me?' I asked as innocently as I could.

Brian laughed. 'She's never back until ten,' he said.

'Oh, right!' I commented, 'but you'll come with me if she is?'

'If a miracle happens,' he said, 'and Jean comes home before nine, I'll come with you.'

Brian was nervous when we arrived at the prayer meeting, as he'd never been to one before. Thirty people jammed into someone's lounge is a bit daunting, so he hung back in the hallway as I claimed the only vacant chair in the middle of the room. The meeting was soon under way and after five minutes I completely forgot about Brian.

People blessed God and praised him and thanked him, and as they did a dark cloud came over me. It was a new and painful experience. Words formed in my mind alongside the pain: 'They are saying peace when there is no peace. Someone here is oppressed. Stop the meeting and ask that person to kneel at your feet for ministry.' I may have had a 'word' at a gate, an automatic blurt, and successfully backed a holy hunch, but this was something else; this was public. John Finney and Felicity Lawson[2] (co-authors of *Saints Alive*) were present, as were leading charismatics from the parish and fellow students from St John's College. These thoughts were crazy and I would have nothing to do with them.

The depression and the pain would not go away, however, so I tried to reason it through: 'Had the meeting bound the power of Satan that night?' Whatever that means, we had. Our experience had been that prayer meetings which started by coming against Satan and his demons had gone better than those which had not. On this occasion authority over Satan had been claimed. 'Is this a "word" that I myself would like to give?' This was not an easy question but generally speaking I know myself quite well and knew that I emphatically did not want to give this message. 'Then where has the thought come from?' If a 'word' does not come from Satan or from self, then the obvious answer is God, and though I spent some time searching for more subtle answers, I could find none.

To a British Christian, however, to know logically that something is likely to be right and of God is no guarantee it will be acted upon. I have only recently begun to realise the size of my emotional hang-ups and culture-clamps by travelling abroad and meeting Christians from other lands. In that prayer meeting I felt sick. I totally refused to obey what was going on in my mind and would not have done so if God had left it there. But my heart-beat suddenly increased and pounded against the walls of my chest with such ferocity that I either had to give the 'word' or leave the room.

'You are saying peace when there is no peace,' I began, shaking all over with my eyes firmly shut. 'Someone here is oppressed. I think that person should kneel at my feet for ministry.'

Nothing happened and time went by; it seemed as if there was silence in heaven for half an hour. I panicked: 'Will no one come forward for God's healing?' I pleaded, but the silence continued. Just as I was about to die with embarrassment and be carried out like Ananias and Sapphira (Acts 5:1-11), there was a commotion. I opened my eyes and saw Brian kneeling at my feet with tears streaming down his face. I laid hands on his head, though I've no idea to this day what I prayed, and Brian returned to his place.

During this encounter I was aware of John and Felicity supporting me with their love, and in many ways it was their encouragement in the preceding months which had given me the freedom to try and, if necessary, fail at this moment. Their authority over the meeting was not in question and they could have interrupted proceedings at any point. That they didn't, and supported us both afterwards, speaks volumes of their love, maturity and leadership, for which I will always be grateful.

I asked Brian later why he had come forward. 'It was the heart-beat,' he said. 'As you spoke it became so hard and fast I felt I'd either have to kneel at your feet or leave the room.' As I write, Brian has now been church warden at St Margaret's Aspley for a number of years and has spoken of his faith in Christ to many people.

During the next term I accompanied my friends from Aspley to the Hayes Conference Centre at Swanwick for their parish weekend away. We shared the facilities with Birmingham Christian Union, and under the grapevine in the table-tennis room I met Carol Hamilton, one of their members from Virginia Water. She seemed just right for me. In my final year at theological college Carol and I became engaged and found a curacy near Birmingham University where Carol was studying. I was ordained in September 1976 and married in January 1977.

To hell and back

It seemed at this point in my life that not even the sky was the limit. I had received healing for past hurts, obtained my degree and been ordained, married the right girl for me, heard God speak and been used by him to help people into the kingdom. As yet I had not seen people physically healed, but maybe this was just around the corner? The church I was serving had a conservative evangelical vicar who was open to things of the Spirit, as indeed were many in the congregation, and it must surely be only a matter of time before we set Birmingham alight.

Gradually, almost imperceptibly, the wheels began to come off. I spent a lot of time during my three years as a curate visiting and praying with a young man who had been crippled by an accident. Many of us believed God was going to heal him, but he never did. Every Christian who came his way had another theory as to why God had not yet healed him and we queued up like Job's comforters to give him advice, tell him about his sins or command him to get up and walk. Eventually he and his wife were divorced and their three teenage children lost their faith in the Christ we had presented to them. It was not only failure with a capital 'F' but pain with a capital 'P'.

During this time my father, aged sixty, died suddenly on the golf course without any warning or sign of an illness. I cannot say I had always related to him as well as I would have liked, but things were beginning to improve as I slowly matured, when he died. I had looked forward to a deepening relationship for the next ten or twenty years, particularly as he had recently retired from a very demanding job, but it was not to be.

In my third year as a curate the vicar left for another parish and, as always with vicars, we only fully appreciated how much he had done when he went. One night, while we were still waiting for a new boss, I woke up sweating, worried about all the things I had to remember. Carol persuaded me to write them down and I listed twenty-six things I needed to do the next day, which I had been carrying in my head.

Fortunately, during that time my best friend, Hugh, moved to Birmingham. He had left college a year earlier than I and completed his curacy in Southsea before coming to Crowther Hall en route to Iran. Hugh and I related very well at various levels. We got on well spiritually and could pray with each other, we were well matched at cricket and golf and spent many happy hours together in the sunshine, and we understood one another's problems. I often used to do and say embarrassing things at parties which frequently meant patching up and apologising afterwards. Hugh had learned to anticipate these aberrations and to tread on my foot or lock me in a cupboard as the need arose; it was a great comfort having him around.

In December 1979 I became Vicar of Christ Church, Burney Lane and Hugh counselled me each week on the golf course. By then the revolution in Iran had taken place and Hugh was somewhat depressed about his own future, though a lady friend had arrived on the scene to brighten up his winter.

Just after Easter we spent a week together golfing at St Anne's in Lancashire. Each day we read the Bible and prayed, and it seemed to be working because on the Thursday his golf reached a very high standard.

On the Saturday morning Hugh took his own life with a shotgun.

His father rang to tell me about it and to ask why. Hugh had left a suicide note saying I would be able to explain why he had done it, but there was no real reason other than a biological depression which had plagued him since his teens. Just another person for whose healing I had prayed who was now dead. Only this time it was my best friend, aged thirty-three.

I carried on, of course. A middle-aged lady in our choir got cancer so I visited her, laid on hands and prayed, and she died. I developed a very good funeral ministry. People said that however many I upset with my strange sense of humour, I made up for it with my sensitive conducting of funerals. But such events and failures took their toll on me. It might not have been so bad but for my Aspley experiences. If I had never met the God who speaks and saves it would not have been so painful to meet a God who does not heal. On the other hand, if God had carried on speaking and saving while others were dying, I think I would have coped better, but all supernatural activity seemed to have been suspended and I sank lower into the mire.

I am told that depression occurs when we suppress our true feelings. When a false mask is presented to the outside world the inner turmoil increases, and the natural energy given by God to wage war on life's problems triggers the self-destruct button. Week after week I stood up in church and read and preached about a Jesus who heals, while inwardly I was screaming out to God who didn't seem to support his own words with action. I had prayed for four people who had died and one young cripple who was still in a wheelchair but now divorced and alone, and yet I was struggling to believe and preach something else.

Difficulties arose in my own life at this time, which only my wife Carol knew about, and in the August of 1985, while my family were away, the thought flashed through my mind of following my friend Hugh home. I was afraid to go on living, but fortunately I was also afraid to die. Friends gave me details about the John Wimber conference in Sheffield and though it was taking place when our third child was due, Carol and I saw this as a new hope for me. So many people had told us so much about it, especially our Baptist friends, that I filled in the form and posted it, virtually with an ultimatum to God.

When I arrived for the beginning of the Signs and Wonders conference I chose my seat carefully near the exit. I had heard horror stories of people receiving 'words' from God about sins in their lives at previous meetings and I was determined, if this started, to be able to escape swiftly and surely. In the evening John began giving 'words' about physical problems, some of which are documented in the appendix to his *Power Healing*,[3] and I was amazed to see people being physically healed. Physical healing seemed pretty safe. Late in the evening he said, 'There's somebody here whose testicle did not drop as a child; on the right side. They may be too embarrassed to come up now. They'd better come and see me at the end of the meeting.' My mind began to buzz with questions.

Before going to Sheffield I had seen a doctor for a check-up and been advised to have a minor operation. My left testicle had never dropped as a child and I was advised to have something done about it to avoid the risk of cancer. The specialist had managed to book me a bed in the hospital for when I returned from the conference.

Was this 'word' for me or for someone else? How common a problem is it? I don't normally ask the men I meet if they're unbalanced like me. Could John Wimber be wrong? Did he mean left when he said right? Would he still see me and pray for me anyway? I knew so little about 'words' from God.

But I was already encouraged by slight inaccuracies earlier: John had given a 'word' for a woman aged thirty-two whose name began with 'L'. A woman named Linda responded, but was adamant her age was thirty-one, not thirty-two. Ladies are usually very sure about their age, but despite the slight error Linda was healed. I also felt more confident about sharing personal problems with an American who was crossing the Atlantic next week, than with his English counterpart. This was far too good an opportunity to miss, and if I confessed now in confidence I would surely then be immunised against possible attacks from discerning Americans later on in the conference.

At the end of the meeting I made my way up on to the stage which by this time was crowded with those receiving ministry. Some were 'resting in the Spirit' horizontally and I hoped it wouldn't happen to me; it didn't look very Anglican. But search as I could, John Wimber had gone. All I could find was a Church of England curate. 'I'm sorry,' he said, 'John appears to have gone. Will I do?' We had plenty of Church of England curates at home in Birmingham; I'd been one myself.

I felt as if I'd gone to a show to see the star, only to discover that an understudy had stepped in at the last moment. But most people, having gone to the trouble of getting there, normally stay rather than ask for their money back, so I stayed. He was great. I heard myself saying, 'I'm claiming a "word" about a physical condition, but that isn't my real problem.' I did receive prayer for my left testicle at the conference, but to no avail; I had it surgically removed when I returned home.

The curate listened, cared, didn't judge, and prayed. I remained upright. After half an hour he said, 'I'd like you to see David. Can you make it at lunch time tomorrow?'

I could. 'Maybe this will be an American,' I thought.

As if a Church of England curate wasn't bad enough, David turned out to be a Church of England bishop. He too was great. He did much the same as the curate, I cried a little and felt much better. 'I feel forgiven and loved and I want to start again,' I said, 'but how do I stay healed?'

'Do the stuff,' replied the bishop. I have met a fair few 'right reverends' in my time, but this was certainly different. 'The stuff' is short for 'the stuff in God's Book', or 'the stuff Jesus did'. Briefly, it means proclaiming the kingdom, healing the sick and casting out demons. I wanted to be healed and stay healed. I suppose I wanted God to remove temptation from me and I was rather disappointed at this response, but David challenged me to find my healing in doing what the conference had been equipping me to do.

Motivated by having been to hell and back, educated by the teaching and demonstrations of the conference, I now resolved to go home and do as I had been told, whatever it cost. I decided to do what the bishop had said, what John Wimber had said and what Jesus had said and see if it worked for me.

Notes

1. Jimmy and Carol Owens, *Come Together* (Lexicon Music Inc: Distributed by Word (UK) Ltd, 1972).
2. John Finney and Felicity Lawson, *Saints Alive!* (Moorley's Bible & Bookshop Ltd on behalf of Anglican Renewal Ministries: Ilkeston, 1981).
3. John Wimber and Kevin Springer, *Power Healing* (Hodder & Stoughton: London, 1986).

2

The God Who Speaks

I roared home from Sheffield, determined to 'do the stuff'. I studied John Wimber very carefully and convinced myself that 'doing the stuff' in practical terms meant standing at the front of a meeting and saying, 'Come, Holy Spirit.' I thought I could manage that. I came home before the end of the conference on the Wednesday to check Carol's well-being (Hazel was born the following Tuesday) and to prepare for an East Birmingham Alive meeting in our church on the Thursday night. Our new Bishop of Aston was the guest speaker and I was hopeful that, with persuasion, he might let me have a go at the ministry. I need not have worried as he had met John Wimber earlier in the year and was very encouraging and supportive.

After the bishop had preached, I stood at the front, invited everyone to stand and said, 'Come, Holy Spirit.' Nothing happened, not a murmur nor a shake nor even the faintest flutter of an eyelid. I was sure I'd got the words right. After a while the bishop looked at me as if to say, 'Is that it?', and it did seem to be, but I didn't give up immediately. One or two people shared a few pictures which nobody could understand, and this time it definitely was it. Suddenly, as I was about to dismiss everyone I got a twinge in my left thumb.

The speakers in Sheffield had said pain in our bodies can

sometimes be a 'word' from God for somebody he wants to heal, so I tried it.[1] I'd have tried anything at that point. 'Is there anyone here who has something wrong with their left thumb?' I asked hopefully. You would have thought in a group of 150 people somebody would have had something wrong with a left thumb, but apparently not. The bishop looked at me again and this time I let him give the blessing and dismiss the crowd.

As people began filing out a young man made his way forward to see me. 'I cut my left thumb opening a tin,' he said apologetically, 'but I didn't like to mention it in front of all those people.'

'Go away,' I thought, 'it's no good now.' Inwardly I was screaming, 'Come back, everyone, the thumb's here!' but it was too late. Face to face I thanked him for coming forward, prayed for him and then crawled home, mumbling to myself as I went, 'His thumb was getting better anyway; I don't expect it was God speaking.'

Greg, from our church, rang to encourage me the next day which was totally unexpected and very welcome as I'd thought I might be looking for a new job. Thus reaffirmed, I tried again with our young people on the Sunday night. We all closed our eyes and I said, 'Come, Holy Spirit.' Nothing happened. At least this was a slightly more comfortable 'nothing' as we were all seated in a lounge, but I was still fed up. I started moaning to God and immediately the thought came into my head, 'Open your eyes.' I remembered being taught to keep my eyes open to see what the Father was doing so I opened them to behold a wondrous sight: one young man had slid up the armchair. I've since seen many people slide down chairs when the Spirit comes, but this guy had gone up and over the top and was hanging over the edge backwards with his beaming face pointing to the ceiling. 'Having a good time Stephen?' I enquired, greatly relieved to see something going on.

'Yeah man,' he said, 'amazing.'

Thus encouraged I tried it again the following Sunday

night. Roger Jones, our director of music, had come to talk to the young people, and after he'd finished we repeated the ministry. Immediately thoughts flashed into my mind: 'Toe; back; eye.' This was crazy stuff. Here was a young people's meeting and there were only nine or ten present. If I'd received such 'words' at our over-sixties I'd have felt more confident. At this point Roger began to cough painfully and I knew he often suffered from a sore throat, so I said to God, 'What about this man, Lord?' The thought came back to me, 'Not on the agenda.' I opened my eyes, but no one was crawling on the ceiling or swinging from the light, so I gave it a try: 'Anyone here with a pain in the toe, back or eye?' I asked, feeling very unsure of myself. Three teenage lads claimed one each. We divided up to have a go on them, and registered total failure.

The one with the pain in the back said he'd only felt pain when he sat on the chair in the room. We were very slow to realise these three were our most sceptical members, with two of them claiming to be unbelievers. It was like the 'word' from God for me in Sheffield about a physical complaint when my biggest problem had been something else. With hindsight and more experience I can now say I believe God gave those three 'words' about very small complaints to show to three people, who in varying degrees were struggling with unbelief, how much he loved them. Clearly, if I'd had a 'word' about two unbelievers and a sceptic everyone would have said I knew that anyway. No one knew of the physical complaints mentioned, especially as one had only cropped up at the time, and had we not been so dimwitted we might have used God's 'words' more lovingly and profitably.

Nevertheless, I was encouraged. We carried on with the ministry on Sunday evenings and in our small mid-week meetings, beginning to learn not to 'despise the day of small things' (Zech 4:10). I enthused about the conference and shared with my friends whenever God showed up and did something significant among us. Occasionally people received a picture, a sense of peace or a little touch of power, and together in our small groups we became less afraid of silence.

I shared a few of these things with an acquaintance from another church and then half-jokingly said, 'Get me an invitation to one of your services and I'll come and do a Wimber on your congregation.' This was a very silly thing to say. She took me seriously and a letter duly arrived from her vicar inviting me to speak and minister at a Thursday night celebration in January; I was too embarrassed to refuse.

I meditated upon the problem. I was once told how the art of ministering to a group of people you've never met before is to keep remembering they don't know what you don't know. Perhaps this would work: if I could just convince them I knew what I was doing maybe they would become confident God was going to show up and things would happen.

I ransacked my library in search of confidence-boosting fodder. I needed some quotations to add authenticity to my message and eventually my eyes rested on a book by Archbishop Stuart Blanch.[2] Like most of the books in my study I hadn't read it, but I thought a casual aside from an archbishop or two would sound impressive. I read the first eleven pages, usually enough to find a decent quote, but then found myself putting it down in total amazement. One sentence stopped me in my tracks. This is what a former Archbishop of York had written: 'The Bible.... rests on the assumption that God speaks.'

This was for me what John Finney describes as a 'blob' experience – a moment of insight, a sudden encounter with truth.[3] In the past fourteen years I had been thrilled to hear God speaking to me five or six times, and had paraded my stories in the pulpit like a centenarian with a telegram from the Queen. Most of us think God may from time to time beam in with a special 'word' on special occasions for special people. Believing this myself, I had exhibited my 'words' from God as trophies or rewards for good conduct, as evidence of my high spiritual standing, but suddenly that lie was exposed. God is a God who speaks. Just as I am a man who eats, God is a God who speaks. Nobody asks me on Sundays if I've eaten anything in the past week; everyone assumes I have. I am a man who eats; it is part of my very nature as a man and something I do almost without thinking. God is a God who speaks; the Bible declares it from beginning to end. I could no more claim credit for hearing God than for listening to the Queen's speech on Christmas Day.

As the penny dropped I recognised in myself a wrong-thinking about God. People are inconsistent. Even the mature saint fails to do good all the time. We cannot always discern accurately who a person is from what he does. If a Christian preacher confesses to spending a night with a prostitute, as some have done recently, we cannot easily tell if it is the confession of a 'con-man' who has been found out, or a sinner who is repentant. There are two kingdoms at war within us and at different moments either might be seen to have the upper hand.

But God is not like that. His nature is perfect, incorruptible and totally consistent. His true character is always revealed in everything he does. We may not interpret all he does correctly because we see through a glass darkly due to our sinful natures, but when so many believers over so many centuries have encountered the God who speaks, it seems right to conclude this is not just a comment on what God has done, but who he is. The Bible rests on the assumption that God is a God who speaks.

My whole being thrilled to this new concept, but with the excitement came a twinge of fear. 'If this is true,' I thought, 'then I can expect God to speak to me regularly. And if I preach it as true, the congregation will expect God to speak to them.' This became for me a moment of truth! I began to realise why some of my ancestors had denied the present-day existence of spiritual gifts and settled for a more comfortable way of life. It is always much easier to claim God has spoken and God will speak, than God speaks. All my past hurts, fears, rejections and psychological hang-ups surfaced at once, as my yearning for security sought to bury this simple luminous truth in the ground, like the man in the Bible did with his one talent. As a vicar I had always sought to hide my insecure emotions by commenting on life rather than risk playing the game. And yet I couldn't bear the thought of spending the rest of my days running away from truth in search of a quiet life.

I decided to think through this new concept and prepare my sermon accordingly, trusting that if it were true, it would come true. If God is a God who speaks I would expect him to validate his word. I asked myself three important questions:

1. Does the Bible rest on the assumption that God speaks?

The Bible begins, 'In the beginning God created ....' and the way he created was by speaking. 'God said, "Let there be light," and there was light' (Gen 1:3). As the psalmist says, 'The heavens declare the glory of God' (Ps 19:1).

As soon as mankind appears, God speaks to them. He speaks to Adam and Eve and family, to Noah, to Abraham and the patriarchs. From Moses to Malachi, the prophets thunder, 'Thus says the Lord.'

He speaks to the world through Jesus, the Word of God. Hebrews 1:1–2 (RSV) says, 'In many and various ways God spoke of old to our fathers by the prophets; but in these last days he has spoken to us by a Son.' On the day of Pentecost the Spirit of God is poured out for all believers: 'The promise is for you and your children and for all who are far off – for all whom the Lord our God will call' (Acts 2:39), and it is through the spiritual gift of languages, God speaking, that the world is alerted to this truth.

Paul assures us that God, the God who loves to speak, is now dwelling in every believer. 'We were all baptised by one Spirit' (1 Cor 12:13); 'You are the body of Christ' (1 Cor 12:27). The gifts of the Spirit that Paul talks about are nearly all gifts which enable us to hear God speaking or discern what he is doing.

The final book of the Bible continues on the same theme: 'He who has an ear, let him hear what the Spirit says to the churches' (Rev 2:7).

And this biblical revelation about God is not only present from beginning to end but is present as a powerful truth. If we compare the statement 'God speaks' with other biblical statements like 'God heals' or 'God loves' or 'God forgives', we can appreciate its strength. Anyone who says, 'God heals' has to have something to say about the plagues he sent upon Egypt (Ex 9:8–11; 12:29), the leprosy he gave to Gehazi (2 Kings 5:27) and the blindness he gave to Elymas (Acts 13:9-12). Even Revelation tells us that at the end of history God will not heal everyone (Rev 20:11–15).

Anyone who says 'God forgives' has to have something to say about 'God judges', and those who claim, 'God loves sinners' can never forget that 'God hates sin'. It is far easier to claim that God 'speaks' than God heals, forgives or loves. Whether he is saving Daniel (Dan 6:22) or killing Ananias and Sapphira (Acts 5:5,10); forgiving a woman caught in the act of adultery (Jn 8:11b); stoning a man to death for collecting sticks on the Sabbath (Num 15:32–36); whipping the money-changers with thongs (Jn 2:15), or accepting lashes himself (Mk 15:15), God is speaking. Even when he is silent there is often communication: 'Again the Israelites did evil in the eyes of the Lord and for seven years he gave them into the hands of the Midianites' (Judg 6:1). Verse 7 continues, 'When the Israelites cried to the Lord because of Midian, he sent them a prophet.'

There are times in Scripture and in the history of the church when the word of the Lord has been rare with not many visions (eg 1 Sam 3:1), but it seems more likely to have been the result of people's sin than God's unwillingness to speak (1 Sam 2:12-36). In Genesis chapters 1 and 2 Adam and Eve have fellowship with God, but after they have sinned in chapter 3 they hide from him. It appears that sin causes us to turn our backs on God, while the salvation activity of God enables us to turn round, face him, and call him Father. God has recalled us into fellowship through his Son, Jesus Christ (1 Cor 1:9); Paul prays for the 'fellowship of the Holy Spirit' to be with the Corinthians (2 Cor 13:14); and John says, 'Our fellowship is with the Father and with his Son, Jesus Christ' (1 Jn 1:3). The desire of God is to have fellowship with his children, and salvation through Jesus enables us to be restored into that fellowship. A God who creates us for fellowship and calls us back into fellowship through repentance and faith when we sin is a God who loves to communicate with his children.

In Psalm 115:4–5 and Psalm 135:15–16 we read how 'the idols of the nations are silver and gold, made by the hands of men. They have mouths, but cannot speak.'

Habakkuk 2:18 asks, 'Of what value is an idol, since a man has carved it?... For he who makes it trusts in his own creation; he makes idols that cannot speak.'

Jeremiah says, 'Like a scarecrow in a melon patch their idols cannot speak' (Jer 10:5).

Paul begins his teaching on spiritual gifts in 1 Corinthians 12 by saying, 'You know that when you were pagans, somehow or other you were influenced and led astray to mute idols.'

In contrast, Psalm 115 and Psalm 135 set the lifeless idols against the activities of God; similarly Jeremiah 10:10 says, 'But the Lord is the true God; he is the living God;' and Paul teaches about God's spiritual gifts which enable us to discern his activity and hear his voice.

The God of Isaiah (Is 37:17), Jeremiah (Jer 23:36), Daniel (Dan 6:26), Hosea (Hos 1:10), Jesus (Jn 6:57), Peter (Mt 16:16), Paul (Acts 14:15), the writer to the Hebrews (Heb 12:22) and John (Rev 7:2) is a 'living God'. He is not a dumb idol but a God who speaks.

If we accept the biblical revelation, it seems we are on pretty firm ground when we claim that the living Christian God, who lives in all believers, is a God who speaks.

2. Does God speak today?

In a world of changing pressures and insecurities, the Bible has always been very precious to me. The foundation of my Christian faith has been the Scriptures ever since my conversion at fourteen, and I firmly believe in a God who speaks to us today through them. Every day I try to spend some time reading from the Bible, asking the Holy Spirit to speak to me through God's word.

Most Christians would accept this, but some would go on to say God speaks to us today *only* through the Bible. It is this 'only' which concerns me. I was brought up to believe in a God who has spoken and will one day speak again, but for the present only speaks through his written word lest we should be tossed about by every whim and fancy. I believe the main way God speaks to us today is through the Bible, but I do not believe it is the only way God speaks. I spent some time thinking about this and found three reasons why I could no longer accept that God speaks today only through Scripture.

Logic

We present an enormous credibility gap to our secular age if we preach a different God from the one found in the Bible. It is very difficult to convince the world about a God who spoke directly to Moses and Elijah, Peter and Paul but will not speak directly to us today. If people read of a God who is the same yesterday, today and for ever and who speaks directly to people for several thousand years, but are then told he has stopped speaking because he's had a book published, it is not surprising if they turn away from God. The unbeliever is often very quick to see through logical inconsistency. If a book cannot be validated by experience it is normally classified as 'fiction'. If the Bible rests on the assumption that God speaks, it seems logical to believe he still speaks today unless the Bible has told us otherwise.[4]

Experience

Historical and contemporary experience supports the view that God did not stop speaking when the New Testament was completed. George Fox, founder of the Quakers,[5] Evan Roberts, used by God in the Welsh Revival of 1904,[6] Smith Wigglesworth who brought pentecostal revival to many,[7] and Paul Yonggi Cho, pastor of today's largest church[8] are just four of the many people who claimed to have heard God speaking with signs following. The faith of all of these men was rooted in the Bible; Smith Wigglesworth would read no other book. All could be classed as Bible-based believers, teachers and preachers, but none of them as Bible-only people. Their experience validated the Bible and the Bible validated their experience. They all found the God who speaks in the Bible and in their own Christian lives.

The Bible

Biblical Christianity is about being sons and daughters of the King; being brides of Christ; having communion with God; knowing God and being known by him. Through the Spirit we may know God (Heb 8:11), know his voice (Jn 10:4), know the truth (Jn 16:3) and know the mind of Christ (1 Cor 2:16). I was unable to find anything in the New Testament to suggest the promises God made to the disciples and the early church are not meant for us as well. When we see God face to face, then the spiritual gifts will cease (1 Cor 13), but the New Testament gives no indication of this occurring before then.

The Canon of Scripture is closed.[9] This means the promises and teaching of the New Testament must apply to us for today, otherwise we would need a third set of canonical writings to explain to us the new rules. The people in the Old Testament lived under the Old Covenant. The people of the New Testament lived under the New Covenant. As there has not yet been a third covenant between God and his people, it is right to assume we also live under the New Covenant sealed by the blood of Jesus Christ. This must surely mean the promises and teachings of the New Covenant apply to all Christians for today.

To say the New Testament teachings no longer apply to us is to add a new interpretation to Scripture, invariably based on experience or lack of it rather than what the Bible teaches. 'I have not heard God speak,' so God does not speak. 'I have not healed the sick,' so God no longer heals the sick. 'I do not speak in tongues,' so the gift has died out.[10]

Such statements are not New Testament statements and I believe they are to be rejected. The New Testament teaches that anyone who has faith in Jesus will do what he did (Jn 14:12); the Holy Spirit is promised to 'everyone who calls on the name of the Lord ... for you and your children and for all who are far off' (Acts 2:21,39); and all under the New Covenant will know God 'from the least of them to the greatest' (Heb 8:11).

I believe in the Bible. I believe God speaks to us today through the Scriptures. I believe God also speaks to us today by his Holy Spirit.[11]

3. In what way does God speak today?

Having decided I believed in a God who speaks today I began to feel the ground shaking a little beneath my feet. If God speaks today, does this undermine the authority of Scripture? What is the relationship between the written word of God and the living Word of God? Do we attribute equal importance to a 'word' from the Lord today as we give to the Bible? I recognised some of the dangers immediately.

In the last book of the Bible we read these words:

> I warn everyone who hears the words of the prophecy of this book: If anyone adds anything to them, God will add to him the plagues described in this book. And if anyone takes words away from this book of prophecy, God will take away from him his share in the tree of life and in the holy city, which are described

in this book (Rev 22:18–19).

It is right and proper that we should be very cautious about anyone who claims to have subsequent revelations from the Holy Spirit which either add to or take away from Scripture. Muhammad[12] and Joseph Smith[13] claimed subsequent revelations from God which produced the Koran and the Book of Mormon respectively, and the list of today's self-styled cultic prophets who seek to lead people away from God's truth is endless. Being warned by the New Testament against adding to its message or taking away from it, I turned to it again in an attempt to understand the relationship between the word of God and a 'word' from God.

> The holy Scriptures ... are able to make you wise for salvation through faith in Christ Jesus. All Scripture is God-breathed and is useful for teaching, rebuking, correcting and training in righteousness, so that the man of God may be thoroughly equipped for every good work (2 Tim 3:15–17).

The Holy Spirit inspires the writing of Scripture for the purposes of doctrine and teaching, especially the way of salvation through faith in Jesus. This is the word of God. It is God-breathed and therefore carries the authority of God himself (cf 2 Pet 1:20–21; 1 Cor 2:13), but as well as Scripture being inspired by the Holy Spirit, there is another reason for treating the Bible as authoritative.

> We did not follow cleverly invented stories when we told you about the power and coming of our Lord Jesus Christ, but we were eye witnesses of his majesty.... We ourselves heard this voice that came from heaven when we were with him on the sacred mountain (2 Pet 1:16,18).

'That which was from the beginning, which we have heard, which we have seen with our eyes, which we have looked at and our hands have touched – this we proclaim concerning the Word of life' (1 Jn 1:1).

The second letter of Peter and the first letter of John appear to have been written at a time when false teachers and prophets were becoming active (2 Pet 2; 1 Jn 4:1). It was no longer sufficient to say their writings had the authority of the Holy Spirit who told them what to write because many other heretical teachers were claiming the same thing. Their unique authority was the inspiration of the Holy Spirit plus their credibility as eye-witnesses to the earthly Jesus. They could match up the words of the risen Lord Jesus given by the Spirit with those of the earthly Lord Jesus whom they had known and loved. Until the Second Coming of Jesus this unique authority can never be repeated.

The Canon of Scripture is closed because it carries the unique authority of Jesus himself. The Old Testament anticipates and prepares for his coming, the gospels describe his coming and the Epistles testify to the effect of his coming as recorded by those in touch with the early disciples who knew the earthly Jesus.[14]

In Acts chapter one Peter outlines the necessary requirements for someone to be elected as an apostle:

> It is necessary to choose one of the men who have been with us the whole time the Lord Jesus went in and out among us, beginning from John's baptism to the time when Jesus was taken up from us. For one of these must become a witness with us of his resurrection (Acts 1:21–22).

An apostle therefore had to be an eye-witness of the life and Resurrection of the Lord Jesus Christ. They were the special people whose role was to teach (Acts 2:42; 4:2) and to be guardians of the faith (eg Acts 15:2). There are obviously no such eye-witnesses alive today and the Canon of Scripture is closed.

This means the word of God has the authority of the earthly Jesus whose teaching the apostles faithfully recorded and passed on, plus the authority of the Holy Spirit who enabled them to do this. The same Holy Spirit is present

among us today as in the early church, but the earthly Jesus
and witnesses of his earthly life are no longer present. Jesus
is here by his Spirit, but not in the flesh; we cannot see him
face to face so 'words' from God cannot be tested except by
Scripture. This means a 'word' from God today must not
contain any new teaching; neither must it add to nor take
away from the doctrines of the Bible. It seems right to say
that a 'word' from God may therefore illustrate Scripture,
help to apply Scripture, enable Christians to fulfil the commands of Scripture and authenticate Scripture, but must
always be tested by Scripture. This enables us to understand
the different purposes behind the word of God and a 'word'
from God.

In Romans 10:9 Paul writes, 'If you confess with your
mouth, "Jesus is Lord," and believe in your heart that God
raised him from the dead, you will be saved.' This is doctrine
and teaches us especially the way of salvation. This is one of
the main purposes of the word of God.

In Acts 8:29 God says to Philip, 'Go to that chariot and
stay near it.' Although it is part of the word of God and
teaches us the value of letting God be the director of
evangelism, this is also an illustration of a 'word' from God.
It is a piece of local and particular guidance given to Philip
by the Holy Spirit for one man in one place at one time. It is
a 'word' from God which enables Philip to fulfil the word of
God in witnessing to the Ethiopian and leading him to faith
in Christ.

Through the Bible God speaks about the way to be saved
and to live as Christians, and through his Spirit God applies
that truth to the right person in the right place at the right
time. We could say a *'word' from God* released by the Holy
Spirit supports *the word of God*, helping Christians to live
out its principles.

The examples of 'words' from God which I mentioned in
the previous chapter illustrate my beliefs well. The Bible tells
us to proclaim the kingdom, heal the sick and cast out
demons, and this is what John Finney sent me out to do in

Jesus' name in Aspley. The Bible did not tell me to visit Lucy
Fox at a certain address on a certain day in June 1974; I
needed a 'word' from God to tell me that. The Bible gives the
general guidelines, whereas God sends a specific 'word' to
give particular guidance. The Bible is therefore to be kept,
studied and taught regularly. A 'word' from God is to be
thrown away once the message has been acted upon. The
Bible teaches us doctrine and basic truths and God speaks
today to help us put those biblical truths into practice. Anything that contradicts Scripture or takes away from it is to be
discarded at once as not of God, but a current 'word' or
nudge from God by his Spirit can help us to apply the teaching of the Bible to our daily lives. A 'word' from God can
therefore be expected to support the word of God and be
tested by it.

My thinking and my sermon were now complete. Biblically,
logically, theologically and, in a limited way, experientially I
knew God to be a God who speaks and I knew that God
wanted me to proclaim this truth when I visited St Thomas'
Church in Aldridge at the end of January.

   I had completed my sermon preparation for the meeting
by the end of December and at the beginning of January God
began his preparation of me. As I was going to sleep one
night an awful thought crept into my head. 'Go and tell
George and Alice [not their real names] that if they don't
stop sleeping together they'll never find me.' I ignored it of
course and went to sleep, but it was waiting for me when I
awoke. I tried to shake it off all day, busying myself with
good works, but the thought remained and nothing I could
say or do would make it leave. Eventually I went to see
George and Alice on a Tuesday night, stayed until midnight,
but didn't even discover if they were going out with each
other.

   On the following Wednesday night there were fourteen at
our mid-week fellowship and when I asked the Holy Spirit
to come among us there was plenty going on. People began

prophesying and sharing pictures and I was beginning to relax when some more of those thoughts attacked me. 'There's somebody here with pain at the base of the spine; one with pain in the right knee; trouble with a nose, a tooth and an ear.'

I wasn't really in the mood for such intrusions, as the meeting was going well. I was well acquainted with every single person present and since I knew no one who had any of these problems I ignored the original thought and was just beginning to relax when an even nastier thought clobbered me. 'You've disobeyed me once this week already. How many more times?' I'd promised to obey God whatever he said or did and I knew this was a turning point. With sheer embarrassment I tried to carry it off with a laugh: 'I don't suppose there's anybody here with a pain in the back, right knee, or trouble with a nose, tooth or ear? No, I thought not.' But there was, and slowly they were all claimed.

Brian had damaged the base of his spine two days before and I could have kicked myself for just saying 'pain in the back'. John was in such trouble with his right knee that he was contemplating giving up work. Greg had suffered with a blocked nose for many years, Jennifer was booked in at the dentist for a troublesome milk tooth, while Angela's right ear had started burning when I asked the Spirit to come. This was like the pain in the back which one of our unbelievers had received on the earlier occasion after he had come into the room. It seems to be a physical symptom that God can give by his Spirit in order to pinpoint a person to whom he wishes to minister, and it is an encouragement to all that God is present and active. We ministered to everyone that night, discovering various non-physical problems as well, affirming one another and God's love for all of us. There were no dramatic physical healings, but two-and-a-half years later John is still at work.

The biggest encouragement or worry was that I seemed to have heard God speaking. Although the 'words' were not specifically detailed, five out of five in a group of fourteen for

conditions I did not know people had was a reasonable confirmation. This meant the other part was likely to be of God
as well: 'You've disobeyed me once this week already.' It
had to be referring to George and Alice, and I knew it.

People often ask how I know it is of God. One of the
assurances I have that such 'words' are from God seems to
be the incredible pain I feel, coupled with apathy, dry mouth
and an insatiable desire to be one thousand miles away playing golf. This time, as well as that, I was trapped by 'words'
that confirmed a 'word' and so eventually, two days before
visiting Aldridge, I went for it.

'Forgive me if I'm wrong but ... I believe God may be saying ... if you don't stop sleeping together you'll never find
him.'

George looked at the floor. Alice said, 'What do you
mean?'

Well, I thought I knew what I meant, but could only mut-
ter, 'I've just given the "words" as I've received them' – an
important lesson, this one.[15]

'The truth is,' explained Alice, 'we've been sleeping in the
same bed together but never had sex.'

Alice has now found God and in fact was the first person
on whom I laid hands who 'crumpled' in the Spirit. George
never came to church again.

Struggling with God and wrestling with myself prepared
me without my realising it for what was to come next. I felt
no great thrill in being right as it was hardly a 'successful'
evening, but afterwards I found that a quiet confidence in
God had begun to grow within me and a little bit more faith
than before was now present. There are times when we
experience the true depths of God's graciousness.

At a quarter to two on the same day as the meeting at
Aldridge I parked my car outside the crematorium chapel
prior to doing a two o'clock funeral, and switched the
engine off. As I sat for a moment to compose myself a wave
of heat came across my forehead, so I closed my eyes and
asked God what was happening. The physical sensations of

heat and power which indicated to me the presence of the Holy Spirit were accompanied by a 'knowing' in my mind that God was going to give me 'words' for physical healing. Immediately I was imagining a human body and, working my way upwards in my own mind, thought of a big toe, bowels, chest, mouth and the head.

People always want to know what it's like hearing God speak and are usually disappointed when I cannot testify to blinding flashes, writing on the wall or audible voices, though I do not deny this may be the experience of others. The physical sensations were just like those many of us experience when we ask God to send his Holy Spirit upon us. Some people experience warmth, tingling, fluttering eyelids, a change in breathing rhythm, shaking or falling, and so on, all of which can be some of the physical phenomena that occur when the power of the Holy Spirit comes upon us.[16] Such phenomena are not of themselves important – there is no advantage in lying on the floor as opposed to standing or sitting – but after a little experience of such things they can be useful pointers that God is present in a particular way to do a particular work. I do not always experience physical phenomena when God is speaking, but on this occasion I did and it was helpful in recognising God's activity.

The 'knowing' that 'words' for physical healing were then on the agenda is not so easy to describe, but it is a common, everyday experience for many people. It is no different from ordinary premonitions such as, 'I knew this was going to happen,' or, 'I sensed my mother was ill,' or, 'I just felt it in my bones.' Outside the 'religious experience' arena we frequently talk of hunches, intuitions or uncanny feelings; my 'knowing' seemed no different from these.[17]

The words in my mind then came like the thinking through of a problem or the making up of things out of my own imagination. So often people looking for 'words' from God are looking for something apart from themselves or outside their normal experience, but the Holy Spirit indwells the believer, enabling us to develop the mind of Christ who is in us, as we are in him. Satan and his demons seek to take us over and possess us, but the Spirit of God comes to free us that we might become more truly ourselves. Very serious religious people frequently find that God speaks to them in serious tones, while those with a wicked sense of humour often find God has the last laugh. I believe we need to look for God most often within our experience and not outside it.

After I had thought up my five bits of the body I pointed out to God there was rather insufficient detail for a meeting of about ninety people. From then on the thinking through followed a question and answer pattern which went something like this:

Q. 'Tell me more about this big toe on the right foot.'

A. 'It's a man with an ingrowing toe nail that is black and blue.'

Q. 'But Lord, I suffer from an ingrowing toe nail and it never goes black and blue.'

A. Silence

Q. 'What about the bowels then?'

A. 'A lady with a serious bowel complaint.'

(I wondered if it might be cancer but this was never discussed and I merely noted the condition was more than a problem with diarrhoea.)

Q. 'What is the problem with the chest?'

A. 'Inter-ventricular.'

(This was very odd. It's always worth noting unusual words, particularly as I didn't think I'd ever heard this one before.) I thought it was for a lady and had something to do with the lungs.

Q. 'The mouth?'

A. 'Mouth ulcer.'

Q. 'Which sex?'

A. Silence

Q. 'The head?'

A. 'A severe headache.'

Q. 'Any more details?'

A. 'It's time for the funeral.'

I looked at my watch and rushed into the chapel just in time. It wasn't the easiest cremation I'd ever done but, relying heavily on experience, I saw it through as sensitively as I could and went home.

I was too embarrassed to share the 'words' I'd received with Carol. It felt as though I'd been playing a silly game and pretending to be some super-spiritual giant who could hear God. I needed to remind myself of my own sermon: 'Our God is a God who speaks and lives in every believer.' Encouraged but still very much afraid I reached for the dictionary and was overjoyed to find that 'ventricular' really was a word, but to do with the heart rather than the lungs.

I decided to take it all seriously and tackle head-on the problem of giving 'words' from God to a Church of England congregation. They tend to creep up afterwards and say, 'That "word" was for me, but I didn't like to claim it in front of all these people.' I decided to tell them all about the bishop and the man with the thumb, and how I felt about it at the time, then to give all the 'words' at once, before asking everyone to come forward together. That seemed fine, but supposing they were there and did come forward, what would I do next? 'Lord,' I said, hoping he hadn't given up on me, 'the people I'm taking with me from our own church have even less clue than I do; how shall we pray?' Again the thoughts in my head felt a little like having a conversation with myself: 'The big toe is not the man's main problem; minister as led. The bowel problem is serious. The heart is a physical problem I want to heal. The mouth ulcer is something more than that, and the headache will be healed by laying hands on the back.'

Eventually I shared all this information with Carol who appreciated my fears: 'You'll get loads of mouth ulcers,' she said. 'I've got one myself at present.'

We arrived at ten to eight to find nobody was there except the music group so we slipped into the back room to pray. Almost immediately I found my throat seized up and I couldn't speak. Everyone prayed for me with the laying-on of hands but to no avail until the thought came to me, 'They need to tell it to go – to cast it out.' Before I could whisper it to anyone Greg put his hand on my throat and commanded the affliction to leave in Jesus' name, and as he did I felt a loosening in my throat. Greg then told me I would be fine by the time I got up to speak and I was, not even needing a glass of water.

As I stood at the side during worship a deep peace came over me. The previous six hours had been a mixture of excitement and paralysing fear but now the presence of God took over and I knew all I had was from him. From then on the proceedings felt like the acting out of something already written.

I preached about the God who speaks and those who don't claim their 'words' from him when given, and then gave out my five 'words'. As I gave the 'word' about the toe, Charles looked at his wife in disbelief. While at work he'd banged the toe on his right foot, which had aggravated his ingrowing toe nail problem. He'd called his wife into the bathroom at six o'clock to look at his black and blue nail as he tackled it with scissors. When I gave the 'word' about the toe, a lady was saying to herself, 'I bet there are loads of people here with bad toes.' Two years previously she'd narrowly avoided a very serious bowel operation and had been lucky to survive. She knew the second 'word' when it came was for her.

While all this was going on Jan Coleman was in agony. Two or three times a week she suffered very painful palpitations due to a damaged left ventricle, and she was having one now. This is Jan's account of what happened:

Towards the end of the last chorus before the ministry began, the palpitations started and so did the chest pain which became quite severe – legs were trembling and weakness spread throughout my body. No one else in the church knew that I was actually having an attack then, but a few friends knew of the problem. I slumped into the chair in the hope that no one would notice what was happening to me, also because my physical strength seemed to desert me. When Peter gave the word 'interventricular' it was as if God was calling me by name. I was upset that he had allowed this to happen in church and started to weep. Several people who knew I had this complaint reached towards me and said, 'That's you Jan, go on.' Although my desire was to hide – I didn't want to be exposed – I couldn't fight it and it was not with my own strength that I rose and struggled forward. I was really surprised when I found myself heading towards the front of the church.

I mentioned the mouth ulcer and headache and everyone assembled at the front. There were three people claiming bad headaches so I said to the first man, 'I thought the Lord was saying the headache would be healed by laying hands on the back.' He laughed: the day before a specialist had diagnosed that the severe permanent headache he had was due to a form of rheumatism in the spine.

When people laid hands on Jan Coleman power seemed to go right across her chest and her heart stopped beating. 'I'm dead,' she thought, but realised it was just the palpitations stopping. She hasn't had any since.

The lady for whom Sarah prayed, who was claiming the 'word' about the serious bowel complaint, kindly sent me the following account:

I went to this meeting somewhat wary of the whole basis of the 'Signs and Wonders' ministry, having read a book critical of it. Hence I was not especially expectant.

During the meeting Peter mentioned various ailments which he believed God was revealing to him, as being suffered by particular people present. Some of these were very specific, including one which related to my own condition. Had it been a very vague description I would not have gone forward for prayer.

I went to a side room with a young girl of Peter's team. She said it was the first time she had ever done this sort of thing so, coupled with my own neutral if not negative feelings about the whole procedure, this did not seem to bode well.

She prayed one very short and simple prayer and so did I. To my surprise I did experience a very sudden inrushing of the Spirit, creating a physical sensation I have only experienced twice before in the last fifteen years. It was very powerful though, lasting only a couple of minutes.

Later in the evening, I went to pray with someone who requested prayer, without specifying a problem. I prayed quite calmly and briefly, but there was a violent reaction. The person went into a sort of convulsion, losing control, and several people were needed to restrain her. The minister felt it was some sort of emotional crisis.

It must be said that this lady experienced no physical healing that night.

Charles wrote to me afterwards telling me what happened to him. This is what he said:

I was an original doubting Thomas, I did not believe God spoke to people directly. However, that Thursday night was the start for me to seek a new and much deeper relationship with God. If God cared enough to use my bruised big toe to speak to me, then how much more I needed to listen to him speak directly to me about how I lived my whole life... I did not start to grow as a Christian until I listened to God speak directly to me.

Andrew was the only one to claim a mouth ulcer and he felt he had to come forward after what I'd said in my sermon about claiming God's 'words'.

The man with rheumatism really had a back and neck problem rather than just a severe headache. Following ministry to him on the night he testifies that since then the problem occurs less frequently, though it is still there. However, he now regularly goes for prayer at St Thomas' own healing services.

The experienced eye will probably discern how God seemed to be tackling cynicism and disbelief that night as much as bodies – not least my own. I have heard some people describe so-called 'words' from God as mere psychic impulses which some receive when they are in the same room as the sick or needy person. I can only say that on several other occasions besides this one, God has graciously given me 'words' well in advance of meetings, helping me to avoid the intrusion of my own thoughts. I cannot believe that receiving 'words' at a quarter to two in the afternoon for an evening meeting about people I had never met before could be interpreted as psychic impulses, especially as one person had suffered for over two years, two for several months, one only quite recently, while one had not yet banged his toe when I received the 'word' about it. It must also be noted that those who were healed were prayed for in the name of Jesus and no other name, so it is unlikely the information received had a demonic source. As far as I am concerned God himself validated the claim that he is a God who speaks.

I went home and laughed. I'd just 'done a Wimber' on the congregation. How silly we Christians are in making heroes out of people! God showed up and I had virtually nothing to do. If God hadn't shown up there was nothing I could have done. Ministering in the power of the Holy Spirit is all about asking God to come, and giving him space to do what he wants to do; because our God is one who loves to speak he is unlikely to turn down many invitations.

My experience at Aldridge was for me something of a watershed and I'm delighted to say God has often turned up since. The five 'words' from God seemed to confirm the word of God which declares from beginning to end that God is a God who speaks. Following the advice of Bishop David – to 'do the stuff' – seemed to be working and I found myself moving away from my problems as I entered a new area of ministry.

Notes

1. See David Pytches, *Come Holy Spirit* (Hodder & Stoughton: London, 1985), p 106, no 3 for more teaching on this subject.
2. Stuart Y Blanch, *The World Our Orphanage* (The Epworth

Press: London, 1972), p 7.

3. From a lecture given by John Finney on 'The Changing Church' course at Queen's College, Birmingham, August 1986.

4. In the 1960s Thomas J J Altizer and William Hamilton asserted that God was once alive and is now dead. See 'The Death of God Theologies' in Altizer and Hamilton, *Radical Theology and the Death of God* (Penguin Books, 1968). If the Church preaches a God who once spoke but no longer does, is it surprising someone will conclude, 'God is dead'?

5. A Lion Handbook, *The History of Christianity* (Lion Publishing: Berkhamsted, 1977), pp 480,481.

6. Eifion Evans, *The Welsh Revival of 1904* (Evangelical Press of Wales: Bridgend, 1969), ch 5 etc.

7. Jack Hywel-Davies, *Baptism by Fire* (Hodder & Stoughton: London, 1987).

8. See Paul Yonggi Cho, *Suffering... Why Me?* (Bridge Publishing, Inc: South Plainfield, NJ 07080, 1986), p 92.

9. F F Bruce has written an excellent book on the Canon of Scripture which gives a useful historical survey as well as looking at the relevant theological views. F F Bruce, *The Canon of Scripture* (Chapter House Ltd: Glasgow, 1988).

10. Archbishop Michael Ramsey in his article on the authority of the Bible in *Peake's Commentary* reminds us it is not the experience and teaching of the church which is ultimately authoritative but the word of God: 'Though the Church made the Canon of the New Testament, it was not thereby conferring authority on the Books. Rather was it acknowledging the Books to possess authority in virtue of what they were, and it was an authority supreme and divine.' *Peake's Commentary on the Bible* (Thomas Nelson and Sons Ltd: London, 1962), p 5.

11. See Clark H Pinnock, *The Scripture Principle* (Hodder & Stoughton: London, 1985) for helpful discussion on the relationship between the Bible and the Holy Spirit.

12. Penguin Classics, *The Koran* (Penguin Books: Harmondsworth, 1956), pp 9–12.

13. *The Book of Mormon* (The Church of Jesus Christ of Latter-day Saints: London, 1966). 'The Testimony of Three Witnesses' found at the beginning says, 'And we also know that they

have been translated by the gift and power of God ... and not of man.'

14. Archbishop Michael Ramsey says this *op cit*, p 1:

> The central fact of Christianity is not a Book but a Person – Jesus Christ, himself described as the Word of God. The books of the Old Testament came to have authority within the Church because Jesus Christ set the seal of his own authority upon them and interpreted them as preparing the way for himself. The books of the New Testament came to have authority because the Church recognised in them the testimony of the apostles to Jesus Christ. It is the relation of the books to the person which makes them very different from a collection of oracles such as itself provides the basis for a religion. Indeed, both in the Jewish Church and in the Christian Church, the religion preceded the making and the canonisation of the books.

15. It is always important to give the 'word' God gives you. Twice we gave out the 'word' 'waterworks' as from God and on both occasions people with a bladder problem claimed them. On a third occasion, however, our organist gave a 'word' about a technician with problems connected to waterworks. This time the waterworks were of a different kind: the 'word' was for an employee of the Severn Trent Water Board.

16. Pytches, *op cit*, p 145. David lists various other physical phenomena which sometimes accompany a movement of the Holy Spirit.

17. *ibid*, pp 106–107 for comments on 'knowing' a 'word' from God.

3

Prayer

Once I had rediscovered the God who speaks, prayer became an exciting new adventure in seeking God. Our group of young people continued to meet with me on Sunday nights and these little gatherings became for us an experiment in prayer. We continued praying for people and needs, petitioning God in the traditional way, but we also made room for God to come and speak, minister or do whatever he wanted to do. We would sit, eyes closed, welcome him and then wait.

On one occasion we began waiting upon God at about nine-thirty in the evening and gradually those present experienced the power of the Holy Spirit. Some felt heat, a few started shaking gently and one young man slid off his chair and on to the floor where he stayed, beaming, for some time. People laid hands on one another and together we shared God's love. By ten o'clock everything had died down and the meeting dispersed as the youngsters and leaders made their way home; all, that is, except Jo.

As everyone else gathered their belongings and left, Jo remained seated, eyes closed, with her hands together on her lap. Her parents arrived ready to take her home in the car, but had to wait as they sensed with me that something more important than an early night's sleep was taking place. We tried laying on hands and blessing what the Father was doing, but nothing we did made any difference, so eventually we just sat, watched and waited.

At ten-thirty I asked God quietly what was happening and he told me that Jo was having a vision and not to interfere. Five minutes later her hands separated, the palms turned upwards and her arms very slowly lifted up. Her left hand began to shake and one solitary tear made its way down her face. At five to eleven I felt God telling me to be prepared with pen and paper to write down what Jo had seen, and at eleven o'clock she opened her eyes.

'What's been happening, Jo?' I asked gently.

'You've no idea,' she began falteringly. 'You've no idea how much God loves us.'

It seemed strange that a sixteen-year-old girl should be saying this to a middle-aged vicar, but it was true. This is what we wrote down:

> At first it was as if I was physically bolted to the floor. Then I felt I was being lifted up – transported past pillars of silver. I could see the colours of the rainbow and there was a very bright light around all the time. I saw the side of a golden throne, but the light seemed to prevent me seeing the whole of it. There were steps leading up to the throne and in my vision I fell down – it was so powerful. I was still in the light when I saw through the shape of an eye the cross and Jesus. The feeling of love was tremendous. God's love and power was overwhelming; it just cannot be described adequately.

It must be said that Jo is not a very emotional person. She had struggled with God all day as nothing ever happened to her and was amazed when I later showed her the rainbows of Ezekiel and Revelation: she did not know the rainbow she saw was in Scripture. When her friends at school asked her the next day how she had spent the weekend, they did not expect to be told that Jo had spent an hour and a half with God, nor that it was the most exciting hour and a half of her weekend.

This new experiment in prayer was beginning to put my

old Christian life in the shade. Prayer had previously been a chore and a lifeless discipline, bringing along my agenda and shopping list, saying 'Amen' and getting up to go without waiting for an answer. But now I was beginning to discover the thrill and the excitement of prayer in the answer.

The gospels tell us that Jesus himself experienced this in his Father's response while praying: 'As he was praying, heaven was opened and the Holy Spirit descended on him in bodily form like a dove. And a voice came from heaven: "You are my Son, whom I love; with you I am well pleased"' (Lk 3:21–22).

'As he was praying, the appearance of his face changed, and his clothes became as bright as a flash of lightning ... A voice came from the cloud, saying, "This is my Son, whom I have chosen; listen to him"' (Lk 9:29,35).

'"Now my heart is troubled, and what shall I say? 'Father, save me from this hour'? No, it was for this very reason I came to this hour. Father, glorify your name!' Then a voice came from heaven, "I have glorified it, and will glorify it again"' (Jn 12:27–28).

And whatever Jesus did yesterday his disciples do today: 'Peter began and explained everything to them precisely as it had happened: "I was in the city of Joppa praying, and in a trance I saw a vision"' (Acts 11:4–5).

Then Paul said: 'When I returned to Jerusalem and was praying at the temple, I fell into a trance and saw the Lord speaking' (Acts 22:17–18).

Sometimes when God speaks he confirms the truth of Scripture by blessing us and assuring us of his love. This is the relationship the Father of love and mercy wants to have with his children and there are moments when God desires to spend quality time with us, listening and talking, sharing and affirming as any loving father enjoys doing with his children. This may happen as we worship, read the Bible, pray or wait silently in his presence, as Jo did. It could be said this is the most important aspect of hearing God speak; it helps us to know God and to enjoy him for ever.

Often we are so busy doing, we never have any time for being. When I look for God it is normally the hand of God rather than his face that I seek: what he can do for me rather than who he is. Prayer is useful; it can get things done. The purpose of prayer is life. But when I read in the gospels of Jesus at prayer he seems to have such an intimate relationship with his Father that everything is turned upside down. For Jesus the purpose of life seems to be prayer. If the end of this life is the gateway to an eternity spent enjoying God face to face and worshipping him, then maybe prayer is not the necessary chore that leads to a more fulfilled and 'successful' Christian life, but the ultimate goal towards which we are all striving. Experiencing God in prayer can be the first-fruit and foretaste of the glory that is yet to come.

Edie Matthews was one in a million. She had suffered as a child from infantile rheumatoid arthritis and as a result was a small person – not a dwarf because her body was perfectly proportioned, but even when she was seven years old she could run under a table without ducking. At twenty-one she was confined to a wheelchair in which she spent the rest of her life. For her last thirty years she lived with her friend Edith who was also confined to a wheelchair, and together they worked, lived and looked after each other.

I used to take communion to them once a month until the City Council gave us a minibus with a tail-lift and then we were able to bring them regularly to church. At the age of sixty-seven Edie Matthews was admitted to hospital in some discomfort and I visited her on the ward. Wearing my clerical collar I was able to go in twenty minutes before visiting hours and after a brief conversation I made an offer to pray with her, which was gratefully received. At this point I felt rather awkward: it was a very long ward full of patients and the visitors were due in soon so I hesitatingly put a hand on her forehead and asked God to do all he wanted to do.

It took me by surprise when the power of the Lord came on Edie. She was already seated in a chair, but now her head went back, her arms went up, she started shaking and her face began to glow. I looked furtively around, but no one else seemed to be noticing so I just sat it out. 'Bless you, Lord; pain be gone; keep doing all you're doing,' I kept whispering, and anything else which came into my head. This went on for fifteen minutes but despite my fears we were totally uninterrupted; I think the nurses were delayed and late in letting the hordes in.

When she came round Edie was beaming. 'Edith believes in this sort of thing,' she said, 'but I don't ... didn't'.

'How do you feel?' I asked.

'A million dollars,' she said. 'The pain's all gone. You know, Peter,' she carried on, 'I reckon dying must be like this; it's glorious.'

I was thrilled, and encouraged her to let me pray for her again the next time I visited her. Edie was not used to the lay-ing-on of hands.

The hospital diagnosed a narrowed and restricted bowel as the problem, advised against an operation and sent Edie home with pain-killers. It was not their fault they made a mistake: Edie had been used to pain all her life and no one knew how seriously ill she was. The real problem was cancer at an advanced stage.

A little while later Edie was re-admitted in pain to the hos-pital, where I visited her and prayed again, but by now she was more heavily drugged and nothing visible occurred. Three weeks after my first hospital visit I had a little nudge from the Lord. I was in my study at about lunch-time and sensed I ought to ring the ward and find out how Edie was doing. The sister who answered told me she'd had a very good morning and there was nothing to worry about at pres-ent. I gave her my phone number and told her who I was as Edie did not have any relatives nearby.

'Win some, lose some,' I thought and went over to church to prepare for an afternoon meeting. I was sure God had told me to ring but it seemed on this occasion I was wrong. I had been gone only ten minutes when Carol came running over from the vicarage to find me. 'The sister went to check Edie after you rang,' she said. 'She's deteriorating fast.'

I went straight away, collecting Edith and her wheelchair on the way. When we reached the ward Edie's relative had just arrived from Essex and all together we went in to see her behind the curtains. Edith held her hand and a little tear of recognition came on to her friend's cheek. I laid my hand on her forehead, saying, 'Come, Holy Spirit and do all that you want to do.' As I was saying this short prayer Edie died. Edith squeezed her hand and said, 'There's no wheelchairs in heaven Edie.'

I believe Edie was feeling a million dollars as she died, and still is. As I had prayed the first time, three weeks before, she experienced the presence of God, and as I prayed this second time she experienced the nearer presence of God. The thrill of prayer is in the answer. In prayer we hear God and receive God and know God. The purpose of life is God.

But even so prayer that waits expectantly until the voice of God breaks through is prayer that cannot fall short of action. Jesus emerged after forty days in the wilderness, where he presumably prayed as well as fasted, full of power and authority to defeat the works of Satan (Lk 4:36). I believe the key to this power and authority was not his divinity, as some suppose, but his prayer relationship with the Father and his obedience to him.[1] Like the Roman centurion he was not so much a man *in* authority as a man *under* authority (Mt 8:9). If this is so then we can learn from Jesus, seek to follow him, and expect to minister as he did in the power of the Holy Spirit with the authority of God the Father.

Power

There are a number of phrases in Scripture which suggest Jesus had human limitations. He was hungry (Mt 4:2), tired (Jn 4:6), thirsty (Jn 19:28), sleepy (Mt 8:24), sorrowful, troubled (Mt 26:37) and tempted (Mk 1:13). He wept (Lk 19:41), sweated in anguish (Lk 22:44) and on one occasion

at least, power went out from him (Mk 5:30; Lk 8:46).
Eventually he died (Jn 19:33) and blood and water flowed
from his side (Jn 19:34).

But if Jesus was fully human and to some degree limited,
it is right to ask where his supernatural power came from.
How did he still the storm, for example?

'[Jesus] got up, rebuked the wind and said to the waves,
"Quiet! Be still!" Then the wind died down and it was completely calm' (Mk 4:39).

There are indications in the gospels that on occasions
Jesus' Father provided supernatural power by his Holy
Spirit: in Matthew 12:28 Jesus says, 'If I drive out demons
by the Spirit of God, then the kingdom of God has come
upon you.' In Luke 5:17 it says, 'The power of the Lord was
present for [Jesus] to heal the sick.' Although Jesus drove out
demons and healed the sick in his own name, the power
seems to have come from God. Jesus explains it in John
5:19, 'I tell you the truth, the Son can do nothing by himself;
he can do only what he sees his Father doing.'

In John's Gospel we read of a Jesus who was 'with God in
the beginning. Through him all things were made; without
him nothing was made that has been made' (Jn 1:2–3).
From the lips of Jesus we hear the declaration, 'before
Abraham was born, I am!' (Jn 8:58), and towards the end of
the Gospel Jesus accepts Thomas' confession, 'My Lord and
my God!' (Jn 20:28,29). And yet it is in John's Gospel that
Jesus' dependency on his Father is most clearly seen. Jesus
says, 'By myself I can do nothing' (Jn 5:30a) and, 'I have
shown you many great miracles from the Father' (Jn
10:32).[2]

I believe there is sufficient negative evidence in all the Gospels pertaining to things Jesus could not do, and sufficient
positive evidence in John's Gospel of Jesus' dependency
upon his Father to agree with David Pytches when he says
that Jesus 'voluntarily and deliberately laid aside his
omnipotence'.[3] It is impossible to say what natural spiritual
power a man who has never sinned possesses (1 Pet 2:21–

22), and I would in no way want to say Jesus was spiritually impotent, but it does seem reasonably certain from Scripture that when Jesus became flesh he was no longer all-powerful.

At the very least I think we can say Jesus could do no mighty work *apart* from the Father, and was dependent upon him. But this is sufficient to conclude that in the realm of spiritual power Jesus was different from us in degree and not kind, thus presenting us with the ideal model to copy. Through Jesus we have access to the same heavenly Father who pours out the same Holy Spirit on all believers.

This argument is supported by the fact that Jesus' disciples were able to do all that he had been able to do even when he was no longer with them.[4] They healed the sick (Acts 3:16), cast out demons (Acts 5:16), raised the dead (Acts 9:41), escaped from prison (Acts 16:26), and survived snake bites (Acts 28:3–6). It is also worth noting that Jesus was not the only one to walk on water (Mt 14:29).

Although Jesus did not lay aside his nature or his character it does seem that to some degree he laid aside his power when he came to earth. He had human limitations, was dependent on his Father, and his disciples were able to do many of the mighty works he had done. We might even ask to what extent Jesus could have claimed to be fully human if he was still omnipotent. And this conclusion is very important. It means in the realm of power we can model ourselves on the example of Christ, and expect to do the things he did in the power of the Holy Spirit (Jn 14:12).

We have not yet raised the dead or walked on water but from time to time we have been able to witness God's power being released among us.

Peter Reed, once our church warden, recently retired from work. For some months he was sorely troubled with a trapped sciatic nerve in his back, and torn muscles. The doctor, physiotherapist and osteopath did all they could and the medical verdict said his body might or might not heal itself. In the meantime pain-killers were prescribed on a regular basis.

We prayed for Peter three or four times when he requested it and each time as I laid my hand on the affected area he and I felt great heat. Asking God to come and heal was rather like switching on a sun-ray lamp and on one occasion Peter felt healed for two days before the pain returned. I think he became too embarrassed to keep asking us to pray and we didn't like to push ourselves too much, being British. As a result the pain grew worse and worse. For three months Peter's wife Peggy put his shoes on for him and the list of things he was unable to do for himself grew longer.

No one outside the family knew how bad life had become until one Saturday he cancelled his seat on a coach to a Christian day conference because he was too ill to sit for any length of time. On the Sunday morning I saw Peter bent over double in pain trying to put the communion vessels out for the nine o'clock service. He was grateful for my offer to pray for him afterwards.

Susan, a member of our healing team who was present at the service, joined me in laying hands on Peter's back and we asked God to send the power of his Holy Spirit upon him to heal him. On this occasion we did not have time to discover if the 'sun-ray lamp' came on or not because within seconds Peter fell over in the power of the Spirit and landed in the bishop's chair. He was positioned horizontally with his back resting on the edge of the chair, making it impossible for us to keep laying hands on the affected area. I simply said, 'Lord, we bless you for what you are doing and ask you to go on doing it.' Almost immediately the right leg started dancing by itself as if someone had hold of the foot and was pulling it or jerking it in an attempt to lengthen it or release a trapped nerve. Susan and I saw the leg being jolted without either of us touching it, for nearly fifteen minutes.

I reminded God after a while of the approaching eleven o'clock service but waited patiently until he'd finished. Slowly Peter came round, stood up and then walked about as if he were trying on a new pair of shoes. 'That's better,' he said, as if he'd just swopped a pair of size sevens for a pair of

size eights. Peter knew nothing of the dancing leg, but
testified to a feeling of extreme cold going all down the
affected right side. That was nearly two years ago and ever
since then he has done up his own shoes, dug the church gar-
dens, stopped taking the tablets and felt no pain.

I do not know why Peter felt heat on some occasions and
cold on another, nor why he was healed at the fifth attempt.[5]
Susan and I do not have power to heal the sick and we didn't
feel power when we came into church nor when we left it.
All I know is that when we prayed the power of the Lord was
present to heal and Peter was healed. I suggest it was the
same power to heal that was present when Jesus healed the
sick (Lk 5:17).

Authority

A servant ministers with his master's authority when he
hears his master's voice and obeys his commands. It appears
Jesus laid aside his omniscience as well as his omnipotence
when he became a man and needed to hear his Father and
obey him in order to minister with his authority.

There are a number of references in the first three Gospels
which suggest Jesus was not all-knowing.

As a child he 'grew in wisdom and stature, and in favour
with God and men' (Lk 2:52). As an adult he responded to
being told things in a spontaneous way. When he heard
what the centurion said, 'he was astonished' (Mt 8:10);
when told of John the Baptist's death, 'he withdrew by boat
privately to a solitary place' (Mt 14:13); 'When Jesus saw
that he [a teacher of the law] had answered wisely, he said to
him, 'You are not far from the kingdom of God' (Mk
12:34). I cannot believe Jesus was pretending or play-acting,
but rather reacting humanly to things he was hearing for the
first time.

In ministry situations Jesus often asked people questions.
He wanted to know how many loaves were available (Mt
15:34); who touched him and was healed (Mk 5:30,32);

whether the man's eyes were healed (Mk 8:23–25); how long a boy had been demonised (Mk 9:16–21); and the name of another demon (Lk 8:29–31).

In death Jesus cried out, 'My God, my God, why have you forsaken me?' (Mk 15:34), and although some people claim to know the date of the consummation of the age Jesus is not one of them. 'No-one knows about that day or hour, not even the angels in heaven, nor the Son, but only the Father' (Mt 24:36).

Each verse on its own may not be totally convincing, but cumulatively I believe there is a strong case for arguing that the Jesus presented in the first three Gospels did not know everything. The people certainly treated him as one who did not know everything. Someone told him, 'Your mother and brothers are standing outside, wanting to speak to you' (Mt 12:47). The Twelve treated him the same way: 'When the apostles returned, they reported to Jesus what they had done' (Lk 9:10).

On the other hand there are many situations when Jesus did know things that ordinary human beings would not have known: 'Take the first fish you catch,' Jesus said to Peter, 'and you will find a four-drachma coin' (Mt 17:27).

If Jesus did not know everything, but to some extent laid aside his omniscience, then it is fair to ask how he knew about the coin in the fish. Just as John's Gospel contains hints of Jesus' dependency on his Father for supernatural power, so it seems that Jesus is also dependent on his Father for supernatural knowledge. He teaches what the Father teaches him (Jn 3:34; 7:16; 8:26,28; 12:49–50), and does what the Father commands him (Jn 10:18; 14:31).

The source of Jesus' supernatural knowledge appears to have been his Father. It seems reasonable to conclude from the evidence in the Gospels of Jesus' limited knowledge and reliance upon God that he did not possess supernatural knowledge independently from his Father. This being the case we can expect the disciples of Jesus, who have access to the same Father through the Holy Spirit, also to receive supernatural knowledge from God, and this is what we find in the Acts of the Apostles. After Jesus had ascended and the Spirit had come, Peter knew about the deceit of Ananias and Sapphira (Acts 5:1–10); another Ananias knew about Saul (Acts 9:10–19); Cornelius knew about Peter and vice versa (Acts 10); and Agabus predicted a famine (Acts 11:27,28) and the arrest of Paul (Acts 21:10,11). If Jesus and his disciples received supernatural knowledge from God when they prayed, waited, listened and watched, then there is no logical reason why we who are also filled with the Holy Spirit, should not expect to be able to do the same from time to time (Jn 14:26).

One Saturday morning as Kay (not her real name) prayed, God said to her, 'Go into town to the Christian Literature Crusade bookshop and there you will meet Peter Lawrence. He is the one to help you with your problems.' Kay does not go to our church, but I had met her a few times and she had been to several meetings at which I was speaking. Kay is a lovely Christian lady, but suffers from shyness. She needed quite a lot of courage to obey this prompting, especially as she didn't think she had any problems at the time.

The strange thing was that I hardly ever go to a bookshop in Birmingham because I have a friend in the trade, another one who works at a Christian bookshop, and several who work in town and are prepared to do my shopping for me. I hadn't been to CLC for quite a while and whenever I do go it is never on a Saturday morning; having more flexible working hours than most people, clergymen do not normally shop in Birmingham on Saturdays when it is crowded. But on this occasion my father-in-law who lives in Spain was staying with us and wanted a particular book. We spent some time in four other shops and the Post Office and five minutes in CLC. Kay had only been there a few minutes when we arrived and was almost too startled to speak when I said, 'Hello.'

From then on Kay came to some of our extra-mural activities which we ran outside normal church hours enabling local people to worship in their own church and still come to us with special needs. On one occasion as we waited on God Kay fell over in the power of the Spirit, later testified to being healed of an addiction to chocolate and, following further ministry, went on to shed over two stones in weight. At another time she began to shake and as people laid hands on her a goitre around the neck which was visible to all completely disappeared. All those who were around Kay at the time actually saw it go as they prayed. Such an encounter with the Holy Spirit encouraged Kay to seek further help privately and as a multiplicity of demons left her so did a number of other physical problems – many connected with the thyroid gland.

Kay certainly did have some of her problems sorted out although on most occasions I was not the one to minister to her. Nevertheless, when Kay prayed she heard God and when she obeyed his voice God's word was fulfilled.

Jesus received supernatural power and knowledge from God the Father through the Holy Spirit and was able to minister with God's authority by doing what the Father was doing and saying what the Father was saying. Jesus said the same power and authority would come to us through faith in him as we pray in his name (Jn 14:12–14).

The prayer of faith

Asking, waiting, listening and receiving is the way we receive supernatural power and knowledge; the prayer of faith offered in trust and obedience is the way we release that power and bring the will of God to fruition. This is the next step in the adventure of prayer: it is a move from the passive 'receiving' to the active 'doing'.

Praying in faith is not believing hard enough that something is going to happen, but praying what God has already told us to pray at the appointed place and time. It is exercising faith in God and not in ourselves, asking what he has told us to ask and not what we have decided to ask. It is not praying, 'If it be your will,' which only expresses faith in the 'God who hears', but praying, 'Your will be done,' after he has told us his will, expressing faith in both the God who hears and the God who speaks. It is cashing in the victory won in the quiet time and always goes hand in hand with obedience. Often it is praying in the situation as opposed to praying at home or in church.

James 5:15 says, 'The prayer offered in faith will make the sick person well.' The meaning of sentences like this in Scripture is not always obvious, but in this instance James goes on to give us an example. If we look carefully at this example we will be able to interpret Scripture with Scripture, and see the prayer of faith in action.

> Elijah was a man just like us. He prayed earnestly that it would not rain, and it did not rain on the land for three and a half years. Again he prayed, and the heavens gave rain, and the earth produced its crops (Jas 5:17–18).

Elijah is a man who offered the prayer of faith, and 1 Kings 18 tells us exactly what this means: 'The word of the Lord came to Elijah: "Go and present yourself to Ahab, and I will send rain on the land." So Elijah went (vv 1–2). Later Elijah receives a 'word' from God as he heard the 'sound of a heavy rain' (18:41). The whole of Elijah's lifestyle is to do and to pray what God had already told him to do and to pray. He prayed for rain because God told him he was going to send rain. The prayer is exercising faith in what God has said.

This can be seen even more clearly in his battle with the prophets of Baal:

> Elijah stepped forward and prayed: 'O Lord, God of Abraham, Isaac and Israel, let it be known today that you are God in Israel and that I am your servant *and have done all these things at your command.* Answer me, O Lord, answer me, so these people will know that you, O Lord, are God, and that you are turning their hearts back again' (1 Kings 18:36–37, my italics).

Then the fire of the Lord fell.

I have heard some people say we should challenge people of other faiths to a contest like Elijah did with the prophets of Baal. I suspect they have missed the whole point. Elijah did it because God told him to do it, not because it was a good idea. He says, 'I am your servant and have done all these things at your command.' Elijah prayed for fire as an act of faith in what God had already said he would do. The fire fell because God said it would if Elijah obeyed and asked him to send it. The prayer of faith is not one when I decide what I would like and then believe it hard enough so that God has no choice but to obey what I have chosen should happen. The prayer of faith is praying what God has told me to pray. Jehoshaphat did this with praise (2 Chron 20); Daniel did this with intercession (Dan 9:2–3); Ananias did this with the laying-on of hands (Acts 9:17); and Jesus did this with thanksgiving (Jn 11:41–42).

The raising of Lazarus in John 11 is a good example of the prayer of faith. Jesus is told, 'The one you love is sick' (v 3). Immediately he responds by saying, 'This sickness will not end in death' (v 4), and stays put for two days. On the way his disciples do not know Lazarus has died, but Jesus does (vv 11–14). Clearly Jesus is in possession of supernatural knowledge and from what we have already argued we can assume his Father has told him what has happened, what he must do and what is going to happen. This is born out by Jesus' prayer at the tomb: 'Father, I thank you that you have heard me. I knew that you always hear me, but I said this for the benefit of the people standing here, that they may believe that you sent me' (vv 41–42). Although it is a 'thanking' prayer and Elijah's was an 'asking' prayer, this is also a prayer of faith. Faith that God is going to do what he has already said he will do. Jesus' command, 'Lazarus, come out!' is said in obedience to what the Father has told him to do, and God backs up Jesus' act with the might of heaven.

I find the prayer of faith is called for most often when I am ministering in public. Elijah prayed for fire in front of others and Jesus had a crowd in front of Lazarus' tomb. Jesus could easily have sneaked into Bethany at night to test out his theory alone and arrived with Lazarus at breakfast, but God wanted to release his power through Jesus in front of others, even though it led to a cross (Jn 11:46–53).

I must confess I find praying the prayer of faith publicly causes me more anxiety and sleepless nights than it should. At such times I find Jesus' sweat in Gethsemane most comforting.

Recently the Reverend Teddy Saunders, our team leader, asked me to lead a time of ministry at a church in East London, South Africa. We flew in on the Sunday morning rather tired and went to bed. 'Lord,' I said, 'I've come several thousand miles to be here; what shall I do?'

'Go to sleep,' he said. 'You'll wake up at four o'clock and I'll tell you then what to do.'

My tiredness was such that I obeyed, although I did set my alarm for 4.30 pm, just in case.

Encouragingly, as I roused from sleep, I noticed it was just four o'clock and in a drowsy half-awake frame of mind thoughts began drifting into my head. 'Ask me to come. Get the shepherds [elders] out at the front to watch. I'll come in power for fifteen minutes.' He then gave me twelve 'words' for healing and told me how to organise it and what to teach as it was happening.

Teddy preached until five past eight and then after a brief preparation I asked God the Father through his Son Jesus to send the power of his Holy Spirit upon us as we stood and waited. This was a prayer of faith allied to obedience. I was doing what I thought the Father had told me to do and praying what I thought the Father was telling me to pray. God came in power: there were about four hundred present and after ten minutes it looked as though less than half were still standing. They didn't fall gently, looking round to find a comfortable spot on which to land, they were virtually all pole-axed. It was like standing at the end of a bowling alley.

I realise that not everyone is familiar with falling in the Spirit and indeed that night I had to minister to one young girl who was worried because she'd seen her father fall over. I asked the Spirit to come on her, he came, she felt him and realised the experience was a good one and not a bad one. The night Jo had her vision Stephen fell to the floor from a sitting position and beamed all over his face. When Peter was relieved of his back trouble and Kay her addiction they both went from vertical to horizontal under the power of the Spirit and were healed.

It is a biblical phenomenon, although many of the instances are unclear as to whether the going down is a voluntary or involuntary action. John 18:6 and Acts 9:4 seem involuntary and it is worth pondering on what happened physically to Peter and Paul as they were praying and 'fell into a trance' (Acts 10:10; 22:17). George Whitefield and Charles and John Wesley also experienced something similar. In his journals John records this from 1st January 1739: 'About three in the morning, as we were continuing instant in prayer, the power of God came mightily upon us, insomuch that many cried out for exceeding joy, and many fell to the ground.'[6] Basically ministry in the power of the Spirit is not a spectator sport and if it has not happened to you, ask those to whom it has. I have twice fallen and once shaken under the Spirit and the inner experience was glorious.[7]

That night in East London the falling in the Spirit was a preliminary activity for the healings which followed. Some found as they fell they were filled or anointed to pray for others and some were being prepared by God to claim 'words' of healing for themselves. When something like that happens and people receive it as from God then faith and expectancy rise and more of his purposes can be fulfilled. The people of East London were tremendously receptive of all that God was doing and had been greatly loved and prepared for this meeting by their Pastor, Chris Venter.

When we do as we are told God backs up our act and the

works of God accompany the 'words' of God. God had said, 'If you ask me to come, I will come in power.' When I stood in front of four hundred people and prayed for God to come, it was a prayer of faith and obedience. God had told me what was going to happen and what to pray, and as I prayed it in fear and trepidation, wondering all the time if I'd made it up out of my own vivid imagination, I was exercising faith in God. The same was true as I gave 'words' from God, though faith had grown a little by then as the first stage seemed to confirm it was God who was speaking that night. He only needs a grain of mustard seed to move a mountain when the idea is his and not ours and our faith is in God and not in ourselves.[8]

As Jesus prayed, God spoke to him. As God spoke he received love and joy, power and direction, authority and knowledge. As Jesus prayed he received guidance on how to pray and strength to do it. As Jesus prayed in the Garden of Gethsemane he already knew his Father's will which he had declared at the Last Supper. His cry, 'Not my will, but yours be done' (Lk 22:42) was the greatest prayer of faith and obedience of all time. Because I believe Jesus was fully human, I feel we can learn to pray as Jesus prayed. Fortunately, we will not have to die for the sins of the whole world as he did, but the same power that defeated the prince of this world on the cross will be released through us to overcome whatever works of darkness we face today.

When we pray, wait and listen, as Jesus and his disciples did, we can expect God to respond, and hearing God speak can help us to pray in faith. Praying helps us to hear God, and hearing God helps us to pray.

Notes

1. In learning to minister as Jesus did the christological question is important. Many Christians assume Jesus did miracles because he was God rather than perfect man anointed with the power of the Holy Spirit, and I believe this needs to be thought

through most carefully.

For those unfamiliar with the historical debate, the article by George S Hendry in *A Dictionary of Christian Theology*, edited by Alan Richardson (SCM Press Ltd: London, 1969) gives a good survey of most of the views and supplies a helpful book list on the subject. I also found *Jesus and the Spirit* by James D G Dunn (SCM Press Ltd: London, 1975) quite helpful.

In arguing that Jesus laid aside his omnipotence and omniscience I must make it clear that I am not advocating the 'kenotic' theory (based on the Greek phrase *heauton ekenosen* in Philippians 2:7, which means literally 'he emptied himself'), which says Jesus completely emptied himself of all his divinity and became only a man. I believe Jesus is fully God and fully man.

Nevertheless, in seeking to minister as Jesus ministered I have found it helpful to ask what the New Testament says about Jesus enabling me to decide in what ways it is right to use Jesus as a model to follow.

2. Raymond Brown says, 'In implicit harmony with the Synoptic tradition, John thinks of the Son acting with the power of the Father in performing his miracles.'

   Raymond E Brown, *The Gospel According to John (i-xii)* (Geoffrey Chapman Ltd: London, 1966), p 526.

3. David Pytches, *Come Holy Spirit* (Hodder & Stoughton: London, 1985), p 47.

4. For a scholarly examination of the way the New Testament sees the early church as a continuation of Jesus' ministry — especially exorcism — see *Christ Triumphant* by Graham Twelftree (Hodder and Stoughton: London, 1985).

5. When I have shared this story some people have been worried with the experience of cold I describe and wonder if it may indicate a demonic healing. Professor Roy Peacock is the author of many scientific papers and in his Christian book *Foolish To Be Wise* describes how God healed him of a fractured skull. A 'line of cold' spread all along the crack for two minutes, after which the fracture was healed. Analysing it scientifically afterwards, he concluded that if a bone was healed quickly the process would be energy-consumptive not energy-productive and the experience would therefore be of coldness rather than heat.

(Roy Peacock, *Foolish To Be Wise* (Kingsway Publications: Eastbourne, 1985), pp 128–129.)

6. John Wesley, *The Journal of John Wesley* (Lion Publishing: Tring, 1966), p 55, Monday 1st January 1739.

7. The manifestations which often occur when God moves in power are well aired by the psychiatrist John White in his book *When The Spirit Comes With Power* (Hodder & Stoughton: London, 1988).

8. In Matthew 21:21–22 Jesus says, 'If you believe you will receive whatever you ask for in prayer.' This is the quotation most likely to be interpreted, 'If I believe I am going to have whatever I ask for, I will receive it.' James 1:5–8 is similar to the Matthew reference, but James himself says in 4:2–3, 'When you ask, you do not receive, because you ask with wrong motives.'

    Can Jesus' words therefore really mean that if I ask to win the National Lottery and believe I'm going to win it, I will? These are the conditions for asking, to be found in some of the other verses of Scripture: 'Ask, seek, knock' (Mt 7:7; Lk 11:9); 'in my name' (Mt 18:19–20; Jn 14:13–14; 16:23–24); 'if you remain in me' (Jn 15:7); 'if you do what I command' (Jn 15:14–16); if 'we obey his commands and do what pleases him' (1 Jn 3:22); and 'if we ask anything according to his will' (1 Jn 5:14–15).

    The key seems to be asking 'in Jesus' name', and what this means is spelled out in John 15:7,14–16: 'If you remain in me and my words remain in you ... If you do what I command ... Then the Father will give you whatever you ask in my name.' I think when all the Bible verses are looked at together and Scripture is allowed to interpret Scripture, then the overwhelming evidence is that we will receive what we ask for only when our faith is 'in Christ', 'in his name', and 'according to his will'. This is why we need to recognise God's voice and obey his commands before we can begin to pray in faith. There is a distinct difference between faith in Christ and faith in our own minds; between the power of the Holy Spirit and the power of positive thinking.

4

Proclaiming the Kingdom

Like so many others, Bill found church dull, boring and largely irrelevant. His wife Margaret is a committed Christian and member of our congregation who prayed regularly for her husband and family to be converted, but with little apparent success. While Margaret went to church Bill stayed at home.

One day Bill became ill, was admitted to hospital for major surgery and I visited him. He seemed pleased to see me and very grateful for the prayers, especially those said for him in church which Margaret had told him about. It didn't seem right to lay hands on him or pray in his presence at the time, so I assured Bill of our love, support and prayers and kept my word. As well as praying for him in meetings quite a few others prayed regularly for him in private and in due course, with nothing spectacular happening, Bill recovered.

At about the same time Bill's business went rapidly downhill and eventually he was declared bankrupt. Unemployment with its loss of dignity and sense of failure left him feeling very empty, so when Margaret nagged Bill for the umpteenth time to come to church, he came.

Evening Prayer was not Bill's scene; he was very uncomfortable with it. He sat still and tried to be good. The only thing he heard was my announcement about an optional time of ministry after the service. We chatted briefly when

Evening Prayer ended and in the course of conversation he asked, 'What happens at this time of ministry?' I was slightly embarrassed, struggling to find the right response, when suddenly three words of Scripture came into my mind. 'Come and see,' I said and, out of curiosity, he joined us in the side-chapel.

There were about fifteen present when I asked the Holy Spirit to come and minister to us. Never having experienced anything like this before, Bill didn't know what to expect, but he saw others standing, eyes closed, hands held out, and did the same. Slowly he became very hot and began to perspire as his hands started shaking from side to side. Bill found he couldn't stop the shaking so he relaxed into this new experience until eventually the sensation began to leave him.

'What was that?' he asked afterwards.

'That was Jesus,' I explained.

'Do you do this every week?'

'Yes,' I said, as that was then our regular practice, 'and you'll be most welcome any time.'

'I didn't like the service much,' he said apologetically, 'but I'll have some more of that.'

Bill came again and again. On one occasion he crashed to the floor and slid under a television we had on a table in the side chapel. About a quarter of an hour later he got to his feet positively glowing. But an even bigger turning point came in his life the night a young married man fell to the floor face down.

As the man lay on the floor demons began tormenting him and he shouted out. I offered to take him out privately, but he said, 'No. Do it here. I don't mind. I just want to be rid of them.'

So we did, with Bill and others watching, like Jesus had done. I commanded the demons in Jesus' name to come out. Eventually three appeared to leave, one at a time, through the mouth. This seems to be a common way for them to leave, either with dry-retching, a cough, a burp or as phlegm, and this occasion was no exception. All who were there could see the manifestations of the demons as they came out, and a change in the young man's face, which finally became very peaceful as the ministry concluded and God blessed him.

From then on Bill read the Bible, attended Bible classes, was confirmed in the church and now leads Bible studies, prayer times and ministry sessions in his own home. He also comes regularly to Evening Prayer and sings in the robed choir. Bill is getting on for sixty, but he's like a child who has suddenly discovered a whole new world and just can't get enough of Jesus. At a recent mid-week meeting we came out of church to find that his car had been stolen. 'Praise the Lord it was mine and not someone else's,' he said. 'I'd have hated anyone not to come back because of this.' It is interesting to note that Bill has not shaken or fallen under the Spirit's power for some time now: it seems that in Bill's case this kind of power from God came on him specifically as part of his conversion experience.

Bill accepted the Lord Jesus Christ as his personal Saviour after experiencing physical healing, the power of the Holy Spirit in his body, power over demons and the word of God that explained it all to him. All of this was a proclamation of the kingdom of God in word, deed, sign and power that encouraged Bill to be born again of the Spirit. He was saved by responding to the word of God in faith but it was the deeds, signs and demonstration of power that opened Bill up to the word and gave him the faith to believe in Jesus.[1]

I was brought up in a church that excelled in preaching the word of God and caring for people with good deeds, but the signs and demonstrations of power which accompanied Jesus' ministry were never experienced in our fellowship. I was sustained in my faith by reading Christian biographies and hearing stories of the great things God did for others in other places at other times. Since then I have constantly struggled in the secular age to convince people of the claims of Christ through 'word and deed', not realising that for most of my life I have been presenting only half the gospel. Many of the churches where I have worshipped find great difficulty in reaching men for Christ following the traditional 'word and deed only' method, and Bill assures me that he would not have been reached either if he had not experienced the power of God for himself. Evangelism has never come easy to me, but since Bill's conversion we have been thrilled to see other men coming to faith in similar ways.[2]

'Signs and wonders' are often seen by some today as an optional extra, but I don't think the New Testament writers saw it the same way. According to the Gospel writers Jesus concentrated on three spiritual tasks and encouraged and empowered his disciples to do the same. When he returned to Galilee in the power of the Spirit (Lk 4:14) he proclaimed the kingdom, healed the sick and cast out demons (Mt 4:23–25).

When Jesus sent out the twelve apostles, 'he gave them power and authority to drive out all demons and to cure diseases, and he sent them out to preach the kingdom of God and to heal the sick' (Lk 9:1–2).

When Jesus sent out the seventy-two he told them to proclaim the kingdom and heal the sick (Lk 10:9) and when they returned they said, 'Lord, even the demons submit to us in your name' (Lk 10:17).

When the Spirit came on the believers at Pentecost Peter proclaimed the King and the kingdom (Acts 2:36–41; 2 Pet 1:11) and went on to heal the sick and cast out demons (Acts 3:1–10; 5;15–16). When Philip was appointed deacon he proclaimed the King and the kingdom, healed the sick and cast out demons (Acts 8:4–13). When Saul was converted and became Paul he proclaimed the King and the kingdom, healed the sick and cast out demons (Acts 28:23; 28:8,9; 16:18).

It is interesting that healing the sick and casting out demons can be seen as different ways of proclaiming the kingdom. Proclaiming the kingdom and casting out demons can be seen as bringing healing to people, and proclaiming the kingdom and healing the sick can be seen as overcoming the works of Satan (Acts 10:38).[3] There is an integral link between all three which, alongside the common scriptural practice of speaking about them together, suggests that God may see all three as belonging to the same package. Since New Testament days Christians have often tried to break up this package on the apparent grounds that all of it was given to the early church, but only part of it is either given to or needed by the present church. I am not sure the Bible supports this argument.

Jesus said, 'Anyone who has faith in me will do what I have been doing' (Jn 14:12). This is a promise to all believers.

Then Jesus came to them and said, 'All authority in heaven and on earth has been given to me. Therefore go and make disciples of all nations ... teaching them to obey everything I have commanded you' (Mt 28:18–20). This is a command to all disciples of Jesus to do everything the apostles did, which includes healing the sick and casting out demons.

> He [Jesus] said to them, 'Go into all the world and preach the good news to all creation. ... And these signs will accompany those who believe: In my name they will drive out demons; they will speak in new tongues; they will pick up snakes with their hands; and when they drink deadly poison, it will not hurt them at all; they will place their hands on sick people, and they will get well' (Mk 16:15,17–18).

'Signs and wonders', especially healing the sick and casting out demons, seem to be an integral part of the commission to proclaim the kingdom which is entrusted to 'those who believe'.

When the early church concentrated on these three main spiritual tasks God spoke to them and in them and through them (Acts 8:29; 9:11–12; 13:9–10). It is as if a 'word' from God is most often given to support *the* word of God, when we are seeking to fulfil his commands. It is certainly our experience that there is a link between obeying the word of

God and receiving a 'word' from God.

Susan approached me one day in church and asked if she could come to see me about a problem.[4] She saw me in my study and wanted to know why others often received 'words' or pictures from God, but nothing ever seemed to come her way. Susan is a faithful born-again worshipper in our church, speaks in tongues, helps with the youth work and belongs to our healing team. I couldn't think of any logical reason why she had never heard God speaking directly to her.

'I've no idea why you have this problem,' I said. 'We'd better ask God to come. If you get anything at all in your mind just speak it out. Maybe it will be from God. I'll do the same.' We closed our eyes, welcomed the Holy Spirit and waited in the silence for God to speak. As we did I felt gently warmed and the thought came into my mind, 'Ask Susan who she is praying for to be saved and who she is praying for to be healed.'

This wasn't quite the answer I was expecting so I wavered a little before speaking. After a while I began to assume that as each name was shared the Lord would give me further guidance. Politely I asked Susan if she had received anything and being told that nothing had come, as usual, I asked the question, 'Who are you praying for to be saved and who are you praying for to be healed?'

'Nobody,' she replied honestly.

'That's it then,' I said immediately. 'You don't need any "words" from God.'

I am pleased to say that Susan is now learning with many of us to pray for people to be saved, healed and set free, and as a result is also beginning to hear God speak. Sometimes God speaks in response to our prayers by sending us out to do these things in his name and sometimes as we go in obedience to the commands of Scripture God speaks to us when we arrive.

Although I see proclaiming the kingdom, healing the sick and casting out demons as belonging to the same package, it is convenient to separate them for the purposes of seeing how a direct 'word' from God can help us with each one. I have found there are a number of different reasons why God may choose to speak to us when we seek to proclaim his kingdom.

Timing

In Acts chapter eight Philip is having a very good time preaching in Samaria where many are being saved, healed and delivered. Suddenly God speaks to him, first by an angel and then by the Spirit, to leave Samaria and go to an Ethiopian official. It is a call against the run of play and not one that could be discerned naturally. No one minds being called somewhere else when things are going badly or not going at all, but when 'all paid close attention to what he said', and 'evil spirits came out of many, and many paralytics and cripples were healed' (8:6–7), it is surprising that God should decide to redeploy him. What is perhaps not surprising is that God sends an angel to tell Philip of this latest decision. And the timing, of course, is perfect. When Philip reaches him the Ethiopian is reading Isaiah 53 and is ripe for the gospel, to which he responds and is baptised.

In Acts chapter nine Ananias is told by God to go to Saul. When he arrives Saul himself has had an amazing vision of Jesus, and receives healing, the Holy Spirit and baptism in one visit.

In Acts chapter ten Peter is told in a vision to go to the house of Cornelius where a number of people receive the Holy Spirit and are baptised, again in just one visit.

The timing on each occasion is such that God has already begun the work before the various disciples arrive. This is God's timing. There are moments when people are ready and moments when they are not. When I went to Bill Fox, his wife Lucy was dying, and when I visited the other Bill he was physically ill and financially bankrupt. With each one I had a 'word' from God or a kind of prompting, and at the

moment when they were most open to the gospel God sent
the gospel to them. I believe we so often fail in trying to proclaim the kingdom to someone because it is the wrong
moment, and then give up all too easily when they respond
negatively. Hearing God speak can help us to proclaim the
King and the kingdom to individuals at the right time.

One Sunday morning as God's Spirit came gently on our
congregation I sensed God prompting me to say that he was
already preparing people for them to evangelise during the
coming week. In faith I said God was about to give us
'words', pictures or visions concerning people with whom
we would be in touch before the following Sunday. I thought
God might also be wanting to tell us what to say in situations
where he wished to do a specific work in people's lives. It
was not the kind of 'word' I had ever given before.

As I said this Elsie began to see a picture in her mind of a
friend of many years' standing who had been in hospital for
about eight weeks. During that time she had seen her once or
twice, but always in the presence of others, thus reducing the
visit to a purely social one. This time it seemed as if God was
wanting Elsie to speak about Jesus, so when she went home
she prayed about it, and was 'told' to say to her friend, 'Jesus
loves you.'

On the Monday after, Elsie was tired. It was raining and
she didn't feel like hospital visiting so decided to go on the
Tuesday instead. But then a persistent thought entered her
head and stayed there: 'Go today, you must go today.' In
pure obedience to what God might be saying Elsie went and
for the first hour of visiting time was alone with her friend.
Apparently she'd been depressed all weekend until about the
time on the Sunday when Elsie felt led to pray for her. At that
moment a feeling of lightness and joy came over her and the
depression lifted. Being told Jesus loved her, and hearing of
Elsie's prayer, released instant tears and with them came a
deeper feeling of peace. Both the words, the prayer and the
experience of the day before confirmed to her this simple
proclamation of the gospel. Before the other visitors came

Elsie's friend also shared how on the following day she was going for further tests and treatment elsewhere and would not have been there had anyone come to visit. Listening to God speak can help us to proclaim the King and the kingdom to individuals at the right time.

A 'word' from God can also help us to proclaim the kingdom to groups of people at the right time. In Luke 10 Jesus sent out the 'seventy-two ... ahead of him to every town and place where he was about to go'. He told them, 'The harvest is plentiful, but the workers are few.' I believe Jesus' timing is often overlooked. He sent out the twelve once and the seventy-two once, and on both occasions they met with success. Mark 6:12–13 says of the twelve, 'They went out and preached that people should repent. They drove out many demons and anointed many sick people with oil and healed them.' Luke 10:17–18 says, 'The seventy-two returned with joy, and said, "Lord, even the demons submit to us in your name." He replied, "I saw Satan fall like lightning from heaven."'

Although Jesus instructed his disciples about coping with failure and rejection, this was probably meant for the future when he would no longer be with them. They were certainly not flogged or executed on this occasion when Jesus said the harvest was plentiful, and I suspect Jesus sent them out initially to fields ready for reaping. We know the harvest was not plentiful in Nazareth (Mt 10:13), in the region of the Gerasenes (Lk 8:37), in Korazin and Bethsaida (Lk 10:13) and even Capernaum (10:15), but it was abundant in the villages to which Jesus sent the seventy-two, and Jesus said beforehand that it would be. It is interesting that a Samaritan village rejects Jesus (Lk 9:51–56), but Philip meets with enormous success in Samaria at a different time (Acts 8). Jerusalem rejects Jesus and crucifies him, but just before the Ascension, the disciples are told to stay and wait in Jerusalem. Possibly some of the three thousand who were saved on the day of Pentecost had shouted, 'Crucify him!' a few weeks earlier. Listening to God speak can help us to proclaim the kingdom to groups of people at the right time.

Our evening service only attracts between thirty and forty people on a regular basis, and virtually all of them are regulars who know the gospel and know the Lord. It is not therefore appropriate to preach an evangelistic sermon on most occasions, but to seek rather to feed and challenge the flock. But as I was preparing in prayer for one Sunday evening service I felt God tell me to preach the gospel and ask people to put up their hands if they wanted to accept Jesus as their personal Saviour. I then sensed he was saying we should pray for three people to respond. As a few of us gathered to pray before the service I shared what I thought God had said and we prayed accordingly.

I find it particularly difficult when among people I know well to give a 'word' which may be from God, but I obeyed the thoughts in my head and, without my mentioning any numbers or exerting any manipulative pressure, three regular worshippers raised their hands. We were overjoyed to talk and pray with them afterwards. Hearing God speak can help us to proclaim the kingdom to groups of people and individuals at the right time.

Place

Very closely related to discovering *when* to proclaim the kingdom is deciding *where* to proclaim it. If we are to be fishers of men we need to fish at the right time, in the right place, and put the net on the right side of the boat. In Mark 1:21–34 Jesus has an amazing response to his first sermon in Capernaum, but the following morning while it is still dark he slips away alone to pray (Mk 1:35–39). Most of us know how much we need to pray before ministry, but Jesus knows how much he needs to pray after ministry. Simon and his companions seek him out and enthuse about the ministry in Capernaum, but Jesus replies, 'Let us go somewhere else' (Mk 1:38). A few days later Jesus returns to Capernaum (Mk 2:1). After all we have said about Jesus hearing the

Father and doing what his Father tells him to do, I think we can assume that through his prayer relationship God told Jesus where to proclaim the kingdom.

This is more obviously spelled out in the missionary journeys of St Paul:

> While they were worshipping the Lord and fasting, the Holy Spirit said, 'Set apart for me Barnabas and Saul for the work to which I have called them.' So after they had fasted and prayed, they placed their hands on them and sent them off. The two of them, sent on their way by the Holy Spirit, went down to Seleucia and sailed from there to Cyprus (Acts 13:2–4).

God calls Paul and Barnabas to go and proclaim the kingdom, and by his Holy Spirit directs them to Seleucia and Cyprus. In Acts 16:6 Paul is 'kept by the Holy Spirit from preaching the word in the province of Asia' and also Bithynia (v 7), but in verse 9 he receives a vision telling him to go to Macedonia. In Acts 22:17 Paul recalls how earlier while praying he fell into a trance and was told to leave Jerusalem, but in Acts 20:22–23 he is 'compelled by the Spirit' to return to Jerusalem. In Acts 27:24 an angel tells him he will arrive safely in Rome. Hearing God speak can not only help us to proclaim the kingdom at the right time but in the right place too.

Towards the end of 1987 the Diocese of Birmingham offered me a three-months' sabbatical break as I had been in my present parish for eight years. Being blessed with three small children, two of whom were at school, I could not think of a suitable place and project, so I visited Bishop David Pytches at Christmas. After the evening service I asked him what I could do with three months off. Between conversations with other people he said, 'Go with the John Wimber team to South Africa.' Knowing the cost of the venture I thought to myself, 'Poor man, he's tired. He's had a hectic Christmas and everyone's coming at him with their problems.' My wife Carol, however, thought God had been speaking to us through David and continually encouraged me to go to South Africa, even though I was slow to respond.

By the time she persuaded me to try the proper channels I was too late. Those organising the trip from England said I could not go and anyway I couldn't afford it. There were to be other ministry teams to Edinburgh and Frankfurt later in the year so I asked God about them and in the stillness waited for a reply. In a relaxed but serious way the thought came into my head, 'I've written it in my diary.' I asked what was written in the diary and back came the thought, 'South Africa.' From then on whatever I said, or asked of God, the answer never varied or wavered: 'I've written it in my diary.' There was both reprimand and encouragement in such a response, so I wrote to America, the Diocese and two clergy charities in case it was God's 'word', and left it in his hands.

Having received no further news, and not having shared these developments with anyone else locally, I attended a mid-week prayer meeting. In the middle of a time of waiting upon God, Tony had a picture in his mind of a diary with some words of assurance written in it. He had no idea what it meant. I could hardly wait to enlighten him, and welcomed the encouragement.

Over the next few weeks I received permission from America to join the team, permission from the Diocese to go, and all the money I needed for the trip, so I went to South Africa. Such preliminary guidance and the knowledge that people were praying encouraged me to back hunches and nudges more than usual when I arrived. Normally these days I am up at the front leading a time of ministry so it was a good, nerve-wracking experience to be sitting in the congregation waiting to minister as need arose – a position I had put my own people in many times.

At the very first session John Wimber prayed, 'Come, Holy Spirit.' Those who appeared to be engaged by God did not seem to be many. A thought formed in my mind, 'Go up to that man there and minister to him.' Nothing seemed to be happening to him so I asked the Lord what I should say.

'I'll tell you when you get there,' he said. So I went. Uninvited I put my hand on his head and found myself saying, 'You've been hurt by other Christians. God wants to heal you and restore you.' He wept a little: Joseph had travelled with ten or eleven other black people from the Cape to Johannesburg in a minibus which had taken them twenty-two hours. I had travelled from Birmingham to London and then fourteen hours by plane, and here we were together for five minutes.

Joseph had indeed been hurt by other Christians. As a result of this he had recently resigned as a deacon from his local church and the visions and prophecies he and his wife used to receive had dried up. 'Why did you come to me?' he asked, and I said, 'God told me.' He was deeply moved. It felt to him as if God had sent a white Englishman to him and picked him out of a congregation of over 2,000.

Two days later Joseph found me, told me of a vision he'd just received and how during this God reminded him of an earlier prophecy which my coming to him had now fulfilled. He introduced me to his friends and a warm time of fellowship followed.

This pattern was repeated a further nine times and every 'word' God gave me was confirmed by the person and led to ministry. Some had been asking God for spiritual gifts; one was for healing; another was for words of knowledge; one was for tongues; and a missionary working in Swaziland in the midst of witch-doctors wanted to be able to cast out demons. Each time God told me the gift they had been seeking from him and when I shared it with them their faith was lifted. There was immediate confirmation that two out of the four received what God wanted to give them there and then. Some 'words' I gave were for healing, of whom three were immediately healed, and a further 'word' helped me to proclaim the gospel to a non-Christian as she teetered on the brink of making a decision.

But whatever individual 'words' were spoken, each message carried a word of love from God. When someone comes and tells you in the name of Jesus something about yourself that is right, immediately you sense God must be in it. You feel, 'God loves me. God cares about me. God knows about me and wants to help me.' Going up to strangers claiming to have a 'word' from God was not something I had often done in the past and of course it needs to be done with prayer, care and great sensitivity, but it showed me how God's divine 'word' can help us to proclaim the kingdom in the right place. South Africa did seem to be the right place at that time.

Sign

Many of the 'words' from God which Jesus gave acted as signs that encouraged people to believe and to follow him. Jesus joined Simon Peter in his boat and told him to 'put out into deep water, and let down the nets for a catch'. Reluctantly Simon agreed, James and John came in another boat and all were amazed at the large catch of fish – so much so that they 'left everything and followed him' (Lk 5:1–11).

Jesus met Nathaniel and said, 'Here is a true Israelite, in whom there is nothing false.' This aroused Nathaniel's interest and Jesus continued, 'I saw you while you were still under the fig-tree before Philip called you.' Nathaniel then responded, 'You are the Son of God; you are the King of Israel' (Jn 1:43–51).'

Jesus said to a Samaritan woman, 'You have had five husbands, and the man you now have is not your husband.' As a result she believed in Jesus herself, fetched many more from the village to hear him, and they became believers too (Jn 4:18).

It may also be argued that in Luke 19:1-10 Jesus had a 'word' from God about the name and whereabouts of Zacchaeus (v 5) when he was in the sycamore fig-tree. Certainly Jesus sought and found and saved the lost that day (vv 9–10) with very little human effort.

A word of knowledge[5] from God may be interpreted as a

piece of information about somebody, some thing or some event supernaturally given by the Father. It acts as a trigger that arouses interest, encourages belief and leads to the proclamation of the King and the kingdom. It is very noticeable that in all four of these examples the piece of information is itself quite small and unspectacular: 'Let's go fishing'; 'I saw you under the fig-tree'; 'You have had five husbands'; 'Hallo Zacchaeus'. No cynic would have been convinced by these particular 'words', but the Father gives them to those who are seeking and ready to receive his word. They are given to help Jesus once more to do what the Father is doing. Through hearing God speak we are given signs to arouse interest and to build up faith in preparation for receiving the good news.

While I was sitting in a meeting, an invitation to go forward to receive ministry was given and ministers were asked to help. I should have assisted at the front, but God seemed to be saying to me, 'That lady over there would like to go forward for ministry, but she is too afraid. Go and minister to her.' There were plenty of others coping with those who had gone forward so I went over to the lady. On most occasions I would begin an ordinary conversation first, as Jesus did with the woman at the well, but I sensed this was one time to go straight in: 'Excuse me,' I said as gently as I could, 'I thought God was telling me you would like to go forward for ministry, but are too afraid.'

'Yes,' she said, 'that's right.' And so we began.

After a brief discussion I prayed over her, asking the Holy Spirit to come, but nothing visible happened. It was time for lunch, but having breakfasted well, it seemed more appropriate to talk and I found myself conversing for nearly two hours with a deeply hurt, highly intelligent non-Christian lady. Her Christian friends had lovingly cared for her, helping her to perceive in them something she wanted but hadn't yet received. Her sticking point was the emotional difficulty she experienced in trusting anyone, including God, following the number of times other people had let her down in the past. I soon realised she was not going to be rushed or pushed into God's kingdom. She asked me to explain the Trinity and the uniqueness of Christ, why our faith was better than other faiths, what she had to do to become a Christian, and why. There was a great struggle within her to come to Christ through faith rather than works, as she found it easier to trust in her own efforts than the promises of another.

Sometimes people seem to be catapulted into the Christian faith by signs and wonders, but many are the times when proclaiming the King and the kingdom is not at all spectacular or glamorous. My friends saw signs and wonders happening as they ministered at the front and still found time for a hamburger, while I was engaged in dry, academic debate for two hours, missing lunch into the bargain. But God knew this lady needed to talk over important issues and I must have been the best he could find at that moment. By the time we had finished she confessed to feeling much happier and clearer about the options which faced her. She left me, saying she was determined to try Christ for herself and it seemed right to leave the further ministry to her friends who would obviously continue to love and care for her. The 'word' from God was a sign that opened her up for the proclamation of the King and the kingdom.

Warning

God spoke to Jonah and said, 'Go to the great city of Nineveh and preach against it, because its wickedness has come up before me' (Jon 1:2).

The other side of the salvation coin is judgement. We are saved *from* the judgement. When Noah and his family heard God speak, the good news was the ark and the bad news was the rain. I meet many people who will not accept the good news of the kingdom of God because they will not accept the bad news of the kingdom of Satan. When God speaks and sends us out to proclaim the kingdom there are times when he may want us to proclaim good or bad news, according to need. Jesus sends out the twelve 'to preach the kingdom of God' (Lk 9:2) and we are told what they preached: 'They went out and preached that people should repent' (Mk 6:12).

Jonah finally obeyed God and went to Nineveh where he proclaimed, 'Forty more days and Nineveh will be destroyed' (Jon 3:4). I suspect if he had proclaimed, 'God loves you' they might not have repented, but they responded to this solemn warning and God had compassion on them. Whenever God gives a word of judgement it always appears to be with the hope and the intention of arousing repentance which will lead to more of God's blessings. I sometimes find it hard to receive and give such 'words', but bringing a 'word' of judgement to someone and giving it in love may help that person in the long term more than any other 'word'.

A lady who had been going to church for many years came to some of our mid-week meetings. As God's power came she began to realise she had never accepted Jesus as her personal Saviour, and did what she thought was necessary, without telling anyone about it. This was undoubtedly for her the beginning of the salvation event, but greater assurance came a little later. At one meeting she attended I said this: 'I believe God is saying there is a person here who at present is in the middle of an adulterous relationship. No excuses. He wants you to repent — stop it from this moment — receive God's forgiveness — and then tell the person tonight it's all over.' She went away from the meeting that night convicted by God and obeyed his 'word' to her. A day later God's love and assurance came on her in the gift of tongues which she received for the first time. She then came to see me, told me about everything and gave me permission to include it in this book. God sometimes gives us a 'word' to warn people about sin so that we may proclaim more of the kingdom, and they may receive more of his blessings.

Discernment

I find the story about Paul and Silas and the Philippian jailer to be quite extraordinary (Acts 16:16–40). In a climate of Christian persecutions and executions (Acts 12:1–18), when Paul has often fled for his life (Acts 13:50–51, 14:6,19–20), he and Silas are put in prison where they pray and sing hymns at midnight. A violent earthquake flings the prison doors open, *and they stay where they are.* This has to be supernatural discernment, as confirmed by subsequent events. They lead the jailer and his family to the Lord, visit his house for refreshment, and then *return to prison*, demanding that the magistrates come and release them. This is not sensible or rational. After prayer and praise an amazing miracle occurs, presumably an act of God, when an earthquake not only opens the doors but unfastens the chains. What is God doing? Releasing prisoners? Not a bit of it; the magistrates are made to do that. God is saving souls. I can only believe that Paul supernaturally discerned what the Father was doing against all apparent reason. Discerning what the Father is doing can sometimes help us to take the opportunity God creates to proclaim his kingdom.

At one of our Sunday evening meetings I invited Andrew, who was then our lay reader, to come and speak to our young people. After he had led a very entertaining session on the fruits of the Spirit, with pictures of lemons, strawberries and other fruits pinned to us, we welcomed the Holy Spirit into our midst. As we did so Andrew received a picture in his mind of a cross on a grey background a long way away. Nobody seemed to know what it meant so we asked God to come again and give us the interpretation.

This time Andrew saw the cross shining brightly, coming nearer and nearer, and knew what it meant. 'In some of our lives,' he said, 'the cross of Christ is shining brightly and is very near, but for others Jesus is a long way away.' During this session Jane received a picture in which she was in a dark cave like a tomb with only a tiny ray of light coming through a small crack in what was possibly a doorway closed with a large boulder. Andrew immediately discerned that Jane needed to ask Jesus into her life, thus opening the door and allowing the light of the world to come in, and he shared this with her. Reflecting afterwards, Andrew's two pictures or visions were a description of what the Holy Spirit was doing in Jane's life that night. As he came, the cross of Christ drew nearer and grew brighter until eventually Jane welcomed him fully into her life.

Despite going to church for many years, Jane admitted she had never asked Jesus to come into her life, but now wanted to do so. She knelt on the carpet, asked him in and we prayed over her. Over two years later Jane is now a member of our healing team and used to the Holy Spirit flowing through her to touch the lives of others. Discerning what the Father is doing can sometimes help us to take the opportunities God creates for the proclamation of his kingdom.

Encouragement

> The Spirit of God came upon Azariah son of Oded. He went out to meet Asa and said to him, 'Listen to me, Asa and all Judah and Benjamin. The Lord is with you when you are with him. If you seek him, he will be found by you, but if you forsake him, he will forsake you ... be strong and do not give up, for your work will be rewarded' (2 Chron 15:1–7).

This is not a very specific or profound prophecy. In a similar way many prophecies given in meetings today are illustrations of biblical principles and truths which those present know already; but a simple encouragement from God can sometimes have a far-reaching effect.

> When Asa heard these words ... he took courage. He removed the detestable idols ... He repaired the altar of the Lord ... he assembled all Judah and Benjamin and the people from Ephraim, Manasseh and Simeon ... they sacrificed to the Lord ...

> They entered into a covenant to seek the Lord ... They took an
> oath to the Lord with loud acclamation ... They sought God
> eagerly ... There was no more war until the thirty-fifth year of
> Asa's reign (2 Chron 15:8–19).

A 'word' of encouragement from the Lord in season can be
a very powerful proclamation when received in faith. It is a
'word' that frequently encourages us to go on proclaiming
the kingdom.

> One night the Lord spoke to Paul in a vision: 'Do not be afraid;
> keep on speaking, do not be silent. For I am with you, and no-
> one is going to attack and harm you, because I have many
> people in this city.' So Paul stayed for a year and a half, teaching
> them the word of God (Acts 18:9–11).

On 29th October 1984 Lyn received a prophecy from God
which she sent me in the post. Her mother lives in our parish,
but at the time I had not met Lyn who worships at the King's
Centre in Aldershot. This is a part of what she wrote as a
'word' from God:

> I love you and I am pouring my Spirit out on you that you may
> be renewed and led into the paths of righteousness. Do not be
> dismayed ... many seeds have been sown. If you wish these seeds
> to bear fruit follow the path of obedience whatever the cost and
> let the Spirit lead you at all times.

It is always helpful to receive a word of encouragement,
but as there was nothing very specific I soon forgot about it.
I wrote a letter of acknowledgement and filed it away. On
Sunday 11th November 1984 I had a letter from Bridget
from the other side of Birmingham and this is what she
wrote:

> Dear Peter
> I thought I'd write to you 'cos this morning in church I was
> praying for your church and I was given a mini-picture.
> Thought I'd share it with you. I saw a small 'something' at the

heart of your church which was very much alive but very, very small; it might only be two or three people. Then I saw it as a seed, like a grain of wheat or something, which had been there all along, just soaking up moisture and getting warm. Anyway now it has germinated and there was a little bit of root growing out and round the seed.

Don't get too excited 'cos roots grow first and you don't see them. It's only after they've grown a bit that the shoots start. I thought I would tell you, though, in case a bit of encouragement is needed.

Those of you who have read chapter one will know that a bit of encouragement was definitely needed, and greatly appreciated. I don't think I had ever had a letter from Bridget before, nor have I had one since, but it was the matching up of the seed imagery and the message with the one from Lyn, within ten days of each other, that really encouraged me. This convinced me it was God and kept me going through difficult times. A word of encouragement from God can proclaim to us his love and help us in turn to proclaim that love to others.

The narrow road

Enter through the narrow gate. For wide is the gate and broad is the road that leads to destruction, and many enter through it. But small is the gate and narrow the road that leads to life, and only a few find it (Mt 7:13–14).

A word of encouragement can help us to keep going in difficult times, for the moments when evangelism may seem easy are often quite well spaced out. In between these moments there are frequently heartbreaks and tears as we cry out to God for the lost whose hard hearts sometimes break our own. A 'word' from God helps us to proclaim the kingdom, which is our task, but never guarantees the results, which come from people's response to God's grace.

In Mark's Gospel we read of a man who came to Jesus

asking how to inherit eternal life (Mk 10:17–23). There is nothing to suggest that Jesus knew who he was or what he owned, but it says that

> Jesus looked at him and loved him. 'One thing you lack,' he said. 'Go, sell everything you have and give to the poor, and you will have treasure in heaven. Then come, follow me.' At this the man's face fell. He went away sad, because he had great wealth.

It is interesting to compare Jesus' reaction here with the different way he treated Zacchaeus (Lk 19:1–10) and Nicodemus (Jn 3:1–21), who were also wealthy. Jesus never seems to follow a set formula, but always appears to have the right word for each different person and situation. We don't know what happened to the rich young man after the incident, but Jesus seems to pinpoint his problem despite receiving a negative response. Whether the man became a disciple later on or not, the 'word' from God enabled Jesus to proclaim the kingdom. A 'word' from God does not always guarantee a 'successful' result.

My former church warden was off sick from work so I visited him at home. While we were talking, his non-church-going son Robert, who was also unfit, joined us. Apparently there'd been an accident at work and he'd damaged his neck. As we were chatting the thought came strongly into my mind, 'Ask him what he thinks of the healing ministry.'

My instant response was, 'No Lord. It's too soon in the conversation; I'll mention it later, more subtly.' God didn't argue; he just repeated the words, 'Ask him what he thinks of the healing ministry.'

So I gave in. 'What do you think of the healing ministry?' I enquired hesitantly.

Immediately he replied, 'It's funny you should ask that ...' and then proceeded to describe how a Christian friend at work went to church and was involved in the healing ministry like us. One cold day while he was suffering from a bad back his friend had persuaded him to receive the laying-on of hands and prayer outside in a shed. As this was in progress Robert experienced great heat and was healed.

'Fine,' I said, 'shall we lay hands on your neck and do the same?'

'No thanks,' he said. 'I'll call you if I need you.'

But he has not yet done so. The 'word' from God and the earlier sign of his grace enabled me to offer more works of God's kingdom and to share Jesus' love with him. Maybe I was not persistent enough or maybe this was a time to sow and not to reap. We wait prayerfully and patiently with hope for a reaping time to come. A 'word' from God often helps us to proclaim the King and the kingdom, but not always to bring in the harvest.

When God speaks directly to us we may be guided to the right time and place where God is already at work and the soil is prepared for the word of God. When God speaks directly to us he may give us a 'word' about someone that acts as a sign pointing that person to Jesus. When God speaks directly to us he may give a warning against sin or an encouragement to continue following him and doing his work. We do not need a 'word' from God to begin proclaiming the King and the kingdom because we already have words of Scripture, but we often find when we obey the Bible's commands that God speaks to enable us to be more effective. Proclaiming the King and the kingdom helps us to hear God speak, and hearing God speak helps us to proclaim the King and the kingdom.

Notes

1. See John Wimber, *Power Evangelism* (Hodder & Stoughton: London, 1985) for a fuller development of this theme.
2. John Marsh has written a helpful book on how the Holy Spirit equips us for the task of evangelism. John Marsh, *So I Send You* (Monarch Publications: Eastbourne, 1988).
3. Raymond Brown says:
      Let us begin with the Synoptic Gospels, where the miracles

are primarily acts of power (*dynameis*) accompanying the breaking of the reign of God into time. The miracles worked by Jesus are not simply external proofs of his claims, but more fundamentally are acts by which he establishes God's reign and defeats the reign of Satan. Many of the miracles attack Satan directly by driving out demons. Many more heal sickness which is associated with sin and evil. The raising of men to life is an assault on death which is Satan's peculiar realm. Even the nature miracles, like the calming of the storm, are an attack on the disorders introduced into nature by Satan. (Raymond E Brown, *The Gospel According to John (i-xii)* (Geoffrey Chapman Ltd: London, 1966), p 525.)

4. I will normally see a lady on her own confidentially and in private just once, preferably in the study of our house when my wife Carol is around. If we then make another appointment for further ministry I always ask a lady from our church to assist me, and not always the same one.

5. The phrase 'word of knowledge' appears in 1 Corinthians 12:8 (AV). Scripture does not define it for us and as it comes nowhere else in the New Testament, it is hardly surprising that scholars differ in their understanding or interpretation of it. In common usage it is rapidly coming to mean 'a piece of information given supernaturally to a person by God'. Because scholars disagree about the meaning of a 'word of knowledge', I have tended to use the phrase 'word from God' in this book. By this I mean any supernatural, direct communication from God, whether verbal or otherwise. For further discussion on the meaning of 'word of knowledge' see David Pytches' book *Does God Speak Today?* (Hodder and Stoughton: London, 1989), p 12.

5

Healing the Sick

I started praying for the sick by laying hands on a lady with cancer who died. After one healing service where I received no comeback the second person on whom I laid hands also had cancer and also died. My third attempt was with a crippled married man who after much prayer failed to improve and was divorced. My fourth was my best friend with depression who killed himself with a shotgun. As a vicar I laid on hands and prayed for many sick people, mostly with serious illnesses, many of whom died, and none of whom was physically healed. And then at last, after fourteen years of trying, I got one.

It was Lent 1986 and the local Baptist minister and I organised a six-week course in the Methodist church on healing. About fifty people came and after a powerful time of worship, as the Holy Spirit came upon us the word 'waterworks' formed in my mind, so I gave it. Mary, aged seventy-four, very bravely claimed it and came forward. In front of everyone present I laid hands on her head and prayed for her to be healed. Nothing visible happened and she returned to her seat.

Mary had suffered from a bladder complaint for thirty years. She had long ago stopped mentioning it to people, learning to cope with the embarrassment of having to change two or three times a day. It was not the kind of condition you kept asking people to pray for and if there had not been a 'word' from God given that night the situation would not have altered. She was healed from that moment and has not been troubled since. To God be the glory!

A direct 'word' from God given and received in faith helped us to move from theory to reality. Although it was very undramatic and not very convincing for the cynics it was thrilling for us to have received our first healing. We are still beginners in this ministry but we have found a 'word' from God to be of enormous value in seeing more people healed. It has helped us in many different ways to follow the biblical pattern we see in operation as Jesus healed the sick, most of which can be found in Luke 5:17–26 where Jesus heals a paralysed man. I have found five useful principles in this particular account:

1. Love

Mark begins his version of this story by saying: 'A few days later, when Jesus again entered Capernaum, the people heard that he had come home' (Mk 2:1). It looks as though this was Jesus' home for a time. Matthew 4:13 says, 'Leaving Nazareth, [Jesus] went and lived in Capernaum' (cf Mt 9:1). It seems as if the home which was crowded out with teachers of the law and Pharisees was at the very least Jesus' regular lodging place and the roof the four men smashed up might have been his friend's roof or maybe even his own.

After a busy time Jesus came home for a rest, only to be interrupted by important people from Jerusalem who wanted to argue. This was a tense time which required full concentration, when suddenly it appeared as if his home was being broken into by uninvited vandals. My probable reaction in such circumstances would have been unprintable – Jesus' reaction was one of love. If anyone had felt before this incident that they couldn't disturb Jesus with their problems because he was too well known, too tired or too busy, they would have had to think again. When the poor and the needy turned to Jesus for help they were always met with love.

We don't need a special 'word' from God to tell us to love one another because we already have a word of Scripture (Jn 15:12). Love is a natural healer.[1] If a child cries out with toothache in the night a loving touch from Mother or Father will often alleviate the pain. Bishop John V Taylor in *The Go-Between God* says: 'More and more practitioners are coming to recognize that the little-known dynamics of our interpersonal relations are the clue to a great deal of healing. We are rediscovering the therapy of touch, which is a sacrament of acceptance and love.'[2] Since hearing God speak and receiving 'words' from him, I have made many mistakes, but the greatest mistake has always been lack of love. If we could only learn to give 'words' we think are from God with love and sensitivity, it would not matter so much if they were sometimes wrong.

When Christians listen to sick people, spend time with them, pray with them and lay hands lovingly on them, whatever else happens they should always feel loved. Sometimes, however, a 'word' from God can help a sick person to feel specially loved.

One Friday lunch-time I entered the kitchen joyously with a newly written sermon, hoping to receive spiritual encouragement and physical sustenance. Unfortunately my wife Carol was absent putting our youngest to bed and I was left alone with my needs. I put a record of Stainer's *Crucifixion* on the turntable, reclined in an easy chair with my eyes closed, and at once a wave of warmth came over me. A tear slid down my cheek as I sensed the presence of God with me by his Spirit in a special way.

In my mind I saw Jesus in a children's book picture of the Garden of Eden, but there was no snake present. 'This is my world,' he said lovingly, 'Do not be afraid.' For some time almost every moment of every day had been taken up ministering to demonised people and it seemed good to spend time apart with Jesus and rest for a while. I was due to travel that afternoon to Cheltenham to take some seminars on healing in another church.

'When you go to Cheltenham this weekend,' he said, 'I want you to know everything you receive in your mind will be of me, and I will bless all who come. There will be thirty there and here are some 'words' to help you.' On the newspaper lying on the floor I jotted down these 'words':

Bone displacement – hip.

Lady with blurred vision in left eye.

Bladder complaint.

Epilepsy.

Each of the series of meetings had a different attendance, ranging from twenty-four to thirty-three, but on the afternoon when I felt it right to give the four 'words', all of them were claimed. A lady suffered from pain in the hip due to the bone continually slipping out of place. As people laid hands on her the pain went. Another lady began to see more clearly in the left eye as friends in Christ prayed over her. Yet another lady with a minor bladder complaint was grateful for prayer which eventually concentrated on her more serious emotional problems.

Rob had epilepsy. Thirty years ago he had been preparing to enter the ministry when he had an accident and fell twenty feet onto his head. His wife was told he would not live more than a couple of hours, but as she drove to the hospital she felt God saying he would survive, and he did. Unfortunately, the operation on his brain left him with epilepsy, causing him to abandon plans for the ministry and remain unemployed for thirty years. In all that time he and his wife kept their faith in God, but not once at any of the meetings they attended was he ever called out to the front by a special 'word' for prayer.

As we prayed for him he was overcome with God's love. It seemed almost too much for Rob that God had given a special 'word' just for him. Heat came upon his head which went backwards under God's power as a tear or two trickled down his face, just as they had on mine the previous day. Rob had another fit soon after we prayed for him and then no more for some time, but maybe the most important thing after thirty years was the special love I know he felt from God. A special 'word' from God often helps us to feel his great love for us.

2. Authority

Having suffered a hole in the roof, Jesus is then confronted with an atmosphere of scepticism and antagonism from those who challenged his authority. Before he heals the paralytic, Jesus says, 'But that you may know that the Son of Man has authority' (Lk 5:24).

Jesus demonstrates his authority to forgive sins by healing the crippled man, thereby proving simultaneously his authority to heal the sick. We need to be sure we have the authority of God to heal the sick. I have found there is the general authority which can be seen in Scripture, but there is also a particular authority which frequently comes with a 'word' from God and, because Jesus has passed on his authority through the twelve to us (Mt 28:18), there is also ecclesiastical authority. It must always be remembered, however, that a soldier only has the authority of the General to do what the General has told him to do, either in the manual or directly on the spot. God's authority in us is always dependent on our obedience to him.

Scriptural authority

In Luke 9:1–2 Jesus gives the twelve authority to cure diseases and then sends them out to heal the sick. In Luke 10:1 Jesus appoints seventy-two others and sends them out to heal the sick (10:9). That makes a total of eighty-four given authority to heal. In Acts chapter one, also written by Luke, we read there are 120 believers gathered together which suggests the number authorised to heal the sick may have been a sizeable majority.

I have already mentioned how in Matthew 28 Jesus tells his disciples to teach new disciples to do all Jesus had told them to do (v 20). This includes healing the sick. In Mark 16 Jesus says those who believe 'will place their hands on sick people, and they will get well' (v 18). In John 14:12 Jesus says, 'Anyone who has faith in me will do what I have been doing.' It appears that all Christians, all who have been born again by water and his Spirit (Jn 3:5), have been given the general authority of Scripture to heal the sick.

At one meeting I sensed the Lord saying to me, 'That lady over there wants to be used in the healing ministry; go and release her into it.' So I went over and cautiously said, 'Excuse me, I think the Lord may have asked me to come to you. Have you been seeking him lately about something you want to do for him?' Among Christians this is not too difficult an approach. If she had said 'no' it wouldn't have been too embarrassing to withdraw apologetically, but she replied, 'Yes I have, but I can't make up my mind if it should be teaching or healing.'

'I think it's healing,' I said and she became ecstatic, clapping her hands and beaming like a child on Christmas Day. Despite this introduction it soon became apparent to me that this was in fact a mature Christian lady who needed only to be led into this gift. I laid hands on her and began to ask God to anoint her and release her into his ministry of healing, but as I was praying somebody else signalled urgently for me to join them. I said, 'Go on receiving the Spirit and I'll be back in a minute,' and then I slipped away. Less than five minutes later I came back only to find she'd gone. 'Oh dear, I've blown it!' I thought, and started chatting to someone else, but in a few moments the lady returned to tell me she had been to the front and laid hands on a sick person who was apparently instantly healed! I'm not altogether sure what 'anointing', 'empowering' or 'releasing' means, but I'm certain this lady only needed encouragement to realise the power Jesus was giving her at that moment, confirming the authority she already had from Scripture to heal the sick.

Particular authority

In John chapter five Jesus pays a visit to the local 'hospital'. In his day it was called 'the Pool of Bethesda' – a place where 'a

great number of disabled people used to lie' (Jn 5:3). This is
one of the few occasions recorded when there were many sick
present, and Jesus seems to heal only one man (5:5). It is
worth asking why Jesus healed him and no other. It wasn't
because he was a good man. Jesus said to him, 'See, you are
well again. Stop sinning or something worse may happen to
you' (5:14). It wasn't because he had a lot of faith: 'The man
who was healed had no idea who it was' (5:13) who healed
him. Jesus says this afterwards: 'I tell you the truth, the Son
can do nothing by himself; he can do only what he sees his
Father doing, because whatever the Father does the Son also
does' (5:19). He healed him apparently because it was what
the Father was doing. Although Jesus had general authority
to heal the sick, it is probable he needed a direct 'word' from
God to know he was to heal this man on this occasion. A
direct 'word' from God can bring the general authority of
Scripture into focus for one person in one place at one time.

In one healing meeting I felt God was saying to me, 'The
lady sitting in front of you has a serious illness. I want you to
minister to her.' When all you can see is someone's back, it
isn't easy to see if they look ill and from all I could see she
looked fine. At the end of the meeting 'words' were given for
various conditions and people who wanted prayer were
invited forward but this lady remained seated. In due course I
went up to her. 'I think the Lord may be saying you have some
kind of an illness and would like prayer,' I said. 'I have a
chronic illness,' she replied, 'and I'd love to have prayer.'

Sonja Botha is the founder and director of the Happiness
Chinese Mission in Johannesburg and had suffered severe
stomach and back pains for twenty years. She had undergone
four major operations without any success and many Christians had counselled her and prayed with her. She is a super
Christian lady, but had suffered cruelly at the hands of others
most of her life. I listened, counselled and prayed for as long
as seemed appropriate and she became no better. I then went
to a prayer meeting where others ministered to me and I burst
into tears – I don't fully know why. That night Sonja's pain

increased, but I managed to see her again the next day at our final session.

I really didn't know how to minister, but felt it right to have another go. I asked God to send his Spirit on Sonja and show us what to do. After a few minutes she said, 'There are two people I have to forgive,' and then did so. After that two ladies joined me, laid hands on the affected area, commanded the pain to go in Jesus' name, and it went.

A few days later the pain returned so Sonja went for a medical check-up. What I didn't know was that she suffered from curvature of the spine, which the doctors were amazed to discover was now perfectly straight. Following further tests they found the spinal problem had masked an intestinal disorder which was correctable, Sonja was assured, with surgery. Don't ask me why God did not heal that in the same way at the same time. The more we are involved in healing the more we have to acknowledge the mysteries surrounding this ministry, but it was thrilling to receive her letter after I returned to England, testifying to God's healing.

Human authority

James 5:14–16 says:

> Is any one of you sick? He should call the elders of the church to pray over him and anoint him with oil in the name of the Lord. And the prayer offered in faith will make the sick person well; the Lord will raise him up. If he has sinned, he will be forgiven. Therefore confess your sins to each other and pray for each other so that you may be healed. The prayer of a righteous man is powerful and effective.

Unfortunately this passage is often used by Christians to let them off the hook. 'We are not elders,' they say. 'We don't have to pray for the sick.' I interpret the passage in this way: the elders pray for those who call them to come round and as a result of confession of sin, anointing in oil and praying for the sick person in faith, 'the Lord will raise him up' (Jas 5:14–15). The word for 'raising' him up is the same word used for raising Lazarus from the dead (Jn 12:1,9,17). The implication is that those who are seriously ill, maybe at death's door, and definitely not well enough to come to a meeting, should ask the elders to go round and pray for them. James goes on to say, 'Therefore confess your sins to each other and pray for each other so that you may be healed' (5:16). This appears to be everyone praying for one another at meetings – presumably those who are not so seriously ill.

I like to encourage everyone to start on colds, sore throats, aches and pains. I have felt personally discouraged by starting with difficult conditions, with little apparent result. Had I started with less serious problems and seen some of the positive results we have experienced recently, I am sure my faith in God's healing would have grown more quickly.

In our church we informed our bishop and used an adapted Diocesan service to commission a healing team of twelve. I then put their names and addresses in our magazine and said they had my authority as elders to visit and pray for people in their homes. They are encouraged to take others with them and whenever anyone else shows an aptitude for ministry to the sick we give them official recognition. This is important because our churches are often full of damaged people, especially when the healing of Jesus is offered, and sometimes people who are very damaged do not relate well in a healing team and could, in fact, do harm if they ministered without supervision.

When the human authority in our churches is obeyed, God often uses those in charge to fulfil his purposes. One Saturday morning I called in at Chorleywood with some others from our church on my way home from my mother's to take a wedding in Birmingham.[3] Bishop David Pytches was leading the meeting and at the end of the talk he asked the Spirit to minister to us. Nothing much seemed to be happening to me so I opened my eyes and at that point David saw me and said, 'Peter, please feel free to minister.' Even though David knows me I wouldn't have felt able to minister without that human authority. All sorts of people go to the services at

Chorleywood and if the ministry team has to be worried about who else is trying to get in on the act, they would not feel free themselves to minister.

I had rather hoped to slip away unnoticed at that point, but as David had publicly authorised me I thought I ought to pray for at least one person on the way out. I approached a young man who was standing still, where nothing much was happening. I don't know why I went to him: there were plenty of other people around for whom quite a lot was happening. I put my hand on his head, tried to relax him – telling him God loved him and so on – and then probably because my arm was aching, I put my hand on his chest. At this moment I thought to myself, 'He's got a serious illness – incurable.' So I said, 'Nothing is impossible for God. Just believe and let him come.' As I said this the young lady standing next to him collapsed in the chair and began sobbing.

Realising I would be late for the wedding if I stayed longer, I called my church warden John and his wife Pauline over to help me, as they were staying all day. I passed on the authority David had given to me – both of them are in our healing team in Birmingham – and left. Pauline is a physiotherapist, knew all about terminal cystic-fibrosis which the young man had, and was able to minister love into the situation. He shared his side of the story with her. He'd felt rejected by God and somewhat hurt by Christian friends and said, 'Lord if you really love me send someone to me and get him to lay hands on my chest.' When I arrived and put my hands on his head he said to God, 'OK, but I bet he doesn't put his hand on my chest.' Apparently at that very moment I put my hand on his chest, and his wife who had come with him and knew everything collapsed in the chair.

David didn't know God was speaking through him; he was just following correct procedures. I had no idea how God was using me; I was just obeying orders and doing what seemed right at the time. There are times as we go in his name with his authority following the guidelines of Scripture, when God simply uses us as he wishes, not always needing to tell us what he is doing. But in any local situation we need the authority of those in charge before ministering, that everything might be done decently and in order, with love.

3. Power

Luke records that on the occasion when the four men lowered their friend through the roof Jesus not only had God's authority but also his power to heal the man: 'And the power of the Lord was present for [Jesus] to heal the sick' (Lk 5:17). As Luke takes the trouble to mention this it seems likely Jesus did not always have the power to heal the sick although there are a number of occasions when such power from God was flowing through him. Luke says, 'The people all tried to touch him, because power was coming from him and healing them all' (Lk 6:19).

At healing meetings, services and conferences there are times when there is a lot of power about and a number of people are healed. I remember one meeting led by Blaine Cook when so many people seemed to be healed that I wished I was sick because I was missing out. The times when God's healing power is manifested for all to see are very precious and need to be treasured.

There are many other occasions, however, when we have to start from cold to pray for the sick, not knowing if God's power is going to be released or not. On one occasion a woman 'who had been subject to bleeding for twelve years', touched the edge of Jesus' cloak and was healed (Lk 8:43–48). Jesus said, 'Someone touched me; I know that power has gone out from me' (Lk 8:46). This means Jesus could feel the flow of God's power in his body, and this is often the way we know when the power of the Lord is present to heal (cf Lk 6:19). It is God anointing us for a specific occasion with power, which may come in the form of heat or tingling in the hands, or some other similar phenomenon, that can help us to recognise his presence and activity. Such power sometimes comes before we start praying for someone, as an encouragement to us, or during the ministry.

In the course of one cold winter's afternoon and evening I prayed for five different people called Mary.[4] On the first four occasions my hands heated up quite considerably as I prayed. When I came to the fifth I was feeling full of faith and very pleased to pray for this lady who was needing prayer for a bladder complaint. I placed my hands on her head and asked God to come to her. Nothing happened! My hands felt cold, reflecting the temperature of the room. 'Lord,' I said, 'nothing is happening. Why have you turned the power off?' Then I sensed him telling me to lead her in a time of repentance, which I did, finding myself praying against fear and loneliness. At this moment my hands heated up like a kettle, becoming far hotter than they had been all day. Mary said afterwards, 'How did you know? How did you know my problem was fear and loneliness? No one knows that!' The following week the bladder was as bad as ever but the fear and loneliness had gone. The power of the Lord was present for this lady on that night to be healed emotionally and I was guided how to minister by feeling God's power in my hands.

4. Discernment

'When Jesus saw their faith, he said "Friend, your sins are forgiven"' (Lk 5:20). Later, 'He said to the paralysed man, "I tell you, get up, take your mat and go home."' (5:24).

Once we have welcomed a sick person with love, received authority and sensed the anointing of the Lord's presence to heal the sick, we then need discernment as to how to minister. Here is an amazing statement: 'When Jesus saw their faith, he said "Friend, your sins are forgiven"' (Lk 5:20). A more logical account would have read, 'When Jesus saw their faith, he said, "Get up, take your mat and go home."' Presumably Jesus discerned the man needed to have his sins forgiven before being healed. Maybe he was a bad sinner; maybe people had accused him of being a bad sinner because he was crippled; maybe he had a low self-image and thought he was a bad sinner; maybe Jesus needed to forgive him in order to heal him; maybe Jesus needed to forgive him first so that he might know how to keep his healing afterwards. Whatever the reason, Jesus discerned the need for forgiveness before he healed him. I suspect this was revealed to him supernaturally for they were the first words in the conversation.

I can find no other instance in the Gospels where Jesus forgave someone's sins before healing their sickness, although in John 5:14 he says to the former invalid, 'See, you are well again. Stop sinning or something worse may happen to you.' Jesus does, however, often listen to people first (cf Mt 8:1–4; 20:29–34; 9:27–31), which may have helped him by natural or supernatural means to discern how to minister.

At one meeting a 'word' was given for a person with pain in the right ear and a young Christian man came forward to claim it. On being interviewed he said his main problem was catarrh which had lately been troublesome, the worst pain being in the right ear. I asked him how long he'd suffered from catarrh and my faith dropped drastically as he replied, 'Since birth.'

As I was about to panic the thought came into my head, 'Don't forget the "word" that was given.' This at least gave me my next question: 'The "word" given was for the right ear,' I said, 'How long has the right ear been troubling you?'

'Since we had the drums in church,' he replied without thinking. This was much more hopeful. His was an Anglican church. Drums in the chancel played at certain services had antagonised a few people. This young man was the drummer.

A lady from his church helped me to minister to him. She had been one who initially opposed the drums, but now found his sensitive playing an aid to worship, and she shared this with him. I then asked the Holy Spirit to come and show him what Jesus thought of drums in church and his playing. In a few moments he was laughing; clearly Jesus did not think the same about drums in church as some others did. He felt much better, but the pain in his ear was still there.

Believing we were being led by the Holy Spirit, we placed

our hands on his head and ear and commanded the pain to go in Jesus' name, and it went. I am sure it was the discernment God gave us about the drums, and the ministry of forgiveness and reconciliation which followed that led to the ear being healed.

Discernment is also sometimes needed in knowing how to bring about effective healing. What must I do or say? What must the sick person do or say? In the story of the crippled man Jesus said, 'Get up, take your mat and go home' (Lk 5:24) and when the man obeyed he was healed. This may not have been totally straightforward; it may have been as he stood that his legs were healed, which requires greater faith and obedience than if strength came as he was lying down. Jesus used a considerable variety of different approaches in healing the sick.

He healed from a distance with a declaration of healing (Mt 8:5–13; Jn 4:46–54).

Jesus said to the man with the shrivelled hand, 'Stand up in front of everyone ... Stretch out your hand' (Mk 3:1–5).

Jesus touched a leper and said, 'Be clean!' (Mt 8:3).

Jesus told ten lepers to go and show themselves to the priests. 'As they went, they were cleansed' (Lk 17:14).

Jesus put a paste from soil and spittle on a blind man's eyes and told him to wash it off (Jn 9:6–7).

'After he took him aside, away from the crowd, Jesus put his fingers into the man's ears. Then he spat and touched the man's tongue. He looked up to heaven and with a deep sigh said to him, "*Ephphatha!*" (which means "Be opened!")' (Mk 7:33–34).

After Peter had cut off Malchus' ear Jesus 'touched the man's ear and healed him' (Lk 22:50–51).

Uninvited, Jesus touched a coffin and told a dead man to get up (Lk 7:14).

He said to four-days-dead Lazarus, 'Come out!' (Jn 11:43).

A woman touched his cloak and was healed (Mk 5:27) and all who touched him were healed (Mt 14:36).

Jesus touched one leper, but not the ten; he touched some, while healing others from a distance; he made mud paste, spat and stuck fingers in ears; he made one person stand up publicly and took another away from the crowd. Sometimes people ask me when Jesus needed or used a 'word' from God to heal the sick and I say I think it must have been all the time. The disciples even saw effective healing with shadows (Acts 5:15) and handkerchiefs (Acts 19:12) among other approaches.

In 1987, while visiting Carol's parents in Spain, I attended a house group Bible study of about a dozen people, most of whom I had not met before. During a time of prayer and ministry I said, 'I think there is a lady here with a lump in the breast who has already had two removed previously. I believe the Lord is saying you need not be afraid, but go to the doctors and have it treated medically.'

In 1989 when I visited Spain again Wendy shared with me how the 'word' had fitted her condition exactly, except she was not aware at the time of having another lump. When she returned home after the meeting and examined herself she discovered it, subsequently saw the doctor, had it removed surgically and when I saw her was fine.

I do not always understand the different ways God sometimes chooses to heal, but there are occasions when God may speak to give us discernment as to how to minister to the sick.

5. Faith

Jesus began this ministry to the paralytic 'when [he] saw their faith' (Lk 5:20). Faith can be present in the person ministering (Lk 7:11–17; 22:50–51) or in the sick person (Mk 5:25–34; Acts 14:8–10) or in some other person or friends (Mt 8:5–13).[5] Faith in God and his power and willingness to heal through Jesus by his Spirit normally needs to be present somewhere for someone to be supernaturally healed by God. Faith can come when people experience the presence of the power of God but I have to say that many are the times when my hands have felt hot or the person has shaken in the power of the Spirit and they have not been healed. As well as love, authority, power and discernment there usually needs to be faith.

Receiving the gift of faith

How do we come by faith? How did the four friends who lowered the paralytic through the roof get their faith? Mark begins his account like this: 'A few days later, when Jesus again entered Capernaum, the people heard that he had come home' (Mk 2:1). The implication in Mark's Gospel is that a crowd gathered because of what had happened a few days earlier: 'That evening after sunset the people brought to Jesus all the sick and demon-possessed. The whole town gathered at the door, and Jesus healed many who had various diseases' (Mk 1:32–34). So the whole town had already seen Jesus heal the sick. At the very least I suspect these four would have been present and seen Jesus healing people, but sick people did not normally have many able-bodied friends. One wonders if the four friends had themselves been among the sick whom Jesus had healed? People often receive faith to do for others what has been done for them.

It is interesting that Paul's first miracle (Acts 13:6–12), which led to the proconsul of Paphos becoming a believer, was to give Elymas the sorcerer blindness. When Paul himself was converted on the road to Damascus (Acts 9:1–19) he was struck with blindness and became a believer. Paul obviously had the faith and the experience to believe that this miracle could happen and he also knew it could be the best thing for the kingdom of God and for Elymas. It meant that Elymas, like Paul, could no longer persecute Christians for a while and it also meant he would experience a miracle which would challenge him to believe in Jesus. I suspect most Christians would have been very loath to inflict blindness on anyone else unless they had experienced it themselves as Paul had.

It is sometimes easier to have specific faith to do for someone else what God has done for you. Audrey is a Christian friend who suffered for a long time with back trouble. At

many of our mid-week meetings we would find her standing
against a pillar in agony, unable to sit for long on our wooden
seats. She also suffered severe pain when she stood for any
length of time. She attended a conference in Brighton where
she heard Terry Virgo share how one of his legs had been
lengthened after prayer, healing the pain he often suffered
when standing at football matches. Terry was offering to
pray for anyone present with sciatic problems. Audrey did
not know whether one of her legs was shorter than the other
but she went forward, was measured up, and Terry prayed
for her. As he did so one leg grew a quarter of an inch, and all
the back pain went.

On the following Sunday Audrey, now full of faith, prayed
for someone in Birmingham with a similar complaint and his
leg grew as well. People who have been healed themselves by
God are usually the best to train and authorise to pray for the
sick.

Obedience can lead to faith

I have always felt sympathy for Naaman the Syrian who
appeared to be given a very rough ride considering the seriousness of his illness. This great commander in the Syrian
army believes a Jewish servant girl when she tells him a
prophet in the enemy camp can heal his leprosy. Armed with
silver and gold and a letter from his king he goes to the king of
Israel who directs him to Elisha. After all this effort the
prophet does not even grant him an audience, but sends his
servant with a message to go and wash in the Jordan.

Naaman had the faith to believe he could be cured by the
wave of a hand or a word from Elisha, but not by taking a
bath in front of his servants (2 Kings 5:11–12). Sometimes,
however, when faith is lacking, obedience will do. Naaman
swallowed his pride, did as he was told, and was completely
healed. Obedience to a direct 'word' from God brought healing and led to faith in the God of Israel (2 Kings 5:15).

At a meeting of about forty or fifty people the Lord gave me
four different 'words' and three people responded to them.

While our ministry team was interviewing them I went looking for the fourth. It was a 'word' for a married lady with an irritable bowel complaint who was very worried about her son.

Sitting in the front row was a friend of mine with two other ladies. 'I bet it's one of you,' I said, thinking I was joking. My friend immediately pointed discreetly to the lady sitting next to her. I tried to be sensitive in approaching her but failed. 'Have you got an irritable bowel complaint, Madam?' I asked.

'Yes,' she said, 'but it won't be healed; I've had it for years.'

'Are you worried about your son?' I continued, trying to remind myself this was an interview not an interrogation.

'Yes,' she admitted, 'he's going through a divorce at the moment.'

Her own minister was with her, heard this part of the conversation and was able to minister into this problem later. I felt it right at the time to concentrate mainly on the physical problem.

'Come out here, then,' I said, 'and we'll pray for you.' The lady did as she was told. A friend with me prayed for her, she fell over in the Spirit and was healed. I'm not sure who was the more surprised, she or I.

Some time later I visited her church and during the ministry time noticed she was in some physical distress with a different condition. As I laid hands on her head I now detected faith in her and she was healed. Obedience to a 'word' from God can sometimes lead to healing and faith.

The faith of friends

A centurion came to Jesus and asked him to heal his servant. He came out of compassionate love for another who was suffering; he recognised in Jesus the authority and power to heal (Mt 8:9); he discerned that Jesus did not need to come under his roof, but only to say the word (v 8); but it was his 'great faith' that Jesus praised (vv 10,13).

When Peter Reed, once our church warden, fell over in the bishop's chair he not only received physical healing but the spiritual gift of faith as well. Recently he became ill with shingles which showed itself as a five inch band of red around his stomach and caused him great pain. He sent for me and I prayed that the Spirit should come upon him. Immediately he fell over again, the pain went and within two hours his bright red sash faded and disappeared. It is so easy praying for people with faith.

Peter's former next-door-neighbour then retired from work and developed eye trouble. Mick went to the doctor, then the hospital and was told he had a mole at the back of the eye which was totally inoperable and would almost certainly lead eventually to complete blindness in that eye. Mick was no longer allowed to drive a car. Peter heard about it, enthused to him about Jesus' power to heal, and dragged him along to our church. Daisy and Greg prayed for him and he felt better. The next day his sight appeared to be improved so he returned to the hospital where he was examined and duly told the mole had gone. He was immediately fitted up with new spectacles and allowed to drive a car. It is encouraging to have medical evidence that a healing has occurred. Several weeks later he was able to read the smallest print on the eye-test card at the opticians.

Peter started a home group of five, but news soon spread. All kinds of people who wouldn't normally go to church started coming and being healed. A lady who'd suffered for two years with a painful swollen foot saw it go down as they prayed for her, and skipped down the path when her husband came to collect her. A young man with a pain and a lump in the back lost the pain and the lump as the Spirit came upon him. A very young child covered with an eczema rash since birth improved tremendously, and several other long-standing back aches, neck aches, leg aches, and so on all went as local people experienced the power of God, many for the first time. This all began to happen while I was on sabbatical for three months and soon Peter's home became too small to hold everyone. The faith of friends in God can be very precious.

Faith in the sick person

> In Lystra there sat a man crippled in his feet, who was lame from birth and had never walked. He listened to Paul as he was speaking. Paul looked directly at him, saw that he had faith to be healed and called out, 'Stand up on your feet!' At that, the man jumped up and began to walk (Acts 14:8–10).

Faith seemed to come to this man as he heard the word of God being preached, and he believed. It is never easy for a sick person himself to have faith to be healed which is why a 'word' from God can be so helpful.

Julia has sometimes suffered from a bad back. On one occasion her family prayed for her, she went over in the Spirit at home and was healed. Unfortunately, some time later the back trouble returned and no amount of praying or ministering from several people would shift it. Each time people prayed Julia felt blessed, loved and a little better for a short while, but not healed.

During my visit to South Africa Christine, our lay-reader, was left in charge of the monthly Sunday healing service and, just like the woman in the Bible, Julia kept saying to herself, 'If only I go forward at the healing service I will be healed.' Faith grew inside her to the point where she testified afterwards, 'I just knew I was going to be healed.' This is the work of God. This is a 'word' from God. This is faith in God. It is not a person deciding for herself what to do and believing it – the initiative comes from God. Touching cloaks, handkerchiefs or shadows, receiving communion or anointing with oil is nothing to do with magic, special things or special places. All these things stimulate faith because of their associations which help people to believe and receive what God is doing. The children of Israel were not saved by blood on the doorposts. They were saved by God, but their obedience to him by smearing the doorposts was an act of faith which released God's saving and healing power.

Julia had several times received appropriate 'words' for others, and this seemed to be one for herself. At the healing service Christine invited people to come forward to the altar rail for prayer; nobody moved. This is the moment of faith. Julia led the way and others followed. She found it very painful kneeling and even though she felt God's anointing as Mary and Alicia prayed, her back became no better, so they stopped. This is the test of faith: imagine kneeling in agony at an altar rail with two ladies the other side praying, feeling that God has said he wants to heal, but getting no better. 'You need to lay hands on my back,' said Julia. So Mary leaned over the rail and put her hand in the right place. As they commanded the pain to go in Jesus' name Alicia felt something move, and Julia's back was healed.

Next morning the pain was back just as before. Now came a bigger test of faith! Because Julia was still convinced God had spoken and was speaking, she continued to resist Satan and the pain in the back and fought in prayer for a whole week. After that the pain left and has not returned. I am now looking forward to seeing Julia pray for people with bad backs. God sometimes arouses faith to be healed in the sick person.

Faith in those ministering

Faith can also be aroused in the person ministering by a 'word' from God. Ananias heard the Lord speaking in a vision, telling him to go and lay hands on Saul who was blind (Acts 9:1–19). He knew about Saul and argued, 'But the Lord said to Ananias, "Go!"', so he went (v 15). As Ananias laid hands on his head, 'Immediately, something like scales fell from Saul's eyes, and he could see again' (v 18). Hearing God speak like this can be a tremendous faith-builder.

When I first started ministering to demonised people I really didn't know much about it. Three of us ministered to one lady until late at night, at which point we still didn't know if anything had left or not. The next day I was tired and depressed and poured it all out to the Lord: 'I need to know, Lord,' I began. 'I need to know if we're getting it right, if we're being helpful and if anything has gone.'

He told me a demon had gone.

'How do I know that?' I asked. 'How do I know it is you saying that and not just wishful thinking?'

He stopped me in my tracks. 'Ask me for anything you want and I will grant your request – this will be a sign to you that a demon has left.'

God has said this sort of thing to me two or three times. It is always an awesome experience and I always know what to ask. Afterwards I wonder why I didn't ask for a Mercedes Benz or a large donation to church funds, but at the time it's never like that. When the Spirit is present and I'm praying in the Spirit I find myself asking what the Spirit wants me to ask. I'm sure this is what all the New Testament verses on asking and receiving are about: asking in his name in the power of his Spirit according to his will.

That night I was due to visit Michael and Sandra in their home with Patricia for an informal Bible study. We had started sending people out from our church two by two to meet in members' homes for fellowship as not many people came to centrally organised mid-week meetings. Before leaving I prayed, 'Lord, I want your Spirit to come powerfully on Michael and Sandra.' I sensed God saying, 'Make room for me in your meeting. Ask me to come and I will come.' That rather stunned me! I'd landed myself in it again. I think I was rather tired and depressed at the time, but I went in numbed obedience. By the time I arrived with Pat I felt God's confidence growing inside me as he anointed me with the gift of faith. By now I knew that God was going to come, and by doing so to verify the 'word' about the demon, but little did I suspect what he was really intending to accomplish.

Chatting beforehand, Mike and Sandy shared how they were planning to adopt a baby. Having consulted all sorts of specialists, they had finally been told by the medical authorities, who had put them both through every test imaginable, that they would be unable to have children of their own. Very sensibly they accepted their situation as it was, and were now looking forward to making a home and giving a new life to an unwanted child.

We went through our Bible study. Afterwards I explained a little about waiting on God and asking him to come, as they hadn't experienced this ministry much before, and then I asked God to come. They were both sitting on the sofa with their eyes closed and slowly God's power came on them as it also did on Pat. Sandy's face began to shine and then her hands shook from side to side. She said afterwards she would have fallen over if she had been standing. But what happened to Michael was quite extraordinary: his hands started lifting until they were outstretched above his head and as I went over to him and put my hands on his head he began shaking all over. This went on for some time and even when his hands came down and his eyes opened he was still shaking.

'How do you stop it?' he asked.

'Oh it never lasts for more than a week,' I said jokingly, not really knowing what was happening or what to do about it.

'I thought you said God would never do anything to us against our will,' he said. 'I can't stop it.'

Although I didn't understand what was taking place I knew it was not an unpleasant experience. 'You said 'yes' to God,' I reminded him.

'Only initially,' he replied, but I sensed he was secretly enjoying it and deep down we were all a shade awestruck by what God was doing. Michael tried to pour out some cornflakes into a bowl for me, but spilled them all over the floor.

While this was going on Pat experienced God's power and at one stage saw a picture of a baby. It began to dawn on me what God might have been doing. These shakings were similar to the time Peter Reed was being healed. 'I think you two may well end up with your own baby,' I said.

Michael and Sandra went ahead and adopted a beautiful baby girl, but now they also have their own baby boy.

God told me he was going to come in power on Michael and Sandra and as I began to obey him he anointed me and gave me the gift of faith. On this occasion it was not the gift of knowledge as I had no idea that God was going to heal

Michael, but obedience and faith were sufficient for God to fulfil his purposes. Faith is not learned but grown; not taught but caught. There is very little value in telling people to have more faith. In the West, with our modern scientific worldview, it is often particularly difficult to grow faith. Hearing God speak and obeying his voice can be the start of our growing enough faith to heal the sick.[6]

The ingredients for healing the sick seem to be love, authority, power, discernment and most especially the gift of faith. When we seek to obey the commands of Scripture and the 'words' God speaks to us directly, we often find the Holy Spirit begins to grow within us those gifts we need to heal the sick.

When we seek to heal the sick we frequently hear God speak, and hearing God speak can help us to heal the sick.

Notes

1. Andy and Audrey Arbuthnot who work full time at the London Healing Mission find this to be true and have written a helpful book entitled *Love That Heals* (Marshall Morgan and Scott Publications Ltd: Basingstoke, 1986).
2. John V Taylor, *The Go-Between God* (SCM Press Ltd: London, 1972), p 212.
3. St Andrew's, Chorleywood, Herts.
4. There are several ladies in our church called Mary; most of my stories about someone called Mary therefore concern different people.
5. Despite what some scholars have said there appears to be ample scriptural support for ministering Christ's healing to Christians. Many of those Jesus healed had faith, that is, they were believers in Jesus.
6. Dr Paul Yonggi Cho has some very interesting things to say about faith for healing in his two books *The Fourth Dimension Volume One* (Bridge Publishing Inc: South Plainfield, New Jersey, 1979) and *The Fourth Dimension Volume Two* (Bridge Publishing Inc: South Plainfield, New Jersey, 1983).

6

Casting out Demons

One week after seventy-four-year-old Mary's healing I met my first demon. The story began when a fifteen-year-old boy with Pakistani ancestry and a Birmingham accent came to my door. Mark spoke quickly in a garbled fashion with a note of panic in his voice and the tale he told went something like this: 'Last night, about midnight, a gang of us were messing about in a local park when this dead woman's spirit overcame Angela, one of the English girls. As this happened a Muslim girl called Shafika went into a swoon. The dead woman spoke through Angela, identifying herself as a prostitute who had been murdered with her daughter and buried in the park. Her daughter also began speaking through Angela and as she did one of the lads found himself being lured towards her. "She fancies you," said the mother. Suddenly the mother began to see murder and blood and warned us that one of our group would be stabbed the following evening. We all went back to one room scared stiff, and most of them are still there. We want you to come and sort it out.'

It was then about three-fifteen in the afternoon. Was it lies, a joke, truth or a mixture of all three? I had never met a ghost before and neither had I been on a 'demonisation' course. Should I ring the bishop, go myself or send someone else round?[1]

A vicar never panics! No – that's not quite true. A vicar

130

panics like everyone else, but doesn't show it.

'When shall I come round?' I asked innocently, trying to sound quite calm.

'Now,' he said, 'before someone gets stabbed.'

I had promised to pick up my daughter Amanda from school and then planned to prepare for the evening healing meeting. I wasn't very keen on being stabbed.

'Why did you come here?' I asked, stalling for time, with a hint of 'Why me, Lord?' in the voice.

'Because you had a Billy Graham poster up last summer and my mum was converted at the crusade. She sent me round,' he informed me.

At least there was another Christian involved. I took down the address and promised to go round shortly. After the school run I sat in the car and prayed for help and guidance.

God seemed to be saying. 'This is just a demon. Don't believe the lies. You can cope. I'll come with you.'

I went to the address in our parish to find the mother, a white lady, in a home full of Muslim children. Mark was there with Shafika and his younger brother Akbar, but the rest, I was told, were in a home five miles away. Would I take them there? I would. Akbar was keen to come too. 'I want to get into faith healing,' he said. 'Can I come and watch?' So Mother, the two teenage lads, Shafika and I left the smaller children with a Muslim lady and drove to find the others.

We arrived at a large house which had been converted into flats and immediately the word went round that the 'faith healer' had arrived! As we climbed upwards it seemed that people came out of every door and followed the Pied Piper up the stairs. 'She's in there,' one of them whispered, pointing to a door. Pause for thought. 'Do what Jesus did,' I said to myself. I remembered Jesus putting out all the unbelievers and hangers-on when he went into the room to minister to Jairus' daughter. The girl was in the room with her live-in lover so I insisted that everyone else stayed out except the Christian mother who came with me into the lion's den.

Virtually everything I knew about demons was limited to

what I had read in the Gospels. I was therefore ready for someone to scream at me as I entered the room, or to be thrown on the floor. What I was not prepared for was a quietly spoken, timid, white teenager sitting clothed and apparently in her right mind. Her boyfriend (Mark and Akbar's elder brother) was with her.

As I talked to Angela I saw nothing that suggested to me the presence of a demon. The others had told her the same story which Mark had unfolded on my doorstep and I had no reason to doubt them, but Angela was unable to remember the incident at all. She was very frightened and wanted help, but could not give me any information about the present problem, so I asked about her past. Angela was a lapsed Roman Catholic who knew something about Jesus and a few years ago had played with a ouija board. On one occasion when they had done this she had been the only one to see the figure of a lady coming down the stairs. I couldn't tell by looking or listening if there was a demon present, but after all Angela had shared, it seemed appropriate to pray over her.

I laid one hand on her head, the Christian lady put a hand on her shoulder and I said, 'Come, Holy Spirit.' Nothing appeared to manifest immediately so I kept quiet and waited. After about a minute she slowly keeled over with her eyes closed and the boys' mother caught her. It was a very gentle movement, like a child going to sleep, without any signs of disturbance or discomfort. In fact I wondered if she had gone to sleep. From then on I said all that I felt the Lord was putting into my mind and did whatever seemed appropriate.

As the mother held her up, I told Angela to open her eyes, which she did. 'What is your name?' I asked. 'Alison,' she said. I took her hand and the slumbering child began to take on the appearance of a tormented animal as she resisted my touch and started to shake. 'This must be a demon pretending to be the dead woman,' I thought, remembering how God had said not to believe everything I was told. I appeared to be no longer talking to Angela. As the shaking grew worse I found myself saying, 'Spirit of murder, I command you in the name of Jesus to leave!' The resistance intensified until suddenly the shaking dramatically ceased as Angela keeled over again. A few moments later she opened her eyes, now looking more peaceful and no longer needing to be propped up. 'What is your name?' I asked. 'Angela,' she said.

I spoke to her about the need for accepting Jesus, turning from sin and not sleeping with her boyfriend. He was not very keen on this, but she accepted it. We prayed again without any demonic manifestations and then the hordes came in to see what had happened. Shafika asked for the laying-on of hands, as did Akbar and they both experienced some heat and blessing as we prayed over them. The boyfriend let us pray for him, but felt nothing. They asked me to pray in different rooms where some of them had felt uneasy, which I did, and afterwards everything seemed to be at peace. I asked Mum to teach them about Christ and to call me if I was needed again, and then I went straight to the healing meeting rather differently prepared than I had anticipated.

Shortly after this Shafika was flown home to an arranged marriage in Pakistan. Akbar and many of our local teenagers came to a number of Christian activities where they experienced the power of God's Spirit on several occasions, but none of them stayed with us – although we do still see them from time to time. I wish we could do more for our local youngsters, but the Christian road is not an easy one and appears for the moment to be too narrow for them. Angela and boyfriend are still together, now with their own baby and it must be admitted that the peace we left behind in the house did not remain for long. The offer of a follow-up visit some weeks later met with a polite refusal.

Reflections

Inexperienced Christians can be very effective at witnessing, and healing the physically sick; sometimes more effective than experienced Christians, but so far I haven't found many to be very good at casting out demons. There are even situations when immature Christians may be harmed or affected badly, especially if ministering alone. I have told the story of Angela and her boyfriend because it was my first encounter with a demon, not because I think what I did was the 'right' way or the 'only' way to proceed in such circumstances. Today I would do things somewhat differently, so it may be helpful, with the benefit of hindsight and subsequent encounters, to share a few thoughts on 'my first time out'.

Emergency Ministry

Whenever possible I believe a Christian with no experience of demonic ministry should be accompanied on their first occasion by someone who has been that way before. All the apostles had seen Jesus cast out demons prior to attempting it themselves. When Mark came to my door I analysed, rightly or wrongly, an emergency situation when there was no time to ring for help, otherwise I would have asked someone who'd dealt with demons before to accompany me. Perhaps more than any other area in Christian ministry this is one where we need to be the most discipled and where those with experience need constantly to be making disciples.

On the other hand, if an emergency does arise God promises to go with us as he did with me. I don't believe as Christians we should ever leave people to suffer at the side of the road just because there is no better qualified help available. Providing we don't march headlong into an emergency situation, wanting simply to improve our macho image, God will not normally leave us comfortless.

In most emergency situations the best course for inexperienced Christians is to bind the demon in the name of Jesus and then seek help. The first time I was called upon to cast out a demon I had been a Christian for over twenty years, but even young, inexperienced Christians can be used by God in an emergency, if they are sensible.

Paul was eighteen and had been a Christian for six months when he came across seven younger teenagers who had been playing with a ouija board behind a supermarket. They had previously experimented with it in a house for about a month. One girl had been badly cut and there was screaming, fear and real panic. Paul knew very little about demons, but he did know he was a son of the King and couldn't leave them, so he marched in speaking in tongues. The whole situation died down completely and he was able to drive the youngsters home in his car before ringing me for help. When we have Jesus we are not as those without hope or power or authority. Normally the same result will be achieved by binding demons in our native tongue, but Paul didn't know that at the time and God used him just as he was.

Christian support

Jesus sent out his disciples two by two to preach the kingdom, heal the sick and cast out demons. In this ministry we need to seek the support of other Christians. When I went to minister to Angela I went with another Christian and my wife Carol rang up friends who prayed as I went into the situation. If Mark's mother had not been a Christian I would have made them wait until I had found someone to go with me. Jesus knew what he was doing when he sent out the apostles two by two.

Speaking about demons

God said to me, as I prayed about the ministry to Angela, 'It is only a demon.' When the worried youngsters in the flats asked me, 'What is it?' I replied, 'It's only a demon.' Being horror-movie addicts they were particularly worried it was a departed spirit or a ghost sent to haunt them and they were relieved to hear me repeat what I believed God had said to me. Often, however, the very mention of evil spirits or demons causes other people to be tense and anxious, and we need to be very careful with our language.

It can also be very hurtful in our society to be told one has a demon when it is untrue. I normally tell someone I think they have a demon only when I have seen it manifest itself or heard it speak, because at that point I will need their co-operation in getting rid of it. A demonised person normally needs to put his will into his deliverance and truly want to be free of the demon before it will go. Some really do not want to do that – especially when having a demon has become part of their identity.

Seeking Jesus not demons

When we meet people with problems, our focus is not on demons, but on how to bring Christ into the situation. I was not looking for demons, but getting on with my ordinary Christian life when Mark knocked at my door. In Scripture, people with problems often sought out Jesus for help and sometimes demons manifested themselves quite incidentally as Jesus went about doing his Father's work. I am sure if we seek Jesus and his kingdom he will send demonised people to us or us to them in his own good time.

A 'word' from God

In building up our faith and encouraging us to attempt new things for him, God often uses our present or past experiences as a launching-pad. When eighteen-year-old Paul encountered the youngsters behind the supermarket he had recently received the gift of tongues so God used that gift to bind the demons. When God thrust me into the deliverance ministry he spoke to me in my mind just as he had done the previous week when Mary had been healed. On that occasion I had been given five 'words' for healing which I spoke out, and all had been claimed, so I had some confidence and experience in the area of hearing God speak. Even so, when the inner voice came again, directing me into uncharted waters, I proceeded nervously and tentatively, testing it whenever I could and as best I knew how.

God's 'word' was particularly helpful to me when I saw a perfectly normal-looking girl and when my prayer over her produced no instant reaction. At the very least the 'word' from God encouraged me to keep going, to be patient and to trust him.

A response from the person

Angela wanted help, was frightened, knew about Jesus, and had used a ouija board for which she was sorry and promised never to do it again. Except in the case of a child, when we would look for the same response in the parent (Mk 7:24–30; 9:14–27), it seems right to pray only with those who ask for help, repent of their sins and are willing to receive Christ. Today, if I am not sure of a person's Christian status I would normally want them to invite Jesus to come into their lives by his Spirit prior to praying for deliverance for them, unless God tells me otherwise.[2] An occult background does not always mean a person is demonised, but in this case it was a helpful pointer, particularly as Angela had seen a figure, and repentance is nearly always necessary before we can begin undoing the damage that has been caused.

Learning from mistakes

When I ministered to Angela and her boyfriend I had no idea how much nurturing and post-deliverance care was needed in helping someone to be healed and remain healed. Neither had I fully understood the importance of becoming a Christian in order to prevent demons from re-entering. I am sure now that I should have asked a Christian experienced in deliverance ministry to visit them soon afterwards to check over what I had done and to assess the situation. I certainly should not have entrusted them solely to their newly-converted mother who lived five miles away.

Demons are invisible spiritual beings and as God can see what we cannot see, communication from him is important in helping the demonised to become free. Hearing God speak not only launched me into the demonic ministry, but has continually assisted me since then in seeking to release the captives and heal the afflicted. I have found the voice of God to be very precious in dealing with demons, especially in the following four areas.

1. Finding demons

Job 'was blameless and upright; he feared God and shunned evil' (Job 1:1). Satan destroyed his sons and daughters and possessions and 'afflicted Job with painful sores from the soles of his feet to the top of his head' (Job 2:7). Job's comforters did not recognise the work of Satan and though Job protested his innocence, they added to his suffering with their false accusations.

Just as Job was afflicted by Satan, so Christians and non-Christians can be afflicted by demons today. Failing to discover them, to discern their activity and to deal with them can leave people suffering as Job suffered. Job's comforters were doing their best with the revelation God had given to them, but we who live the other side of the cross have access to the power of the Spirit and the mind of Christ (1 Cor 2:10–16). Hearing the Father can help us to find demons and deal with them.

The Gerasene demoniac (Lk 8:26–39) did not go looking for Jesus; the Good Shepherd came and found him. He crossed a stormy sea to find him, set him free and then crossed back over the sea. I suspect Jesus was doing what the Father was doing.

About a year after the incident with Angela I spent some time in prayer before a meeting, asking, waiting and listening for instructions, and sensed God tell me to look for a person at the end of the ministry time who had a demon, and to minister accordingly. Consequently, I made sure there was a room available for private ministry in case I had heard God correctly.

As the ministry time drew to a close I wondered how I was expected to find a person with a demon. Maybe I would see the word 'demon' written on someone's forehead? I searched in vain and was about to avail myself of a cup of tea when one of our team asked me to assist in ministering to a lady with a pain in the head. This pain had only arrived after we had welcomed the Holy Spirit, and intensified when people sought to minister to her.

This is the stage in helping people, especially those who may be demonised, which always requires sensitivity and love. Having earlier received what I thought was a 'word' from God about a demon, I invited the lady to come with us to the private room I had reserved for ministry. I would not normally take someone out of a meeting where a lot of other ministry is taking place just for a physical condition, but this seemed the safest thing to do in case I was right and this was the lady concerned. She was pleased to come.

There was no need at this point to declare what I thought God had said to me. We were still trying to deal with a headache and so quite naturally I discussed the possible causes of the physical pain. As she suggested a particular reason for her problem God said to me, 'She's not telling you the whole truth; she needs to repent.' As it transpired, this was a 'word' from God to me about the situation, but it was not easy at that stage to know how to use such information in ministering to the person. I waited prayerfully after she had finished speaking, and God convicted her in the silence. I hardly needed to say, 'Are you sure that is all?' for immediately I finished she poured the truth out to us and repented of her sins.

This lady had in fact received some similar ministry for the same problem before. I asked God to send his Holy Spirit in power on the headache and as I did the pain intensified. The lady was able to recognise the presence of a demon herself, and to identify it for us, so I looked into her eyes and commanded it to go in Jesus' name. There was a mild belch and the headache went. We continued ministering for a while in prayer, as God's peace and blessing came upon her. Hearing God speak can sometimes help us to discern the presence of demons.

2. Finding the entry point of demons

It seems to me that people cannot catch demons like measles. Demons can afflict and damage us as Satan harmed Job, but I don't think they can enter and reside in people unless some door has been opened through serious sin or commitment to Satan. It may be the person's own sin (Rev 9:20), or sin done to them by someone else (Ps 106:37), or their ancestors' sin (Ex 34:7; Deut 23:3–4) but just as the Holy Spirit moves most freely in holiness, so demons appear to thrive on sin. Demons often leave through the same door they came in. Discovering the entry point and dealing with it through repentance and forgiveness helps us to open the door and remove demons more easily.

The New Testament is not very explicit on the way Jesus casts out demons, but in two incidents when he ministers to demonised children there is some helpful implicit information. In both cases he ministers to a parent and does not proceed to expel evil spirits until he has their co-operation and response of faith.

In Matthew 15:21–28 Jesus meets a Canaanite woman. He has ministered previously to a Gentile centurion and praised him for his faith (Mt 8:5–13) but this time he appears to refuse her for reasons of nationality. The four hurdles she is made to jump are quite unusual for Jesus and worth noting:-

(a) The lady cries out, ' "Lord, Son of David, have mercy on me! My daughter is suffering terribly from demon-possession." Jesus did not answer a word' (Mt 15:22–23).

Stage one – Jesus ignores her.

(b) The disciples step in: ' "Send her away, for she keeps crying out after us." [Jesus] answered, "I was sent only to the lost sheep of Israel" ' (vv 23–24).

Stage two – Jesus refuses her for being a foreigner.

(c) 'The woman came and knelt before him. "Lord, help me!" she said. [Jesus] replied, "It is not right to take the children's bread and toss it to their dogs"' (vv 25–26).

Stage three – Jesus refers to her as a 'dog'.

(d) '"Yes, Lord," she said, 'but even the dogs eat the crumbs that fall from the master's table"' (v 27). Then Jesus answered, "Woman, you have great faith!" Your request is granted"' (v 28).

Stage four – Having ignored her, refused her for being a foreigner and referred to her as a 'dog', Jesus finally grants the Canaanite woman's request and the daughter is healed.

This is a strange sequence of events involving the King of Love, but those who are used to helping demonised people might have some clue as to what is happening here. Unless a demonised person is absolutely determined to be free and is repentant of all known sins, it is of little use bothering with the demons; they will not come out. I frequently say to demonised people, 'I will match your determination, but don't expect me to do it for you.' We find children's demons have often entered through a parent's sin, and maybe Jesus could not have freed the girl until her mother's determination and faith had been pushed to the limit. This could well have been the way Jesus encouraged the lady to re-open the door through which the demons had entered.

We meet a similar situation in Mark chapter 9 of a boy with an evil spirit. Earlier Jesus has given the disciples authority over evil spirits (Mk 6:7), but they totally fail to remove this one. This time Jesus asks a lot of questions.

The first question is met with a detailed account of the symptoms, after which they bring the boy to Jesus (Mk 9:16–18). When the spirit saw Jesus, it immediately threw the boy into a convulsion. He fell to the ground and rolled around, foaming at the mouth' (v 20). Clearly the boy is in some distress at the encounter with Jesus, but again Jesus ignores the suffering child and turns to the parent. 'Jesus asked the boy's father, "How long has he been like this?"' (v 21). The boy's father replies, '"From childhood,"' and then begs Jesus for help.

Again Jesus turns to the father, not the boy: '"Everything

is possible for him who believes"' (v 23). The desperate man then exclaims, '"I do believe; help me overcome my unbelief!"' (v 24).

Strangely, the next verse says: 'When Jesus saw that a crowd was running to the scene, he rebuked the evil spirit' (v 25). It almost seems as if the conversation would have continued but for the sudden arrival of the crowd.

We cannot be sure exactly what was happening here, except that Jesus saw the necessity for dialogue with the father before he released the son. As with the Canaanite woman, Jesus only ministers after a response of determination and faith from the parent. If these young children had received demons due to their parents' sin, maybe as their two parents turned to Jesus in faith they were simultaneously turning from the evil which caused the trouble in the first place: such a turning would open the gate and allow the demons to be driven more easily through it.

We had trouble ministering to a lady who experienced extreme physical pain and discomfort whenever we asked God to send his Spirit upon her. There were circulation and breathing problems and severe pain in various parts of the body, especially the heart and brain. We ministered three times when this happened and at the end of each session a demon appeared to leave, but we could not continue in this way because of the physical distress being caused.

Graham, the vicar from my next-door parish, was sharing this ministry with me and on the third occasion he received a picture from God of some pigs in a pen behind a gate that was firmly shut. It seemed to him we were simply dragging the occasional pig out through the railings of the fence, when we really needed to find out how to open the gate to release them all. Recognising the pigs to be the demons, Graham advised the lady to pray on her own to see if God would reveal the gate to her. This was a picture given by God for a particular situation, but I have also found it to be a helpful truth which has application for many situations. It is not easy getting pigs out through railings and if a person exhibits excessive distress and pain when demons leave, it is often worth stopping and looking prayerfully for the gate.

The next day when alone the lady asked the Holy Spirit to come, and spent the whole day weeping for the death of her grandfather who had died when she was four years old. This was unexpected because she imagined she had something much more traumatic to be grieving over. From the age of seven she'd been a victim of incest almost until she married. Other horrific things had happened to her as a teenager and it therefore seemed surprising that an ordinary bereavement could cause such a problem. But her grandfather was the only one she felt had ever really loved her, and he had brought her up for the first four years of her life. No one ever told her properly about his death and from then on she lived in a world of her own, talking to an imaginary person at the bottom of the garden to compensate for the awful feeling of rejection. The incest, it seemed, had not caused as many demonic problems as the loss of her grandfather.

Two days later we had a Christian nurse to help us, who led her through a time of saying goodbye to Grandad. Again there was quite an emotional response, but afterwards the demons almost fell over each other to come out. Many appeared to leave that day without causing anything like the anguish of a few days before.

The greatest distress I have so far encountered in the demonic ministry seems to be caused by Christians telling people their demons have gone when they are still there. We have ministered to several in this category and some have attempted suicide because this wrong information was presented to them as certain truth. 'If my demons are supposed to have left,' said one, 'then I really must be mad and life is definitely not worth living, because I still feel awful.'

The way this frequently comes about is through well-meaning Christian friends with very little experience trying to help. Sometimes they say to the person, 'Christians can't have demons.'[3] Sometimes they manage to cast out more demons than Mary Magdalene had and as they believe no one can have more than she did they declare the person to be free.[4] Most frequently the inexperienced Christians command all demons to leave and, despite nothing visible happening, they still say: 'Just believe they've all gone. We have power over demons in Jesus' name so they cannot stay when we tell them to leave. You're clear now.'

I am afraid it really isn't always that easy and these very understandable mistakes can have very serious consequences. Here are some of the visible and audible signs which convinced people demons had left when Jesus ministered:

'The evil spirit shook the man violently and came out of him with a shriek' (Mk 1:26).

'Then the demon threw the man down before them all and came out without injuring him' (Lk 4:35).

'Demons came out of people, shouting...' (Lk 4:41).

'The evil spirits came out and went into the pigs. The herd, about two thousand in number, rushed down the steep bank into the lake and were drowned' (Mk 5:13).

'The spirit shrieked, convulsed him violently and came out. The boy looked so much like a corpse that many said, "He's dead"' (Mk 9:26).

'And when the demon was driven out, the man who had been mute spoke' (Mt 9:33).

Whatever else we might say, there appears to have been visible and audible evidence to support the evangelists' claims that demons had left on most occasions when Jesus ministered to severely demonised people. My reason for believing many demons came out of the lady following the emotional ministry connected to the death of her grandfather was the physical manifestations accompanying each departure. Sometimes there was shaking, retching, coughing up mucus or a dramatic release of pressure which had built up in the chest, neck and face as the demon surfaced and struggled to remain. Twice the lady was thrown to the floor and once we encountered almost uncontrollable screaming. Not every demon showed itself powerfully or left dramatically, but in every case the lady herself seemed to know when a demon had gone.

Perhaps the greatest long-term evidence which compels me to say demons left in this particular case is the dramatically changed life and lifestyle of the person concerned, but this is just subsequent confirmation of what we saw and heard at the time of the ministry.[5]

A direct 'word' from God may reveal the entry point through which demons entered, enabling us to re-open the gate and drive them out. Finding such a gate often makes casting out demons a much easier and less painful process.[6]

3. Finding the identity

A relative of my wife Carol is a missionary in South America. She has told me of her experience in getting rid of all a person's demons with one command. 'If they don't all go easily,' she said, 'we tell the person we will not continue ministering until they have received the lordship of Christ into every part of their life.' Apparently when they have done this a command in the name of Jesus for all demons to depart is frequently successful.

I am sad to say this has not yet been my experience in England, although I was amazed to find how much more easily demons left people in Malawi than they ever seem to here. I believe my wife's relative, but so far all those who have come to me for help in this country only seem able to put their life right bit by bit. Sometimes we have been able to command a 'head demon' to release a group of demons all at once when a person has given this area of their life to Jesus, but ministry at present is often long, difficult and costly. Those who come to me for assistance seem to have been so damaged by people and demons that I cannot easily bring myself to reject them still further by refusing ministry until the whole of their life has been yielded to the lordship of Christ. In fact God often appears to use demons to help a person to give more of themselves to Jesus and become more mature in Christ, piece by piece. Even so, this means our ministry to demonised people is often a slow and painful process, expelling demon by demon or occasionally group by group.

I have also found I frequently need the identity of a demon before it will leave.[7] Occasionally, I have been able to say, 'Demon of Satan, I command you to leave in the name of Jesus!' and it has gone, and sometimes I have told a 'head demon' to release those under its power and experienced a number leaving without knowing their names.[8] My common experience, however, is that the more stubborn ones will not leave without my knowing their identities. By 'identity' I mean the nature of a demon rather than its name – what it does rather than what it is called.

Recently I cast out a demon called Gregory from someone and the next one to appear claimed to be called Harold. I immediately began to wonder if somebody was having fun at my expense so I insisted on knowing what it did. 'Tiredness,' it confessed. The person in question had been feeling very tired when trying to read the Bible or pray, so we commanded 'tiredness' to leave in Jesus' name. We had to ask God for power, strength and energy, but eventually it left with a wail and a bout of coughing.

Jesus appears to have known the identity of most of his spiritual enemies. In the wilderness he commands Satan to go by name, and he leaves (Mt 4:10–11); he asks Legion his name (Mk 5:9; Lk 8:30);[9] he casts out a 'deaf and mute spirit' (Mk 9:25) and a demon that was mute (Lk 11:14); he deals with a demon that caused a man to be blind and dumb (Mt 12:22); and he recognises that 'a daughter of Abraham' whom he heals has been crippled by a spirit for eighteen years (Lk 13:11). It may have been a gift of discernment that enabled Jesus to recognise the demon or its manifestations in the person, or it may have been a direct 'word' from God in his spirit, but Jesus did seem to know the identity of demons on a number of occasions and not all were immediately obvious. He certainly knew what they did and how to get rid of them.[10]

In the story previously cited in Mark 9:14–32 Jesus healed a boy with an evil spirit. We are told that it 'has robbed him of speech ... it throws him to the ground ... he foams at the mouth, gnashes his teeth and becomes rigid'. It threw him into convulsions and had often thrown him into fire or water to kill him. Many commentators have described him as an 'epileptic boy', but Jesus commands a 'deaf and dumb spirit' to come out. The identity of this demon was not obvious from the boy's actions. It would seem that Jesus discerned the identity of this evil spirit supernaturally rather than naturally.

I ministered briefly to one Christian lady who was much used by God to care and counsel and pray for other people. I can honestly say I was privileged to meet such a beautiful Christian person. When I asked the Spirit to come, horrific demons manifested, growling and snarling and throwing her to the floor. Like so many Christians we find with resident demons, she had been an incest victim. Not everyone we see who has suffered abuse as a child is demonised, but when demons manifest in mature Christians we are not surprised to find a history of abuse, sexual or otherwise. With many such people we also find ancestral demons which have been in the family for generations due to black mass rites and passed on to the child at conception or birth.

We managed to bind the demons and she shared some of her problems with me. Knowing herself that demons were present, she listed a number of areas of difficulty in her life, trying to help me discern what was causing the problem. As I ministered to her the thought came into my head that God wanted me to deal with three demons, of which the first one was bitterness. I enquired about relationships and she told me of a relative who had treated her badly. 'Can you forgive him?' I asked, and she said she didn't think she could. Normally this would be the end of the ministry, but in this case I sensed God saying to me, 'Tell her to say the words.' I asked her if she could at least say a prayer forgiving the relative. 'I could say the words,' she said, 'but I don't think I could mean them.'

There are times when many of us suspect our own motives

and wonder if we can really repent and forgive someone, but a demonised person has even more problems than most of us in this area. Sometimes a person may feel bitter because they are feeling the bitterness of the demon inside masking their own feelings. In my limited experience I have not yet seen demons leave without true repentance and forgiveness from the person, and if demons have entered through the person's own sin they appear only to leave when the person repents of that sin. If demons enter through sins done to the person they only seem to leave when the person forgives those who have sinned against them. But while this may always be necessary, only God knows the truth of someone's heart and his 'word' to me on this occasion released that truth. After I had encouraged her to say the words, the lady prayed a forgiving prayer which was one of the most beautiful and sincere I have ever heard. She didn't think she could forgive her relative but God, who knows us better than we know ourselves, was apparently saying she could.

There was then a powerful confrontation. As I asked God to send his Spirit on her, the head was thrown back, the jaws clamped shut like a strong vice and the skin of the face seemed to be stretched so tightly across the bones that the head looked like a skull. I commanded the demon of 'bitterness' to leave in the name of Jesus and after some violent shaking, the jaws were forced apart dramatically as the demon left. The second demon was less powerful and departed more easily, but the third went in similar fashion to the first. Each time I used the identity I believed God was giving me, and ordered the demon to leave in the name of Jesus.

When a demon manifests, it is sometimes possible to discern its identity from what the person then does or is caused to do. A demon of mockery may laugh and smile insincerely, while a demon of self-destruction may cause the person to hurt themselves with scratching or biting. I once encountered a demon of madness which sang a high-pitched song all about Wranglers jeans and Levis. In the case of the lady who prayed the forgiving prayer, the demons were all of the angry, unforgiving, resentful category, but even so there were sufficient differences in the manifestations to see naturally that each one was a separate and distinct entity. The force with which they came out through the mouth together with the lady's testimony, left us in little doubt that three different demons had departed.

I then prayed again that the Spirit would come upon her, and the most incredible joy and peace came over her; at least the ministry was over for the night. Hearing God speak can sometimes release tremendous power and love. The lady and I believe demons left when I addressed them with the identities that God had given me and on this occasion I did not need to hear them speak.

I have found there to be a tremendous advantage in knowing the identity of demons, both for the deliverance ministry and the follow-up. If a demon will not go and we know it is a demon of lust, we know that the person will need to be forgiven or to forgive in the area of sexual immorality. Similarly, if a demon of lust goes, the person knows how to behave in future in order to resist further demonic attacks and to receive more of Jesus. If a person continues to have problems after demons have been cast out it may be emotional hurt that needs healing; it may be that we did not get rid of all the demons; or it may be that some have come back.[11] Keeping records can sometimes help us to minister more effectively to the person.

If people want to know numbers and names in order to notch up their successes on the door-post, that would be quite wrong, but most people who are sick find it helpful to know what their disease or sickness was, and how to stay well. So many weird and wonderful manifestations are caused by emotional hurts and genuine psychiatric illnesses that I have found it helpful to try to identify the Enemy more precisely. Hearing God speak can sometimes help us to do that.

4. Finding the right way to minister

When Saul had an evil spirit David ministered to him with music (1 Sam 16:23); God used Peter's shadow (Acts 5:15) and Paul's handkerchiefs (Acts 19:12); Jesus resisted the approach of a Syro-Phoenician woman (Mk 7:24–30), took time questioning a boy's father (Mk 9:14–29), asked a demon its name (Mk 5:1–20), refused to let another demon speak (Mk 1:34), and drove out many spirits with a word (Mt 8:16). The variety of ways of ministering to the demonised in Scripture points us once more to the need for discernment and listening to God.

Once Jesus ministered to a 'daughter of Abraham' – a believer – in the synagogue (Lk 13:10–17). I doubt whether anyone knew she was 'crippled by a spirit for eighteen years' until Jesus declared this after he had set her free (v 16). On that occasion Jesus used a two-stage ministry and did not command any demons to leave. It is likely that this was an afflicting spirit as opposed to a resident one. Jesus said, 'Woman, you are set free from your infirmity' (v 12). In my experience this is the kind of language which will often remove an afflicting spirit; maybe this is what Jesus was doing. Luke then records that 'he put his hands on her'. In the Gospel accounts no mention is made of Jesus putting his hands on people when he is getting rid of demons, but it is quite frequently mentioned when he is healing the physically sick. It may be therefore that Jesus was laying on hands in order to heal the crippled back which had been damaged by the demon and needed restoring. This interpretation may not be absolutely correct, but it seems to be yet another example of how Jesus is being guided to minister uniquely to one more demonised person. We also need to be guided by God in the appropriate way to set the captives free.

I visited a non-Christian married couple at their invitation and eventually had the joy of leading them through what I thought was a prayer of commitment to Jesus. As I asked the

Spirit to fill them the wife's eyes began to flutter and her hands to shake gently from side to side. I asked God to give her the gift of tongues and the two of us who were ministering began quietly speaking in tongues ourselves. Immediately she began to speak in tongues in a strong, Scandanavian-sounding language and I was tremendously encouraged. Eventually we stopped speaking in tongues, but she just went on and on, not easily able to stop it. Although there was nothing nasty, horrid or angry in the tongues flowing from her, such a lack of control did not seem to me to be in keeping with the work of the Holy Spirit. Then it dawned on me: 'Demons of Satan,' I said, 'I command you to manifest'.

I wish for the sake of unbelievers I could have recorded on video what then began to happen to a normal, perfectly sane, middle-class housewife. I've seen some pretty hairy things in my time, but never anything like this. Her head was shaken from side to side at colossal speed, like a rag doll shaken by an angry child. Her eyes seemed to rattle in her head and roll around as the eyelids opened and closed at supersonic speed. Simultaneously, a hideous, mocking sneer spread across her face, like a teenager making faces at a monkey behind bars. I commanded it all to stop and while the husband looked on in disbelief his wife asked me, 'What was that?' Others might have their own name for it, but mine was 'demons'. We continued ministering to the woman.[12]

As I ordered the first demon to speak to me the same Scandinavian tongue flowed out so I insisted on English. The demon then spoke to me in English with a Scandinavian accent, but as I repeated the command in Jesus' name it gave the word 'pretence'.

Sometimes the person knows the identity of a demon; sometimes the manifestations reveal clearly what it does; sometimes we receive a 'word' from God and sometimes we discover it by commanding the demon to name itself. Initially evil spirits are not often willing to speak or reveal their nature and even if they do speak will normally lie. Eventually, however, as they are persistently challenged in Jesus' name and the person co-operates, their power wanes and they then frequently give a clue as to their real identity. Just as God and angels, who are spirit, are always true to their natures, so are demons remarkably consistent in being evil in all they do and, if the person is co-operative, do not normally conceal their nature consistently when challenged in Jesus' name.

This one finally said: 'She doesn't really believe in Jesus.' When I asked: 'Are you a demon of pretence?' the demon went beserk; the lady's countenance changed as she snarled like a wounded tiger trapped in a corner. This instant change when the right identity was given was almost unmistakable and is the way I have invariably been able to discern a demon's identity. Sometimes telling a particular demon to go in Jesus' name is all that is then necessary, but sometimes knowing its identity guides us in further ministry to the person. Only very rarely have I found that a demon does not eventually leave when we have discovered its identity, and then it is normally because the person is unwilling or unable to repent or forgive. I believe it is wrong to seek information from a demon, but commanding it to name itself, when successful, seems to be the means of beginning to break its power. Just as there is holy power in Jesus' name, there appears to be evil power in a demon's name.

We stopped engaging the demon for a while and the lady confessed that she hadn't really believed all we had told her about the two kingdoms. The experience of Jesus' power forcing the demon to manifest and then be quiet, however, had begun to confirm for her the truth of what we had read in previous Bible studies together. This time she made a genuine commitment and when we commanded it to go, the demon of pretence departed. Afterwards, when we invoked the Holy Spirit again, the eyes rolled and the head shook, but the sneer was not to be seen.

By now it was late on a Friday so we bound the remaining demons in Jesus' name and ordered them to do no more harm. On the Monday we returned, counselling and praying for the whole morning, but nothing happened: no more rag doll appearances, no more shaking or twitching, rattling or rolling. There was no obvious peace, but no obvious demons. Something was wrong; I was sure I'd seen demons on the Friday.

We closed our eyes, prayed and asked God to give us a word of knowledge and one word came into my mind: 'mother'. I shared this and the lady confessed how over the weekend she'd told her mother all about Friday's happenings. Mother had convinced her it wasn't real, we were crazy and there were no such things as demons. I suppose most mothers wouldn't take too kindly to being told their daughter was demonised. Receiving the word 'mother' from God enabled us to know how to minister in the situation.

Sometimes people who don't believe in demons ask me why they've never seen any.[13] The key that unlocks the door to the spiritual world is faith, and without it the door often remains tightly closed. We managed to open the door again after lunch: we talked and listened, shared the gospel once more and reminded the lady of all that we had seen and experienced the previous Friday. Eventually she accepted the truth about Jesus and demons; this time when we prayed the head was shaken again and the eyes once more began to rattle and roll around as in one of those old-fashioned china dolls.

In the way I have previously described we ascertained that the demon causing the head to be shaken violently was 'anger' and the one affecting the eyes was 'conceit'; both left with a struggle. In each case the lady doubled up in pain and coughed them out through the mouth, feeling sure on both occasions that one had gone. After that, when we asked the Spirit to come, the eyes fluttered nicely, the hands moved from side to side gently, the supernatural language could be spoken with perfect control, and peace and blessing was seen on the face. Hearing God speak can help us to find the right way to minister to someone with demons.

When we go to war and meet the Enemy face to face 'the sword of the Spirit, which is the word of God' comes into its own (Eph 6:17). The word *of* God tells us what to do, and a word *from* God, which comes through the Holy Spirit, sometimes tells us how to do it. When we obey what the Father says there is no shortage of power to fulfil his commands. As we offer ourselves in service to the King there are times, of his choosing, when he will enable us to find demons, their entry points into people, their identity when necessary, and will tell us how to cast them out. When we do in faith what he tells us to do, the power comes and the victory won at Calvary is realised in people's lives even if the war goes on.

Being prepared to cast out demons can help us to hear God speak and hearing God speak can help us to cast out demons.

Notes

1. I keep the bishops of our diocese informed of developments in the deliverance ministry within our parish and from time to time give more detailed reports, as the situation demands.
2. The teaching in Matthew 12:43–45 and Lk 11:24–26 will often help a demonised non-Christian to receive Jesus. Unless God specifically tells me to cast out a demon first because the person will believe after he has seen God's power at work, I like to know the Holy Spirit is in residence prior to the demons leaving.
3. C Peter Wagner makes some helpful points on 'Demons and Christians' in *How To Have A Healing Ministry Without Making Your Church Sick* (Monarch Publications Ltd: Eastbourne, 1988), p 189.

   For a more lengthy discussion on the problem see *Christian Deliverance* by Peter Hobson, especially Book 1, chapter 1. (Full Salvation Fellowship: Australia, 1985).
4. In Mark 5:1–20 we have a story of 'many' demons (v 9) which leave one man and go into some pigs. We are told of the herd, there were 'about two thousand in number'. A Roman legion (cf v 9) numbered from 4,000 to 6,000 men, so without being able to be too precise, I think there is scriptural precedent for more than seven demons.

   See also Graham and Shirley Powell, *Christian Set Yourself*

Free (New Wine Press: Chichester, 1983), p 39, 'Numbers of Demons'.

5. Experienced counsellors may be able to discern demonic presences and remove them with the minimum of manifestations. John and Paula Sandford say, 'Exorcisms can be done by quiet authority and faith, without hyper-emotion or physical demonstrations.' John and Paula Sandford, *Healing the Wounded Spirit* (Victory House Inc: Tulsa, 1985), p 336.)

Graham and Shirley Powell say, 'Many demons leave without any manifestation. When praying for deliverance, we should not look for manifestations or expect that they will always occur.' Powell, *op cit*, p 124.)

These people have years of experience and while they quite rightly do not allow demons to 'perform', they do still give tangible reasons in their books for when they believe demons are present and how they know when demons have gone. I am most concerned with the beginner who, from a purely subjective point of view, claims either that a person has demons or that they have left. I believe there needs to be more objective evidence before Christians can or should make those claims.

Frank and Ida Mae Hammond say, 'When evil spirits depart we normally expect some sort of manifestation.' (Frank and Ida Mae Hammond, *Pigs in the Parlour* (Impact Books Inc: Kirkwood, 1973), p 52.) I think this is the most helpful general truth for inexperienced ministers to bear in mind, especially when ministering to the severely demonised.

6. See John Wimber, *Power Healing* (Hodder & Stoughton: London, 1986), pp 130–132, 'Entry Points'.

7. The following have also testified to the value of knowing a demon's identity:

Francis MacNutt: 'Ordinarily we need to find out the identity of the demon we are driving out ... It is important to realise that these powers are not impersonal forces of evil, but we are dealing with real entities that have a name.' Francis MacNutt, *Healing* (Bantam Books Inc: New York, 1974), pp 222–223.)

John and Paula Sandford: '... it is truly wise and powerful to know a name.' Sandford, *op cit*, p 337.

Frank and Ida Mae Hammond:

Experience has proved that a spirit's power is more readily

broken by forcing it to identify itself. Some spirits are much more stubborn or tenacious than others. In most instances when a stubborn spirit is compelled to name itself it will come out. Its power is broken. (Hammond, *op cit*), p 82.

John Wimber:

When I know that I am dealing with a demon, I will command its attention by looking straight into the demonised person's eyes and saying, 'Look at me!' I will then command the demons to tell me their names (see Mark 5:9). I say, 'In the name of Jesus, I command you, spirit, tell me your name.' (Wimber, *op cit*, p 241.)

Bill Subritzky believes in finding out the names of the head demons in a person: 'Paul knew exactly who was his enemy. We all know it is Satan, but we also need to understand the strong men who are under Satan's authority.'

'With the help of the Holy Spirit we need to seek out the leader of the demon powers within a person.' (Bill Subritzky, *Demons Defeated* (Sovereign World Ltd: Chichester, 1986), pp 26, 208.)

John White, the Christian psychiatrist, says, 'I demand in the name of Jesus that any demon who might be present give me its name. Once the demon does so, I know where I am and can act accordingly.' (John White, *When The Spirit Comes With Power* (Hodder & Stoughton: London, 1989), p 100.)

8. For more information on 'head demons' see Bill Subritzky, *op cit*, p 25, 'The Strong Men'; C Peter Wagner, *op cit*, p 202–204; Hammond, *op cit*, chapter 20, 'Demon Groupings'.

9. For a helpful discussion on whether 'Legion' was the man's name or the identity of the demon, see C E B Cranfield, *The Cambridge Greek Testament Commentary* (Cambridge University Press: London, 1959), p 178.

10. For biblical examples of demons' identities see Powell, *Christian Set Yourself Free*, p 43, 'The Names of Demons'.

11. Very rarely do demons appear to re-enter someone who is seeking ministry unless that person commits serious sin. We have found most heavily demonised people have several demons of the same name, normally under different leader spirits.

12. The psychiatrist John White also describes 'the rapid side-to-side movement of the head that makes the face a blur', which he once assumed 'must be characteristic of demonization'. With more experience since then he confesses to being a little more cautious now in deciding it 'must' be demonic, and I think his caution is worth noting. In this particular case the subsequent ministry appeared to confirm a correct diagnosis. (John White, *When The Spirit Comes With Power* (Hodder & Stoughton: London, 1988), p 99.)

13. I was always unsure of the existence of spiritual beings apart from God until I did a Bible study on angels. I found references in more than half the books of the Bible, numbering 273 in total, and could only conclude that to deny the existence of spiritual beings is to deny the truth of the Bible. Whether they are good angels, bad angels, good spirits, evil spirits or demons seems largely irrelevant. The Bible denies the belief sometimes asserted by human beings that we are 'all there is'.

I personally found the strength of the biblical case on spiritual beings far more helpful and convincing than trying to decide whether all cases of 'demons' in the New Testament were really psychiatric illnesses. The Bible is definite. God has created spiritual beings apart from us.

7

Recognising 'Words' from God

In the summer of 1986 an elderly lady asked if she could make an appointment to come and see me. She came from a slightly different tradition from myself and was used to making formal confessions to another priest on a regular basis, but this time she wanted to see me. Apparently there were things in her past she had not been able to tell anyone about and as the Holy Spirit was now moving powerfully in her life she felt the need for a completely clean slate.

I was brought up to confess my sins to God through Jesus Christ and had not been encouraged to hear confessions, but when God began teaching us about healing I soon realised the value of James' advice to confess our sins to each other (Jas 5:16).[1] I therefore readily agreed to see her. A few days before the lady arrived I received a letter with a list of the major sins in her life spelled out. I suspect she was aware of my inexperience at hearing confessions and wanted to give me the chance to prepare prayerfully beforehand for our appointment by knowing something of what she wished to share. I was grateful for this opportunity and, without revealing any details of the confession, I discussed what to do, with my wife Carol, and we decided I should burn the letter in the lady's presence. I was tempted to borrow a set of formal prayers from my Anglo-Catholic friends, but changed my mind after reading John 20:21–23:

Jesus said, 'Peace be with you! As the Father has sent me, I am sending you.' And with that he breathed on them and said, 'Receive the Holy Spirit. If you forgive anyone his sins, they are forgiven; if you do not forgive them, they are not forgiven.'

I became sure the authority to forgive someone their sins was connected to the receiving of the Holy Spirit. Just as faith to ask God to move mountains is dependent on asking in Jesus' name (Jn 14:12–14) according to his will (1 Jn 5:14), so I came to believe forgiving sins could only be done in Jesus' name according to his will. It is the Holy Spirit who reveals to us the mind of Christ, enabling us to forgive sins in his name.

It was a warm summer's day when the lady came into my study where I was waiting with a baking tray, a box of matches and the letter. It didn't seem necessary to speak out the sins which had been written down, as I had already read them, so we had a general time of prayer and confession before turning our attention to the refiner's fire. The confession had been written on two similar pieces of paper covering three sides so I placed them on top of each other on the baking tray and prepared to set them alight. As I took the matches in my hand the thought came into my head, 'It's not all going to burn. Minister to what is left.'

All the windows were firmly closed as I applied a match to the corner of the pieces of paper. The flame spread across the bottom, burned uniformly halfway up the page, turned left, travelled up the side and across the top before going out, leaving two pieces of paper about three inches by two inches, with writing on three sides. I shared my earlier thoughts which I believed were from God and immediately the lady became curious: 'What's left? Tell me what's left,' she said somewhat urgently.

All the sins of commission, the things the lady had done wrong in her life had burned. Although there was writing left on three sides, the words which remained were all about sins of omission, things she had failed to do or wished she had done in her life.

This lovely Christian lady had received some gifts of the Spirit for the first time after her seventieth birthday, although she had served the Lord most of her days, and deep inside I sensed there was a resentment against God for not giving her more gifts earlier in life. She had been asking for these for many years. This meant, accompanying the repentance for things she had failed to do, was a feeling that if God had given her more gifts she might have done better. It could never be true repentance to confess one's own sins to God while deep down still partly blaming him for them.

'Tell her to repent,' said God. So I did. Recognising the truth of what I said, she agreed and at once crumpled on the floor, head bowed in prayer. A few moments later she popped up and said, 'All done.'

Sensing in my spirit a true repentance had now taken place, I applied a match to the remnant of the confession which was consumed in a flash. Not a word was left. I pronounced God's absolution for the forgiveness of sins with some certainty. I believe the inner thoughts from the Spirit, plus the guidance of the flames, gave me the authority from Jesus to forgive her sins in his name. A few weeks later the lady had an accusing thought about one of her sins which had been on the paper. 'You can't get me with that one,' she said to Satan, 'I've seen it burn.'

In Scripture we find many examples of God communicating with his people through other such external signs and wonders. Most of us are already familiar with some of the more dramatic ones.

Moses saw a burning bush and heard a voice coming from the midst of the flames (Ex 3:1–4); Balaam heard a donkey speaking and met an angel (Num 22:28–31); Daniel saw writing on the wall, and talked to Gabriel (Dan 5:13–17; 9:21–23); Jesus conversed with Moses and Elijah who 'appeared in glorious splendour', and heard the audible voice of God at least three times (Mt 3:17; Lk 9:30–35; Jn 12:27–29); many people saw tongues of fire and heard God speaking to them in their own language on the Day of Pentecost

(Acts 2:1–11); and Paul saw a light from heaven flashing around him, accompanied by the voice of God (Acts 9:3–5). Most of us feel we would recognise God's voice and obey his message if it came to us as an audible voice accompanied by a visible sign, but even the whisper coming to Elijah after the fire had fallen from heaven (1 Kings 19:12) is more than most of us have ever experienced. For many of us the heavens seem strangely silent.

The mini-miracle of the guided flame is the only direct external guidance from God, apart from circumstances, I can ever remember receiving. The inner prompting which came to me before the burning of the written confession is a common and frequent way in which I believe God communicates with me. In the same way I suspect the miraculous communications of God in Scripture may have also been memorable and special rather than normative.

In seeking to hear and recognise communications from the God who loves to speak it is important to look where he has told us for that which he has promised to give us. God has spoken and does speak with external signs and wonders, but this is not what he has promised to do for everyone. Maybe the heavens have remained too silent far too long for many of us simply because it is not in the heavens where we should be looking for the God who speaks.

The inside story

The Book of Jeremiah records this prophecy:

> 'The time is coming,' declares the Lord, 'when I will make a new covenant with the house of Israel and with the house of Judah .... This is the covenant that I will make with the house of Israel after that time,' declares the Lord. 'I will put my law in their minds and write it on their hearts. I will be their God, and they will be my people. No longer will a man teach his neighbour, or a man his brother, saying, "Know the Lord," because they will all know me from the least of them to the greatest"' (Jer 31:31–34; see also Heb 8:8–12).

This is the New Covenant promise of God. Jeremiah declares the Old Covenant has been broken (31:32), but a new one is coming, and this is the solemn promise of God. 'I will put my law in their minds and write it on their hearts. I will be their God and they will be my people.' The result of this is, 'They will all know me, from the least of them to the greatest.'

This is some promise! Instead of a set of laws written on tablets of stone, God is going to make his will known by writing it on people's minds and hearts. And this is not just for special people. All his people from the least to the greatest will know the God who speaks. Under the Old Covenant special people such as prophets spoke with the guidance of the Holy Spirit, but under the New Covenant this promise is for all believers.

Jesus saw himself as the fulfiller of this New Covenant promise: 'This cup is the new covenant in my blood, which is poured out for you' (Lk 22:20; cf Mt 26:28; Mk 14:24; 1 Cor 11:25), and Hebrews chapters 8 and 9 explain it more fully. The death of Christ on the cross opens the door of the New Covenant from God's side and all who believe in Jesus and receive his sacrifice for themselves (Jn 6:53) enter a New Covenant relationship with God through that door. Jesus also re-affirms the promises of God declared through Jeremiah and explains how it will come about:

> I will ask the Father, and he will give you another Counsellor to be with you for ever – the Spirit of truth. The world cannot accept him, because it neither sees him nor knows him. But you know him, for he lives with you and will be in you .... On that day you will realise that I am in my Father, and you are in me, and I am in you (Jn 14:16–17,20).

Jesus says when the Holy Spirit comes, who will teach us all things (v 26), he will be in us, giving us the mind of Christ and enabling us to know God on the inside, just as Jeremiah prophesied.

The New Testament writers were certain this promise came true at Pentecost and was now available to all believers:

'If anyone acknowledges that Jesus is the Son of God, God lives in him and he in God' (1 Jn 4:15).

'We know that we live in him and he in us, because he has given us of his Spirit' (1 Jn 4:13).

'Don't you know that you yourselves are God's temple and that God's Spirit lives in you?' (1 Cor 3:16).

The early Christians experienced several external communications from God such as the occasional angel or voice from heaven, but they seemed to be even more familiar with the Holy Spirit who lived inside each one, speaking to them:

'The Spirit told Philip, "Go to that chariot"' (Acts 8:29).

'While Peter was still thinking about the vision, the Spirit said to him...' (Acts 10:19).

'Agabus stood up and through the Spirit predicted ... a severe famine' (Acts 11:28).

'The Holy Spirit said, "Set apart for me Barnabas and Saul"' (Acts 13:2).

I believe these verses refer to the inner prompting or 'knowing' about which Jeremiah, Jesus and Paul spoke.

The Bible describes external encounters with the living God and his message, as when Mary met the angel Gabriel, but never promises them to believers. They may happen, and indeed they do happen, but Scripture does not say we can expect them to happen to everyone. God does not promise blinding lights and flames of fire to all who turn to him, but he promises to give us a new heart and put a new spirit within us (Ezek 36:26). Jesus does not say that when he has gone to the Father he will send legions of angels to give us our daily instructions, but he promises to send the Spirit that we may be in him, and he in us (Jn 14:16–17). The Spirit does not guarantee to write words on walls, tablets of stone or people's foreheads, but to write his truth in our minds (Heb 8:10). God gives his Holy Spirit to all believers, who can expect to hear him and know him within their innermost being. I believe this is where we should look for God's direct communication to us. It is this subjective experience of God, which calls for faith and risk, that is promised to all in the Bible.

Many Christians are concerned with any emphasis on subjective encounters with God because it is often members of the fanatical fringe in our churches who most regularly claim to have a hot line to God. But even though discerning the inner voice of the Spirit may begin as a subjective experience, an objective verification that such 'words' are most likely from God frequently follows.

I was writing letters one Friday morning when the thought came into my head, 'Go and visit Michael and Sandra.' This was not a prompting I wanted to get wrong as they lived a few miles from the vicarage, so I said to God, 'I'll ring them up first.'

'No good,' said God, 'there's no one in, but there will be by the time you arrive.' That was a very subjective piece of guidance: it could have been my own wishful thinking as they were already on my mind, or it could have been Satan wanting to waste my time on a wild-goose chase. It could also have been God. I repented of my sins, came against the Enemy in Jesus' name, prayed some more and as the thought persisted, I went.

When I arrived at Michael and Sandra's home there was no one there and I felt mildly annoyed. Before returning to my car I put a note through the door: if I had wasted my time driving all the way over to their house I wanted them to know I'd been. As I started the engine God seemed to say to me, 'Wait just five more minutes and someone will come.' Reluctantly I agreed to another five minutes, but not a second more, and took off my wrist watch to time it. God and I then sat quietly. After exactly five minutes I started the engine, engaged reverse gear, looked into the rear-view mirror in order to back out of the drive, but found I couldn't get out because Michael was driving in.

He was very surprised to see me as he didn't normally come home at that time on a Friday. He had taken the afternoon off and decided to pop home for lunch prior to picking up Sandra from the school where she worked. Even had I phoned at precisely the moment he entered the house, there would not have been time for me to reach him before he was due to leave. Unknown to me they had an appointment to see someone together about adopting a child. It was a good time of sharing and I was glad to be able to pray for him at this important moment in his life. Although hearing the inner voice of God is often a very subjective experience, the accuracy of such 'words' can sometimes be tested more objectively.

Recognising God speaking internally

I believe most Christians have heard God speaking to them. The nudges, promptings, premonitions, knowings and feelings in the bones that we so often cynically laugh away or describe as feminine intuitions are probably all from God. I was greatly helped in recognising 'words' from God when I heard from others of the many different ways in which God often chooses to communicate his message.

It is very noticeable if we look at the references I have quoted from the Acts of the Apostles how often we are told, 'The Holy Spirit said ...' without being informed how the person experienced this. Was it a thinking or a seeing, a feeling or a knowing, a doing, a dreaming or a speaking which revealed this particular 'word' from God? Frequently we are left groping in the dark without an answer, but there are hints in Scripture which together with some stories from experience may help us to move towards the light.

1. Thinking

Mark 5:27–28 records this: 'When she heard about Jesus, she came up behind him in the crowd and touched his cloak, because she *thought*, "If I just touch his clothes, I will be healed"' (my italics).

The commonest way I receive a 'word' from God is, I think

it. This lady thought that if she touched Jesus' cloak she would be healed, and she was right. This must have been more than a good thought. This must have been a 'God thought', as God healed her. Because the Holy Spirit is within us there will be times when our thoughts will be God's thoughts.

A little while ago I arranged a few mid-week meetings for members of our own church. As I prayed and planned before the first meeting I wondered how many were going to be there. Previous mid-week meetings and courses had attracted between ten and fifteen people so I thought it would be encouraging to have twenty. Sitting in an armchair in my study with my eyes closed, I offered the whole meeting to the Lord, asking him what to do and how to do it, and the thought in my head grew stronger that twenty people would be present.

At that time in our church this was a welcome thought as we did not normally have so many at meetings. I therefore assumed this was an expression of my own hopes and desires. It was a pleasant thought, but not a very profound one so I stored it away in my memory bank.

Jane was the first person to arrive for the meeting while I was choosing a few choruses and she asked me how many chairs to put out. 'Twenty,' I said. 'There will be twenty people here tonight.' This came out rather more strongly than I intended, but Jane did as she was told without comment or question. Exactly twenty people came and every chair was taken.

It is always easy to be wise after the event so I made sure everyone knew about my previous comment to Jane before beginning the time of ministry. 'I thought God said twenty,' I added, 'as I was praying this afternoon.' One lady came up to me afterwards and shared how a sudden thought had come into her head at about six o'clock to join our meeting. She was a Roman Catholic so rang up two Catholic friends and persuaded them to come with her at the last moment. All three arrived after the start of the meeting, taking us from seventeen to twenty. The encouraging thought was maybe more profound than it seemed at the time. It was one simple 'word' from God which simultaneously said to twenty people, 'I know all about you – your comings and goings – I love you and my hand is on your life.' It also lifted the faith of the group who not only felt individually called and special, but corporately that God was present and moving among us.

The following week I received another thought as I was praying: 'You will need twenty-one chairs tonight.'

'Church growth is coming at last!' I thought to myself.

Jane very carefully put out twenty-one chairs and when we started at half past seven I announced confidently, 'God has told me to have twenty-one chairs put out tonight.' We all looked around at the empty spaces before the fourteen of us who were present sang the first chorus. By eight o'clock there were twenty of us sharing God's word together. Six of them had not been present the previous week, which meant six had not come back. 'Ah well!' I thought. 'Maybe church growth will come next week.' The empty chair haunted us for a further twenty minutes and then my wife Carol arrived. She hadn't promised to come, thinking the children would not be asleep before nine o'clock, but sleep had come early and Carol was able to join us.

The following week everyone wanted to know how many were coming, but the voice of God was silent. God was not into number games or impressive forecasting. He had declared his love for us, demonstrated his presence in our midst and was now moving on. God may speak to us through a thought in the mind, but whenever we try to anticipate the next thought we often find our ways are not his ways. A thought from God is not a rational thinking through of a problem, but an impulse in the brain, often sudden and unexpected. Such a thought can normally be verified only by responding with obedience and faith but there are times, I am sure, when God's thoughts may be our thoughts.

Seeing in the mind – a still picture

'This is what the Sovereign Lord showed me: a basket of ripe fruit' (Amos 8:1).

Amos saw a basket of ripe fruit, just as Jeremiah saw 'the branch of an almond tree' (Jer 1:11) and Peter saw 'a large sheet' (Acts 10:11). This is a picture from God, but before it can be of much use there needs to be an interpretation: '"What do you see, Amos?" he asked. "A basket of ripe fruit," I answered. Then the Lord said to me, "The time is ripe for my people Israel; I will spare them no longer"' (Amos 8:1–2).

In the Old Testament the interpretation of a still picture was normally given to the person who received it, but under the New Covenant there are greater options available as all believers have received the Spirit.

Whenever Roger Jones puts on one of his Christian musicals, the performers always meet beforehand for prayer. At one of these gatherings someone shared a picture they were receiving of a dead tree which was still standing and rooted in the ground. A second person received a picture of a tombstone and a third person felt the interpretation was to do with a recent bereavement and the problem of letting the deceased person go.

Roger gave these words to the audience after the performance and three ladies came forward claiming the 'words' and seeking ministry. They had all been tragically bereaved, losing their menfolk in the same car accident. God's Spirit came powerfully on all three, helping them in their great need. Sometimes God may speak to us through a picture.

Seeing in the mind – A moving picture

Ezekiel saw a valley full of dry bones connecting as he prophesied, gaining flesh and breath and coming to life (Ezek. 37:1–14). It was a 'word' from God about the restoration of Israel who were at that time in exile. I like to differentiate between a vision and a moving picture in the mind for purposes of clarification. Scripture does not often make this distinction so we are not certain if Ezekiel saw the bones in his mind as he prayed, or went to the valley and saw a vision, with his eyes open, of all he described. I call it a vision if the eyes are open, a picture if the eyes are closed and it is seen in the mind, and a dream if the person is asleep.

At one of our small gatherings Greg saw a picture in his mind of a river in the final stages of its journey. Just before it reached the sea it was confronted by a huge shingle bank, causing it to disperse and trickle through the pebbles instead of flowing powerfully to its destination.

'It's a blockage;' they all cried, 'someone's got a blockage. Maybe a problem or a burden or a sin that needs to be released. Who needs to be set free?'

After a brief, silent pause Mary spoke quietly and gave us the correct interpretation. She was listening to the Spirit and not just the words of the picture. 'It isn't a blockage,' she said. 'Someone is having difficulty at present and God wants the person to know the same amount of water is still getting through to the sea.' Of course, that was right. If there had been a blockage Greg would have seen a dam and a flood, but the river was still reaching its goal and fulfilling its purpose.

This picture and interpretation meant a lot to someone who was present, and helped them later in the week.

Seeing in the mind – Real events

'Jesus answered, "I saw you while you were still under the fig-tree before Philip called you"' (Jn 1:48).

Sometimes we see real events for evangelism, as with Nathaniel, or healing (Acts 9:12), or deliverance (Lk 10:18–19) or protection (2 Kings 6:8–23). The commonest reason people see real events at our church seems to be for the healing of past hurts. One lady very kindly wrote down what happened to her at one of our meetings:

Every time I went to the healing course at St John's and they asked the Holy Spirit to come, I would have a picture of a shed flash into my mind. I just didn't understand why this happened. It seemed as if there was some barrier there.

On 21st November 1987 I went to Part Four of the Inner Healing Course at Christ Church. After the coffee break Peter asked the Holy Spirit to come. My hands started to shake and I had the same picture of the shed flash into my mind again. Someone was ministering to me and asked what was happening. I said I could see a shed. I was asked more questions about it. Then I could see myself inside the shed. I was about six years old and I was standing in the dark, crying. When I was asked again what was happening I could see some boys, including my brother, all about twelve to fourteen years old. They were lighting matches. I couldn't get out and I felt very frightened. I was asked if Jesus was there. I said he wasn't. I was told he was there, but I said I was only a little girl. I was told Jesus was there even though I was only little.

Then I felt my arms being held tight, my clothing messed about, my body interfered with. I think I was on the floor and I wanted them to stop, but I didn't know what was happening, I just kept on crying.

I was asked to let Jesus in and then Jesus did open the door slightly, but the boys were in the way. Then Peter came and asked if I was being assaulted and I said, 'Yes.' He then started ministering to me. He asked me to let Jesus in and then the door opened and the sun and the daylight shone in. Jesus picked me up, hugged me tight and told me not to cry. After a while he said, 'My peace I give you, my peace I give you.' He then put me down and I skipped into the garden. The grass was green and I looked at all the beautiful flowers.

The Spirit left me and I opened my eyes. After talking I was able to forgive my brother, although he died fifteen years ago, and the others, even though I couldn't remember who they were.

I left the church and got on a bus into town. I felt quite sad and kept wondering if it had happened, although I knew without any doubt it had because it had been so clear.

There was no doubt in our minds of the reality of the incident or the healing which occurred: the shouting, sobbing and thrashing about of the arms gave way to a beautiful peace when Jesus came.

God's Spirit within us can help us to see in our minds what he wants us to see.

3. Feeling

A message from God is often felt by people in the Bible as well as thought and seen. When God spoke to Jacob he felt it in his body. Whether he dreamed his struggle with God (Gen 32:28) and that 'his hip was wrenched' (Gen 32:25), or literally wrestled with a man is uncertain, but he definitely felt its effect when daybreak came: 'So Jacob called the place Peniel, saying, "It is because I saw God face to face, and yet my life was spared." The sun rose above him as he passed Peniel, and he was limping because of his hip' (Gen 32:30–31).

Jeremiah also experienced sensations when God's word came to him: 'But if I say, "I will not mention him or speak any more in his name," his word is in my heart like a burning fire, shut up in my bones. I am weary of holding it in; indeed, I cannot' (Jer 20:9).

Fire is a sign of strength and power, but this is not always how Jeremiah felt: 'My heart is broken within me; all my bones tremble. I am like a drunken man, like a man overcome by wine, because of the Lord and his holy words' (Jer 23:9).

Jesus similarly felt some messages from God: 'As he approached Jerusalem and saw the city, he wept over it' (Lk 19:41). He then prophesied over the city: 'They will dash you to the ground, you and the children within your walls. They will not leave one stone on another, because you did not recognise the time of God's coming to you' (Lk 19:44). In the same way Jesus, praying the prayer of faith in Gethsemane, felt the truth of God's message before the arrest: 'And being in anguish, he prayed more earnestly, and his sweat was like drops of blood falling to the ground' (Lk 22:44).

Because God is within us by his Spirit we can expect occasionally to feel messages from him in our emotions and in our bodies.

Hilary suffers from agoraphobia and never travels more than ten miles from home, although she does very well in driving around Birmingham. One morning she rang me to say friends had invited her to travel with them to Bath that night and she thought God was telling her to go. 'What shall I do?' she asked from the other side of the city.

'I think you should find some Christian friends to pray with you an hour before you go,' I said 'and forget about it until then.'

'Right,' she said, 'I'll be round at five.'

This was not quite what I had in mind, but knowing the seriousness of this for Hilary, I agreed. When she arrived, my wife Carol and I laid on hands. I fully expected to be praying for healing and strength and the ability to cope with a long journey. My hands began to heat up and I sensed a nudge from God to speak out in his name, but what I said contradicted my expectations: 'I think the Lord is saying there is no need to go. He loves you just as you are. Stay at home and relax.'

This was very dangerous prophesying. Hilary would accept everything I said as from God, which was fine if I was right; but maybe I was wrong and God wanted to heal her? In my uncertainty I asked God for a sign and suddenly a bowel pain came into my body. 'Have you had any trouble with your stomach or bowels today?' I asked as delicately as I could.

'Yes,' she said, 'Normally my trouble is constipation, but today I've had a couple of accidents. I don't remember that ever happening before.'

This did not sound like God's healing. I was reasonably sure God would not want to put Hilary through that kind of torment. This kind of suffering was not to my mind a sign of God's activity and so I interpreted the bringing of it to light as a confirmation of the prophecy I gave. Hilary was tremendously relieved.

Feeling a 'word' from God is the area of God's activity which is easily missed. One afternoon I started receiving short sharp pains in my body as I was driving the car home and for one moment I thought I was dying. I asked God about it and he said each pain represented an illness he wanted to heal at the evening service. I stopped the car and made a note of all my pains. A pain in the left ankle; one in the front of the neck and so on; there were seven altogether. They went from my body as I wrote them down. That night, at a small healing meeting of about forty people, every little pain was claimed by someone present, who then received ministry.

On another occasion I was talking to a group of sixteen people about demonisation. As we stopped to pray someone said, 'I've just received a pain at the top of my neck,' and he pointed to it. 'Does this mean I've got a demon?' he enquired.

'No,' I said, 'it's a "word" from God for someone else here with a pain in the neck who needs healing; it'll probably go away now.' As I was speaking the pain left him and someone else said they suffered from that condition, which was greatly eased as we prayed for her. The man was much encouraged to realise it was probably God speaking to him.

One person in a meeting showed signs of great distress as the Spirit came on him and those ministering were worried about how to proceed. I don't know why but as I looked at him I said, 'You are receiving a 'word' from God about someone else; this is not your pain.'

'That's right,' he said, 'that's absolutely right.' He knew at once what it was, who it was for and how to proceed.

Somebody in our church had a great day and felt marvellous until he came to our little prayer meeting, and then depression came all over him. 'I don't get depressed,' he said.

'No,' I replied, 'but someone else does. This is a "word" from God.' The person feeling depressed claimed it and ministry followed.

On the Sunday morning of a healing service Greg suddenly felt acute pain on both sides of the lumbar region of his back as he came downstairs. Many would have rung for the doctor or taken tablets, but Greg received it as from the Lord and it went away. He shared it as the healing team gathered to pray before the service and John said, 'If no one else claims it in the service, I'll have it'. No one else did claim it, but we were all so busy we forgot about John. On the Tuesday John collapsed at the doctor's with a severe kidney infection – a further painful reminder of the need to act upon a 'word' from God.

Some people feel fear or anger or pain or sickness when demons are present in someone else. Knowing our own bodies and emotions can help us to receive God's 'word' through our feelings. As with pictures, feelings often need a word of interpretation before we understand them, but being aware that we may 'feel' a 'word' from God can sometimes help us to recognise God's guidance when it comes.

Knowing

Whenever we receive a message or 'word' from God we normally know something as a result of information imparted to us. I may know there is someone present in a meeting with a bad leg, because the thought came to me, or I saw a bad leg in my mind, or felt the pain in my own leg. But sometimes there is a direct knowing from the Spirit which is not dependent on receiving prior information. This is when people afterwards say, 'How did you know?' and I can only reply, 'I just *knew*.'

Mark 2:8 says, 'Jesus *knew* in his spirit that this was what they were thinking in their hearts.'

And Jesus says of the Holy Spirit, 'You know him, for he lives with you and will be in you' (Jn 14:17).

When Ananias prophesies over Saul, following his recent conversion, he declares that Saul will 'know' God's will, 'see' Jesus and 'hear' words from his mouth (Acts 22:14). The 'knowing' appears to be a separate activity from the 'seeing' and 'hearing'. Knowing, not because he saw and heard, but knowing inside because of the presence of the Holy Spirit.

Derek and Norma (not their real names) are a married couple doing full-time Christian work, with whom I became well acquainted when they ran a week's holiday club at our own church for teenagers. They worked hard with some of our local youths, many with criminal records, without seeing any visible reward for their efforts at the time. On several occasions we tried praying for the youngsters who came, laying on hands and asking God to send his Spirit on them, but nothing ever seemed to happen.

During the week Norma asked Carol and me to pray for her. She was suffering from continual bleeding from the lining of the womb and was about to see a specialist. He had said previously that he thought the best treatment would be to give her tablets which would stop her periods for six months. Norma asked us to pray, because she not only wanted healing, but to start a family as soon as possible.

As we prayed I received an inner conviction, a knowing, that God was answering our prayers and everything would be all right. Obviously with a condition like this we were unlikely to know 'naturally' on the spot if healing was taking place. Following this prompting I opened my mouth and prophesied they would have a child within a year. The next day the specialist saw Norma, began to prescribe the tablets, and then suddenly changed his mind. 'I think we'll just see if it rights itself,' he said, and dismissed her. There was no more bleeding and ten months later their first child, Lucy, was born.

Derek and Norma subsequently invited me to their Youth Club to speak about healing. I duly arrived at their home to find the Youth Club consisted that night of one ten-year-old girl and two teenage lads. We drank some coffee together and suddenly they rose and left. 'We'll see if we can find any more,' they said. I think at this point I was rather hoping they wouldn't come back, but they did, with one more young girl and three older teenage lads. Looking at them in their leather gear and ear-rings (the lads not the girls), I felt relieved to be meeting them in Derek's kitchen and not in a dark alley at night. Nevertheless, I shared some stories with them whereupon the two girls walked out. It must be said that none of these young people had ever been to church.

At this stage I was ready to thank Derek for the coffee and make my excuses when a horrible kind of 'knowing' spread all over me. I knew if I offered 'ministry' rather than just 'talk' something would happen. Panic began to set in. Having left secular employment twelve years ago I now feel far more comfortable in church than I do in the world. And yet David Pytches has said several times in my presence, 'The meeting place is the learning place for the market place.' I knew he was right theoretically, but practically I still began to doubt the 'knowing'. I had tried several times on our own non-church youngsters without any success. Why should this be any different? But then what was there to lose? These five lads didn't know me and if I asked God to come it was his responsibility not mine. I searched my mind, but could find no valid excuse to run away.

'Shall we ask God to send his Holy Spirit on us?' I enquired.

'What! Now?' one of them asked.

'Are you chicken?' I responded.

'Go on,' they said.

Five tough, quite large, street-wise lads stood up, closed their eyes and held out their hands. I prayed, 'Come, Holy Spirit.' After a few moments they began giggling nervously. Reaching deep into my past experience as a schoolteacher I rebuked them, quietened everything down and slowly the Spirit came on them. One by one four of them fell face down on the kitchen floor where they remained motionless. They were virtually lying on top of one another, but no one moved, twitched or made a sound. By this time the fifth one was shaking and trembling quite violently from head to toe. This seemed the appropriate time to make my exit and leave them in Derek's capable hands, since he is well trained to take God-given opportunities. He reported to me later that they have all since been asking a lot of questions about Christianity. When God's Spirit stirs within us we sometimes 'know' his mind without receiving any specific information.

Doing

Jeremiah buys a linen belt, hides it, digs it up later to discover it is now useless, and then God explains the meaning to him (Jer 13:1–11).

Sometimes a prophet's 'word' from God is given through

actions: Agabus tied his own hands and feet with Paul's belt and then said, '"The Holy Spirit says, 'In this way the Jews of Jerusalem will bind the owner of this belt and will hand him over to the Gentiles'"' (Acts 21:11).

Such actions may just be seen as visual aids accompanying the 'word' from God, but there may be more to them than that. As the people of Israel marched around Jericho, so they became victorious (Josh 6:1–27); as Naaman washed seven times in the Jordan, so he was healed (2 Kings 5:14); as the disciples put out into deep water, so they caught many fish and believed (Lk 5:4–11). Doing what seems right may illustrate a 'word' from God, confirm it or even be the 'word' itself.

At one meeting of about twelve people, as I asked the Holy Spirit to come, I sensed God saying, 'I'm going to do something different tonight.' Little Sister Mary of the nursing sisters of St John the Divine, aged seventy-four at the time, suddenly prayed out loud, 'Lord, I feel all burned out. I've had my life and I'm tired and weary, but if there's anything you still want me to do, I'm here.' I discovered later that the missionary station and hospitals in Namibia, where Sister Mary had spent much of her life, had been burned down in the fighting and it felt to her as though much of her life's work had come to nothing.

There was silence for a while and then suddenly Sister Mary said, 'I've got to get up and dance.' She leapt to her feet and, gathering up her blue habit, twirled like a young ballerina in the middle of the floor. Sister Audrey said, 'I think we should join her.' So working class carpenters and the like, not to mention a 6'2" vicar who could hardly be described as a Rudolph Nureyev, held hands and danced.

Then Sister Mary, with beaming face, said, 'I feel as though I'm sixteen again. All my aches and pains have gone.'

I hardly needed to add the interpretation that God had answered Sister Mary's prayer and spoken, in dance, 'There is much for you still to do.' There was also more prophetic life in the dance than we realised at the time. Sister Mary heard later in the year of the visit of a bishop to the church in Namibia where she had worked and 2,000 attended the service. The dance goes on.

Dreaming

Joseph and Daniel are famous for their interpretations of dreams in the Old Testament, and the other Joseph, guardian of Jesus, was guided by dreams in the New Testament (Mt 1:20; 2:13; 2:19). Joel prophesies that when the Spirit is poured out, 'your old men will dream dreams' (Joel 2:28), but the Acts of the Apostles and the Epistles are strangely silent about dreams. Maybe they were all young men in the early church. The last dream recorded in the Bible is that of Pilate's wife in Matthew 27:19. Nevertheless, the God who lives in us may still speak to us through dreams.

One night Graham quite unexpectedly dreamed about a lady whom I was trying to help. It was revealed to him in his dream how she had been sexually molested as a child, and he shared it with me. The person had not mentioned this, but did so at a later date. When she told me about it I remembered what Graham had said and shared it with her. From then on we involved Graham and his wife in the ministry, which proved to be very helpful. God sometimes speaks to us through dreams.

There can, however, be a dangerous fascination with dreams and their interpretations. If the meaning of a dream is not as immediately obvious as it was in the example I have given, I think we need to heed the words of Joseph. 'Then Joseph said to them, "Do not interpretations belong to God?"' (Gen 40:8). I believe, as Christians, we who are not medically trained should not try to be amateur psychiatrists or seek to interpret dreams unless God reveals the meaning to us as we pray and wait upon him. Interpretation of dreams belongs to God.

Speaking

On the Day of Pentecost the disciples spoke in tongues and

people from sixteen different areas heard them 'declaring the wonders of God' in their own language (Acts 2:8–11).

Occasionally, God may speak through us in tongues to someone of a different nationality. Arriving late one evening at a celebration in a church other than her own, Jan straight away noticed one particular black nun. She seemed to stand out in some way from the others present, although she was not the only black person there. At coffee time afterwards Jan sensed God saying to her, 'Go to her.' As Jan approached her in obedience, God said, 'Speak to her.' Jan had no idea what to say, but put her arms around the surprised nun, obediently opened her mouth and spoke a word which was quite unfamiliar to her in the nun's ear; '*Sawubona*,' Jan said. The nun started to shout and cry. Jan sensed God telling her to say it again, so she did. The nun laughed and cried, raising her arms in the air, exclaiming, 'Oh! You speak Zulu!' Jan said no, she didn't. The nun said, 'You've just greeted me in Zulu.'

Her sisters were preparing to leave for the convent where she was staying, but before leaving she told Jan how very sad she had been feeling that evening. The uncle who had raised her almost alone had recently died. It was he who had led her to the Lord and she had loved him very much. She was also very homesick and had made no friends here. The Zulu word of greeting which God gave Jan for her demonstrated his love in a special way at just the moment she most needed to receive it. Jan said, 'I'll be your friend,' and they exchanged addresses. She continued the ministry of love and acceptance by writing to her afterwards.

Speaking in the power of the Holy Spirit in our own language can be rather like speaking in tongues as the mind is sometimes by-passed, eliminating thinking before speaking. Sometimes the Spirit within us says, 'Open your mouth and I will speak through you,' and we find we are speaking in our own language without thinking first. This is how some prophecies, or 'words' to other people, are given. God speaks through us rather than in us or to us.

Jesus said to his disciples, 'When they arrest you, do not

worry about what to say or how to say it. At that time you will be given what to say, for it will not be you speaking, but the Spirit of your Father speaking through you' (Mt 10:19–20).

This appears to be fulfilled in Acts chapter 4 when Peter and John are arrested and questioned. Luke says. 'Then Peter, filled with the Holy Spirit, said to them ...' (Acts 4:8). The resulting words bring glory to Jesus: 'When they saw the courage of Peter and John and realised that they were unschooled, ordinary men, they were astonished and they took note that these men had been with Jesus' (Acts 4:13).

Fortunately we don't always have to be arrested before God will speak through us to someone. After a healing service in our local Methodist church one Friday night in May, a lady whom I knew by sight came up to me. 'God has told me,' she said, 'that you will tell me my problem and what to do about it.'

It seemed to be a question of gathering nuts in May. I'd preached about the need to be bold in asking God for things, and one chap asked me to pray with him for all the sin in the world to stop, for everyone to be healed and saved, and for all his problems to be solved by the time he woke up next morning. I did my best and then I walked into this one.

I sat in front of her in the minister's vestry, opened my mouth and spoke. I spoke about her husband, even though I didn't know at the time if she was married; how to sort out her relationship with him and balance it with her church activities. I cannot now remember any of the details, but I do remember what she said when I'd finished. During the service in church she'd seen a picture in her mind of the two of them on their wedding day, just as it had taken place, except this time I was the one taking the service in my clerical robes. She had seen God's 'word' as a picture in her mind, received a thought from him about seeing me and then heard God speak as I uttered forth in attempted obedience. I discovered later that this was a very mature Christian lady, and that night she was greatly encouraged to realise it was probably God who was speaking to her.

The God who speaks and lives inside us may make his will known to us with a thought in the head or a seeing in the mind; we may feel his message in our bodies or emotions, or simply know it; it may be God will reveal his will to us as we do something, or speak in the night as we dream; on occasions he may prompt us to speak out in faith so others might also hear his voice.[2] Whichever way God chooses to reveal himself to us, it is the fulfilment of his covenant promise, solemnly made that we shall all know him from the greatest to the least within ourselves. God has promised we shall find him and know him, not in the heavens but in our innermost being.

Recognising God speaking externally

In my experience those who begin to discern the voice of God within themselves are those most likely to discern the communication of God when he comes in other ways. Even when God comes with signs and wonders and demonstrations of power, not everyone recognises his activity or responds with faith. There were some present on the Day of Pentecost who felt the wind and saw the flames, and heard God speaking to them in their own language who 'made fun' of the occasion, and said of the disciples, 'They have had too much wine' (Acts 2:13). The writer of Hebrews says, 'Some people have entertained angels without knowing it' (13:2), and only Paul seemed to discern the activity of God in Philippi when 'everybody's chains came loose' (Acts 16:26).

I have met those who have heard the audible voice of God and seen six-inch-high blue letters written in front of them by the hand of God. I have known those who have encountered angels, witnessed miracles and discerned the activity of God in unusual circumstances and on unlikely occasions. But each one had learned to recognise the inner voice of God first and these other happenings came as special events for special reasons, added to the normal activity of hearing God's inner voice and obeying his promptings with faith and humility. An angel told Philip to go to a desert road, but it was the Spirit who told him which chariot to approach. When the lady made her confession to me the flames which at first left some sins unburned and then consumed them all, revealed to us something of the mind of Christ, but it was the inner prompting of the Spirit which alerted us to the possibility of such unusual guidance.

In our lifetime we may or may not be fortunate enough to see signs in the skies or hear voices in the heavens, but we who are Christians can be thrilled with the good news that we do not worship a God who is somewhere out there. The incredible truth which Scripture declares and experience confirms, is that the God who made the heavens and the earth has chosen to live inside all who will receive him. If the heavens so often seem silent and the skies empty, it may be that we need to come inside and close the door, and begin to look for the God who speaks in the place where he has promised to meet us.

Notes

1. In his book *The Normal Christian Birth* David Pawson says some extremely helpful things about repentance and the importance of confessing specific sins. See especially chapter 2 'Repent of your sins towards God' and chapter 32 'Helping disciples to repent'. (David Pawson, *The Normal Christian Birth* (Hodder & Stoughton: London, 1989).)
2. I have heard people testify to 'hearing' the audible voice of God and 'smelling' the fragrance of the Lord, but as yet I have not personally encountered such phenomena. Whether such experiences are internal or external, revelation from God is not always clear, but I would fully expect God from time to time to make use of all five senses he has given us in communicating his will to us. Some, I know, have felt the loving 'touch' of God's arms around them, although I have yet to hear of 'tasting' God other than as a figure of speech.

8

Receiving 'Words' from God

Christine came to see me one day and asked for help in receiving 'words' from God. At the time she was already a mature Christian seeking to do God's will and has since become our lay-reader. She had been the first person in our church to receive the gift of tongues and was normally open to God's Spirit, so I had no reason to suspect any ministry was necessary apart from the encouragement to ask God and step out in faith.

I immediately invited Christine to join me for prayer prior to a healing meeting I was leading with our Baptist minister in the local Methodist church. I think this was partly a good idea and partly a 'God-idea'. We had been given five 'words' from God at the previous meeting for healing, which were all claimed, and some were healed, so this seemed a good opportunity to help Christine at a time when faith and expectancy were high. My Baptist colleague was unfortunately delayed so we started without him.

'We'll ask God to give us 'words' for healing for tonight's meeting,' I said. 'When his Spirit comes on us feel free to share everything that enters your head, however stupid, and whatever you feel in your body or emotions. I will discern what to do with anything you give me, and be responsible for it.' I said this not because I knew what I was doing but to take the pressure and fear of failure away from Christine.

As soon as I prayed I felt a warm glow and what I took to be 'God thoughts' came into my head. 'I'll give you six "words" for healing,' he said. 'Christine and you will receive three each.' When I thought I knew the identity of my three I opened my eyes and asked Christine how she was doing. 'As soon as you asked the Spirit to come,' she said, 'the word "fibrosis" came into my mind, followed by a pain in my head which moved to my left ear. I'm not sure if "fibrosis" is really a word.'

I had been praying for a lady I knew who was suffering with fibroids and hoped she might come to the meeting. Not being at all medical, I wondered if 'fibrosis' might be for her. En couraged by Christine receiving three promptings to add to my three, I gave all six 'words' in the meeting. Only one of my 'words' was claimed, but someone had problems with pain in the head and another person had deafness and ringing in the left ear, just where Christine had felt uncomfortable sensations.

The fibroid lady, Sandra, didn't appear, but her mother-in-law and daughter came, and as no one else claimed 'fibrosis', I prayed with them on her behalf. We experienced tremendous heat – too much in fact – and had to stop to cool down. A few days later Sandra went to see a specialist and was told the last diagnosis and examination must have been wrong because there was no sign of a large fibroid as written down in the medical records. I asked a doctor friend if fibrosis was in any way connected with fibroids and she said it was not but, being a Christian, was thrilled to hear what had happened.

The others felt the power of God as his love and blessing came upon them, but no dramatic healings were registered. We cannot claim definitely to have heard God that night, but we were greatly encouraged, especially as someone appeared to be healed. Something positive, at least, happened to each of the three people we associated with Christine's three 'words'. This was the first time I tried to help an individual to hear 'words' from God.

Today, whenever anyone asks me to help them in hearing God I always approach the problem, as I did with Christine, from the firm conviction that God wants to speak to *all* his children. According to John chapter 10 Jesus is the Good Shepherd. He knows his sheep by name and they know him. Whoever enters the sheepfold through Jesus belongs to him and will be saved. Jesus says his 'sheep follow him because they know his voice' (Jn 10:4), but there is more than just one access.

The Bible rests on the assumption that God speaks. By nature he is a living God, not a dumb idol, and loves to communicate with all his children. Through the New Covenant sealed with the blood of Jesus, God calls us all back into fellowship with him (1 Cor 1:9; 2 Cor 13:14; 1 Jn 1:3). As a result, *all* will know him, from the least to the greatest (Jer 31:34; Heb 8:11). He will pour his Spirit on *all* people (Joel 2:28; Acts 2:17). This promise is for *all* who are called by God (Acts 2:39). 'If *anyone* acknowledges that Jesus is the Son of God, God lives in him and he in God' (1 Jn 4:15, italics mine). 'If *anyone* does not have the Spirit of Christ, he does not belong to Christ' (Rom: 8:9, italics mine).

These are big statements and big truths. This is the gospel of Jesus Christ. Everyone who turns from their sin and enters into a New Covenant relationship with God through the blood of Jesus Christ will know God because he will live in them by his Holy Spirit. This is a living faith. This is new life. This is eternal life. We are called into a living relationship with the living God. We have fellowship with him – he in us and we in him. The God who loves to speak lives in every Christian. Despite these great biblical doctrines, however, not every Christian believes God wants to communicate directly with them.

Some people have said to me they cannot hear God speaking because they have not received the necessary spiritual gift. In 1 Corinthians 12:8–10 nine spiritual gifts are mentioned and they infer from Paul's teaching at the end of the chapter that not all gifts are available to all Christians. Because they feel missed out by God's distribution of communication gifts (wisdom, knowledge, prophecy, discerning spirits, speaking in tongues and interpreting tongues), such people feel they cannot hear the voice of God or know the mind of Christ. Allied to this feeling is the belief that a Christian can only ever receive one or two spiritual gifts. We need to look at this problem.

This is what Paul says:

> Now you are the body of Christ, and each one of you is a part of it. And in the church God has appointed first of all apostles, second prophets, third teachers, then workers of miracles, also those having gifts of healing, those able to help others, those with gifts of administration, and those speaking in different kinds of tongues. Are all apostles? Are all prophets? Are all teachers? Do all work miracles? Do all have gifts of healing? Do all speak in tongues? Do all interpret? (1 Cor 12:27–30).

The apparent implication of such rhetorical questions is that all do not have gifts of healing, speaking in tongues, etc, which is why some of my Christian friends do not believe they can hear God speaking to them directly. In seeking to understand Paul's meaning, it is helpful to look at Paul's own experience. Paul himself appears to have received more than one or two of these ministries and gifts: apostleship (1 Cor 4:9); prophecy (Acts 20;25); teaching (Acts 18:11); miracles (Acts 28:3–6); healing (Acts 14:8–10); helping (Acts 16:9–10); administrating (2 Cor 8:19–20); and tongues (1 Cor 14:18).

We can also include four other spiritual gifts mentioned in 1 Cor 12:8–10: wisdom (Acts 16:25–40; 1 Cor 2:4–16); knowledge (Acts 9:5–12); faith (Acts 13:9–12); and discerning spirits (Acts 16:16–18).

Could Paul have been teaching that Christians may only receive one or two spiritual gifts when his own experience was something different? It seems unlikely and is not supported by his further teaching in 1 Corinthians 14:5: 'I would like every one of you to speak in tongues, but I would rather have you prophesy.' Lying behind Paul's desire for all to speak in tongues and prophesy seems to be the belief that it is possible for all to do so, as he sees the need for teaching the Corinthians to limit the public use of such gifts.

When Paul teaches about not all speaking in tongues and not all prophesying in 1 Corinthians 14, it comes in the context of 'when you come together' (1 Cor 14:26). Then he says, 'If anyone speaks in a tongue, two – or at the most three – should speak ...' (1 Cor 14:27) and, 'Two or three prophets should speak ...' (1 Cor 14:29). This context can also be seen to fit 1 Corinthians 12 where Paul is talking about the body of Christ coming together, in which case his teaching there may be paraphrased as, 'Do all have gifts of healing when you come together? Do all speak in tongues when you come together?' and so on. Bearing in mind Paul's own experience, and the context of writing this whole letter to a church as opposed to an individual, this is the way I interpret what he says in 1 Corinthians 12.

Paul teaches us that when we come together as a church or group we can expect God to release different gifts in different people for the strengthening of the church. This exercising of different spiritual gifts through different Christians when they meet is a marvellous example of the body of Christ working together in harmony. It would be quite ridiculous, as Paul points out, to expect one person to receive all the gifts when the body of Christ comes together, or for everyone to receive the same gift.

Because of personality, experience and other factors, some people receive some gifts more easily than others and tend to develop ministries in particular areas. Those who frequently receive and give prophecies like Agabus (Acts 11:27–28) may rightly be termed 'prophets', but it does not mean God will never use them to heal the sick. God loves to bring variety to meetings and use people in different ways at different times when he is welcomed and people are open to his Spirit.

When Christians do not come together, however, but visit and pray with individuals, God often releases through them whatever gift is needed for that person at that moment. Wherever Christians go, the Holy Spirit goes with them: he is in them, and when they are open to him he can use them in any way he wishes. This appears to have been Paul's experience in the Acts of the Apostles and this has been our experience.[1]

It seems right to me to interpret the passage in 1 Corinthians

12 by the big truths of Scripture. I believe Christians who are open to the moving of God's Spirit can expect him to release any spiritual gift through them at any time as he chooses, because the God who loves to speak, to be in fellowship with his children and to give good gifts, lives in every believer.

Maybe a reason why some people never hear the voice of God is more to do with their own failure to listen than God's unwillingness to speak. In George Bernard Shaw's *St Joan* the newly-crowned King Charles has this conversation with Joan of Arc:[2]

> CHARLES: Oh, your voices, your voices. Why don't the voices come to me? I am king, not you.
>
> JOAN: They do come to you; but you do not hear them. You have not sat in the field in the evening listening for them. When the angelus rings you cross yourself and have done with it; but if you prayed from your heart, and listened to the thrilling of the bells in the air after they stop ringing, you would hear the voices as well as I do.

Jeremiah in his attack on false prophets asks, 'Which of them has stood in the council of the Lord to see or to hear his word? Who has listened and heard his word?' (Jer 23:18).

To hear God, as Shaw's Joan of Arc or Jeremiah suggest, I believe we need to stop and wait, and learn to listen to him in the quiet time.

The quiet time

Most of us do not find that praying and then listening in silence is easy. We do not live in a very silent world. Maybe we can learn from those who are more used to silence than ourselves. I once heard a sermon based on how a monk organised his prayer time, and have found it very helpful. He was asked what he did with all the time he spent alone in his cell and this is how he replied: 'First it is me and him. Then it is him and me. Then it is only him.'[3]

I try to organise my own time of prayer based on this model.

First it is me and him

I begin my prayer-time with Bible reading and worship — sometimes with a praise cassette — and then I make my needs and requests known to God.

Scripture encourages us to confess our sins (1 Jn 1:9); to pray for ourselves (Phil 4:6); the world (1 Tim 2:1–2) and all God's people (Eph 6:18). Most of us are familiar with this kind of praying, but that does not make it 'second best'. God's response to his children coming to him simply and in faith can be at times quite amazing. Cynthia comes to some of our healing meetings to pray for others and on one occasion shared her own testimony of what God did for her before we met.

Cynthia was over eighty per cent physically disabled and for some time had been deteriorating physically. She had a chronic degenerative spinal condition with neurological disorders and functional impairment. The whole of the motor system of her body did not work properly. She saw double through very narrow tunnel vision, but at times even this was lost through muscle spasms. Cynthia had little use of her limbs and needed a specially stabilised electric wheelchair. There was no known cure for her illness and the doctors said all they could do was to make her as comfortable as possible and give her all the support they could. One doctor gave her only two years to live 'at the outside'.

Many Christians prayed constantly for Cynthia without any evidence of physical improvement until one night she was left on her own in the house. The family saw she was all right and went out at about 7.40 pm. At 8.30 pm Cynthia prayed, 'Oh Lord, forgive my weakness of faith. I believe, help my unbelief.' Suddenly the presence of Christ began to fill the room most powerfully. With head bent, Cynthia was aware of a glow which grew stronger and caused a tremendous brightness. Expecting to see a great light shining through the window, she looked up, but saw instead a vision of Jesus who himself was the source of this light. The overwhelming feeling was one of extreme cleanliness.

Jesus very gently touched Cynthia's head and the glow spread right through her body, giving the sensation of padlocks and chains being sprung loose. Instantly, her sight was restored and the hands, feet, legs and body were straightened and could now be moved without pain. Gradually, the vision faded and Cynthia spring-cleaned the house from top to bottom ready for when her family returned. They were obviously overjoyed when they did and a little fearful it would not last, but they need not have worried. Over two years later she is still fit and active.

Cynthia's healing caused the authorities a few problems: at the time she was receiving a mobility allowance and now had to be investigated and examined by doctors. The verdict was to withdraw her mobility allowance because there had been 'a relevant change of circumstances'. Authorities have a quaint way with words, but it is encouraging to know that simple prayer can bring about such a change.

Simple petitionary prayer is a first-class activity in itself but it can also be a progressive and preparatory act as well. As we bring to God the pain and problems of our world and its needs, and tell God what is on our minds, we are also freeing ourselves from our own agendas. Before anything can be filled it needs to be emptied first, and we can empty ourselves by giving it all to him.

I am convinced many people do not hear God or receive him because their minds are still full of their own baggage. I often used to wonder why Jesus climbed a mountain in order to pray before he was transfigured as I was unhappy with the idea of anyone climbing physically nearer to heaven. I now believe the time it took and the height Jesus reached was important, not in drawing closer to heaven, but in moving further away from the world, like the forty days in the wilderness. We cannot expect to switch instantly from the world to God, and the best way I find is to take time to bring my world to him and leave it there: first it is me and him.

Then it is him and me

We are encouraged by Scripture to ask our heavenly Father for good gifts, but not to fill the entire quiet time with our own ideas and needs (Lk 11:13; Mt 6:7–8).

This is my time for silence, asking God to send his Holy Spirit on me and waiting for him to come. I find the two conditions of openness and concentration are helpful in receiving what God wants to give me.

(a) *Openness.* At one meeting I attended ministers were invited to come forward for prayer, and members of our church who were sitting nearby kindly helped me on my way. The leader asked the Holy Spirit to come on us and everyone seemed to receive something except me. As I opened my eyes to look around clergy were shaking and falling like ninepins as God came upon them, but try as I might my own person remained unmoved.

Suddenly I saw my friend William at a distance and made my way to him for help. It must be said William is no ordinary Anglican vicar. Despite being born with a disability, he has tobogganed down the Cresta Run, surfed in the Indian Ocean and ridden ostriches in South Africa. This, I was sure, was the man to sort me out.

'Nothing ever happens to me, William,' I moaned with some desperation in my voice.

'Close your eyes then,' he said. As I obeyed he placed his hand lightly on my head and prayed, 'Come, Holy Spirit.' I stood with my hands held out and did my best to receive.

'Hallelujah, Lord!' I exclaimed. 'Praise you, Lord!' I'd heard others saying similar things and it seemed appropriate at the time.

William interrupted me. 'Let's stop,' he said, so I stopped speaking and opened my eyes.

'Peter,' he continued.

'Yes, William,' I replied meekly.

'Peter,' he said again, 'shut up!'

'Oh!' I said. 'No "hallelujah, Lord!"; no "praise you Lord!"?'

'No,' he said firmly.

So we tried again. I stood there with my eyes closed and emptied my mind. Suddenly my right hand and arm began to shake as great warmth and power filled my body. I was amazed. I found I couldn't stop the right hand from shaking or make the left one start, but that seemed irrelevant. The feeling of power and love was overwhelming. After a while the man-ifestation quietened down and I returned to my seat over-joyed.

I have since passed on what William taught me to many people – often with profound, helpful and dramatic consequ-ences. To receive the Spirit of Jesus we often need to be empty of self first. This may involve repenting of and confessing sins, or slowly letting the strain and pressures of the day drain away. Then we need to let him come to us: no talking, no sing-ing, no speaking in tongues, no more praying. We simply wel-come him and trust him.

The person waiting to have his gall bladder removed does not need to tell the experienced surgeon what to do. He does not need to say, 'It's here, doctor. Let me show you where it is.' Neither is it helpful if he yells, 'Don't touch it! Not there! It hurts!' God knows what he is doing and we need to trust him as Jesus did on the cross when he prayed, 'Father, into your hands I commit my spirit' (Lk 23:46). I find this attitude a helpful one at the start of receiving any ministry, whether we are seeking physical healing, emotional healing, demonic deliverance or 'words' from God.

Sometimes when I teach this people ask, 'Is there not a danger with passivity?[4] If we clear our minds might we not receive demons?' Personally I find it difficult to believe God will send demons when we ask him in faith for the Holy Spirit.

Which of you fathers, if your son asks for a fish, will give him a snake instead? Or if he asks for an egg, will give him a scorpion? If you then, though you are evil, know how to give good gifts to your children, how much more will your Father in heaven give the Holy Spirit to those who ask him! (Lk 11:11–13).

God would never give anything bad to someone who asked for his Holy Spirit, but I have often known people receive God's healing, gifts of the Spirit, power and blessing which have led to fruits of the Spirit when they have 'let go and let God'. Admittedly, demons sometimes cry out when the Holy Spirit comes, but we have always found them to be long-term trespassers who have been in the person some time. By opening himself to God's Spirit, the person facilitates a power encounter as the evil spirits are forced out of darkness by the Light of the World. Once God has revealed their presence to us we can then deal with them in Jesus' name. I believe openness to God's Spirit can only bring good gifts and good news eventually, even if the fruit is not always immediately obvious.

(b) *Concentration.* When we are engaged by the Holy Spirit there is sometimes a physical sensation which assures us of God's presence. It may be warmth, tingling, fluttering eyelids, gentle shaking, or just a feeling of well-being or knowing. Different people register different experiences but when we become accustomed to praying and waiting with an open frame of mind most people can learn to sense God's presence. Such manifestations are not necessary before we can receive a 'word' from God, but they can be very encouraging and faith-building.

After an initial engagement by God's Spirit a more active use of the mind is often necessary before we can discern God's specific 'word' to us. Some people receive 'words' quickly and easily, but that has not always been my experience. If I am really struggling, but feel God still wants to speak, I ask the Holy Spirit to enable me to see Jesus.

I remember once, before a David Pawson meeting, I was in this position, so I pictured Jesus by Galilee, healing, but God was not in the healing. I pictured him on the cross, but God was not in the suffering. I pictured him rising from the dead, but God was not in the joy. I pictured him ascending into heaven, but God was not in the glory. I pictured him on the judgement seat – God was there. Each time I imagined a different picture there was a negative feeling until the last one when I simply 'knew' it was right. Almost immediately as the final picture faded God gave me ten 'words' of judgement. During the day, David spoke about the importance of signs and wonders in church growth, but in the evening he preached on judgement. The 'words' I received before the meeting seemed to be appropriate as a follow-up to his sermon, and David was happy for me to give them.

It is not often right to ask people to claim 'words' of judgement publicly, consequently the authenticity of these 'words' was difficult to validate. Even so I know of one person who left the meeting and immediately threw some illegally copied tapes into the bin, and several people confessed to me afterwards how they were 'challenged' by what I shared.

For those who have difficulty picturing Jesus I believe reading the Bible imaginatively, by focusing our thoughts on events described in the Gospels, is the best way to learn. St Ignatius used to teach people to pretend to be there, writing in their minds the sights, sounds, smells and feelings.[5] This is a good way of developing a true, biblical image of Christ in our mind's eye which the Holy Spirit can use in helping us to see and hear Jesus.

Sometimes words or pictures come into the mind which of themselves make little or no sense. If this happens I ask questions or try to follow the moving picture. The word 'mother' came into my thoughts the other day. Whose mother? What kind of relationship? What needs to be done? And so on. The response which came was surprising: 'A mother with a loving relationship who means a lot to you. You just need to tell her so right now.' I gave it in a small house group, it fitted someone perfectly and proved to be a great blessing.

This is the time for concentration and determination, not only to ask God to speak but to seek and knock with persistence until the answer is revealed. Because God has given a covenant promise to reveal himself to us within ourselves, we must expect to wrestle internally before we can see God through the dark glass of sin and self. Some assume that if

God wants to speak he will make it crystal clear, but if that were always so, it is more likely he would have promised to send messages by angels, write them on walls or thunder them personally from the heavens. I have found in the vale of soul-making the struggle to find God and hear him frequently requires concentration and determination as well as faith. Just as proclaiming the kingdom, healing the sick and casting out demons does not always meet with instant success, we often need to persevere in prayer to give birth to a 'word' from God.

To hear God I believe we need to pray, stop, wait and listen; to learn to be open and concentrate. When God speaks, the initiative changes hands. Then it is him and me.

Then it is only him

There are times in prayer when words give way to even more meaningful communication:

> When Solomon finished praying, fire came down from heaven and consumed the burnt offering and the sacrifices, and the glory of the Lord filled the temple. The priests could not enter the temple of the Lord because the glory of the Lord filled it (2 Chron 7:1–2).

'When he opened the seventh seal, there was silence in heaven for about half an hour' (Rev 8:1).

Many years ago my mother was in hospital for a little while and we visited her every day. In the bed next to her was an elderly lady whose husband visited her regularly, but spoke very little, even though both of them were well enough to hold a conversation. He would sit there, sometimes for an hour, just holding her hand without speaking. I said to my father that I could see no point in his visits if he never spoke to her. I was quite young at the time. 'Sometimes,' he replied thoughtfully, 'when two people know each other really well, words are unnecessary.' This can also be true of our relationship with God.

On one occasion after we had worshipped and received God's word, the Spirit of God came powerfully upon my wife Carol. She keeled over gently and lay in one position for some time while her face began to glow. 'I expected God to speak to me,' she said, 'to show me something, or to do a work on me or in me or through me. But I saw nothing, heard nothing and in my emotions felt nothing.'

'So what did happen?' I asked.

'It was simply an awesome power and presence,' she said. 'I can't find adequate words to describe it.' Such a deep and lasting communication from God without words can help us to put the world in its true perspective.

Sometimes I find as I sit in silence following times of prayer, worship or Bible study, the presence of God fills the room. Some testify to a special fragrance, while I tend to feel warmth and tingling. Others shake or become weak at the knees, but however God's presence is discerned, there is invariably a timeless feeling of love and power when he comes. Then it is only him.

The busy time

It is good to start the day by worshipping God, reading his word, spending time in prayer and waiting upon him, but even this most vital and crucial part of the Christian life can have its drawbacks and temptations. The danger with 'making time for God' is that we then consider the rest of the time belongs to us: God has his chance to speak each morning for a few minutes and that's it. It is so easy to leave God behind in our 'quiet time' and stop listening to him as soon as we close the front door and travel to work. God can be found in the mountain top experience, but God can also be found in the valley of life.

One day at half-past four I had finished my visiting for the afternoon and was driving home to have tea with my family. I realised I was going past Sally's house (not her real name) and suddenly remembered I wanted to see her about something;

Sally was a sixteen-year-old member of our Youth Fellowship. The house looked empty, without windows open or lights on, and as I looked at my watch I realised I was being stupid because I knew Sally didn't reach home from school until five o'clock.

I was about to continue past when a thought came into my head, 'Go and visit Sally; she's there.'

'Don't be silly,' I replied to the voice in my head, 'she doesn't get home until five and the house is all locked up.'

'Go and visit Sally, she's there.' The thought remained and wouldn't go away.

So I stopped the car and thought it through. 'Nobody with me, no one around, I'm not late for any planned meeting, I can't lose. If it is from God she'll be there. If it isn't, it's not difficult to find out, no one will ever know, I won't look foolish, I can still have tea with the family.' The logic was flawless but even so it was not easy to obey this prompting. Sometimes I find insecurity and fear can almost paralyse me into irrational inactivity. With a considerable effort I left the car and knocked on the door.

Sally answered it in her school uniform. Slightly taken aback, she said instantly, 'How did you know I was going to be here? I skived off the last lesson from school.'

'God told me,' I replied with nonchalant confidence, and went in. Her mother was there and the three of us had a very helpful time sharing with one another about Jesus.

This was one of the first 'words' from God I received in my present parish and it says a lot about God. Here was a 'word' costing nothing which was easy to verify. It was totally private and if it had been completely wrong nobody would ever have known. This was the love of God in action, knowing my unwillingness to look a fool, even for him, in front of others. It shows how God is always with us by his Spirit even if two or three have not gathered together, and I began to realise an individual with no charismatic support group can still learn to hear God when alone.

Christians, and ministers in particular, are very often suspicious of what is called the subjective experience, and it is right for the body of Christ to check and seek to verify guidance if an individual claims it to be from God. But there is a fear that has grown up with this caution which often stops us from experimenting. Sin is often caused not by a lack of facts but by a lack of imagination: youths who can't think of anything better to do than destroy things; criminals who have never been able to imagine what it is like to be the person who has his life savings stolen; insoluble political problems because the Protestant has never sat where the Catholic sits, nor the Jew where the Arab sits, nor the white where the black sits – and vice versa.

I believe it is in developing the imagination, not in being afraid of it, that we may learn to move away from sin and towards hearing the voice of God. Charles Sheldon's classic novel *In his Steps* asks the question, 'What would Jesus do?', and the book is an imaginative exploration of how Christian lives would be changed if they asked themselves this question before everything they did.[6] I would like to take that imaginative journey a little further.

Every child playing with a doll or teddy bear speaks to it and replies on its behalf, thus entering the world of 'let's pretend'. Suppose we do something similar and take an imaginary invisible man with us everywhere we go. He is five feet ten inches tall, wears a white robe and a crown of thorns, and has a beard; we'll call him Jesus. In our heads, or out loud if no one else is around, we begin talking to him: 'I'm thinking of smashing up a phone box today, Jesus. Which one would you recommend?'

'When the children come home from school I'm going to sit them in front of the telly so I don't have to talk to them. Which channel shall I select?'

'I'm too tired to go to church this Sunday. Whom shall I partner at golf?'

I suspect most of us could begin to imagine Jesus' reply, and the more we know Scripture and have fellowship with other Christians, the more we shall know the character and mind of Jesus and the better we shall be at playing the imaginative game. Even if it were all pure fantasy, as in Charles Sheldon's book, I am sure the more we played the game and the more skilled we became at it, the less sinful and more Christ-like we would become. Brother Lawrence called this 'practising the presence of God'.[7] But I have found something even more thrilling than playing a game because what begins in fantasy often turns into reality. Imaginary Jesus says, 'Go and knock at that door, Sally is there,' and as I begin to play the game seriously I find she really is there and there really is an invisible Jesus who is with me always by his Spirit. Remaining open to the presence of God, even in the busy time, can help us to receive 'words' from him.

Helping individuals to receive 'words' from God

When Samuel was a boy God spoke to him for the first time but, being young and inexperienced, he did not recognise the voice or know what to do (1 Sam 3:1–21). He went to Eli, God's priest and Samuel's mentor, who on the third time of asking realised what was happening. Eli did not interfere but encouraged him, telling him what to do, and Samuel received God's message. The guidance and encouragement from a more experienced believer helped Samuel to receive God's 'word' for the first time and to begin a new journey as one of God's prophets.

Before a meeting in a Gospel Hall I prayed with Mary and Sarah whom I had taken with me. I thought God said to me they would receive three 'words' for healing between them and I would also have three. I asked the Holy Spirit to come, having already received my three, but they both claimed to have nothing. The meeting was due to start in five minutes. 'You can't have nothing,' I insisted with some degree of panic. 'Something must have come into your head.'

'Well, all I saw,' said Mary, 'was a pan boiling over on a stove.'

'That's not nothing,' I exclaimed, 'that's high blood pressure.'

I turned to Sarah. 'Tell me about your nothing,' I said as patiently as I could with just two minutes to go.

'I felt a pain here and one here,' she said reluctantly, pointing to two different places.

As I gave Sarah's two 'nothings' I found myself saying, 'These people have had pains here recently, but are not necessarily suffering now,' and both were claimed. As I mentioned the high blood pressure, a tall elderly gentleman with a very red face said, 'Speak up, young man.'

'Do you have high blood pressure, sir?' I asked.

'Yes,' he said.

'Would you like us to pray for you?' I asked.

'No,' he replied, though later he allowed one of his own elders to do so. Two out of three of the 'words' I received were claimed.

Giving guidance and encouragement to someone less experienced is, I think, one of the best ways of helping another person to receive 'words' from God. In Romans 1:11 Paul says, 'I long to see you so that I may impart to you some spiritual gift to make you strong.' Whenever we are seeking anything in the Christian life I always recommend finding someone else with a little more experience in that area, not just for advice, but for practical help and ministry. This is how Jesus trained his disciples. They watched him, learned from him, had a go while he watched them and then launched out on their own, empowered by the Holy Spirit, and I believe he wants us to do the same.

In groups

In Acts 4:23 it says, 'On their release, Peter and John went back to their own people.' The group of like-minded believers who had come together then prayed, after which, 'the place where they were meeting was shaken. And they were all filled with the Holy Spirit and spoke the word of God boldly' (Acts 4:31). It is difficult to tell how many were present at this gathering although we do know the early believers met together 'in the temple courts' and 'in their homes' (Acts

2:46). This meeting place sounds much more like one of their homes (Acts 4:4). As they met together and prayed, God's Spirit came upon them and they all received and spoke the word of God boldly.

I heard a story once of a young lad who was left alone in the house. Looking for something to do he eventually found some ink, a pen and some paper and set about being artistic. Some of the ink went on the floor, some on the dining-room table, some on his clothes and some on the paper. Just as his picture was finished his mother came back, entered the room, saw what had happened and said, 'What a lovely picture you've drawn!' Apparently he then went on to become a famous artist. I wonder how many mothers would have instantly reacted in that way?

Carol and I have been greatly blessed with three lovely daughters who are still quite young. On rainy days in the holidays Carol sometimes suggests painting as an option and they normally greet this idea with enthusiasm. But suppose she were to say to them, 'Today you're going to put on your smart party dresses, do your painting on the best dining-room table without a cloth or newspaper covering it, and I'm going to smack anyone who gets one blob of paint, however small, on the floor, on the table or on their clothes.' They would then reply, 'Mummy, we don't want to do painting today.'

Sadly this second illustration is the one which matches many churches' reaction to spiritual gifts. To break free of this fear I believe it is helpful to create nurseries, secure places of love, where experimenting and making mistakes is not only allowed but encouraged; a place where ministers can love their people and be loved by them. We need to wear old clothes, put on overalls, have easy-to-mop floors and cover the tables with cloths and newspaper. We then say to one another, 'Let us give praise for everything which lands on the paper, and clear up anything that misses without any fuss.' This is how children learn to paint.

One Sunday about seven or eight young people met together with me for informal fellowship. Sensing it might be right, I said, 'I want you to close your eyes and relax, and when I ask God to send his Spirit on us, give me anything you receive in your mind or body, however silly or strange it seems to you.' Somebody received a pain in the left ankle which was confirmed by someone else rolling down his sock and showing us a bandaged left ankle. It had only recently been injured and he assured us no one present knew about it beforehand. Then Peter shared about a room he was seeing with trays full of diamonds. He was hesitant at first, but we encouraged him to share it, after which Sarah confessed to visiting the jewellery quarter in Birmingham that morning instead of coming to church. Peter described exactly some of the things she had seen. We may not have followed it up correctly – there seemed to be no great ministry or healing – but our little nursery was very encouraged.

This was the day of small things, but very exciting to us. I will always be immensely grateful to the small group of young people who created a safe place for a middle-aged vicar to learn by making mistakes. Trial and error is the way we so often learn and in this little group there were many other 'words' and pictures that were right, and many that were wrong or never claimed. But we kept going and kept encouraging and kept learning. At times some of the paint seemed to land on the paper.

If a minister and a small, safe group can come together, then this may be a good place for many to start. It probably needs to be a hand-picked group initially, with not too many Pharisees present. Alternatively, if the minister cannot lovingly be lured in, then a few kindred souls meeting regularly, asking God to give good gifts, and taking risks in a loving atmosphere is likely to help us unpack the paints and use them. The paintings can then be taken to the minister as the prophets of old took 'words' from God to the king.

In church

In 1 Corinthians 12–14 Paul writes about the body of Christ being together and coming together and receiving spiritual gifts. 'When you come together, everyone has a hymn, or a word of instruction, a revelation, a tongue or an interpretation. All of these must be done for the strengthening of the church' (1 Cor 14:26).

I think it is important that the receiving and using of spiritual gifts, if possible, does not always go on in a corner. While the small group is an ideal nursery, and individual ministry can help some to begin, if charismatic gifts are always kept behind locked doors for the benefit of the chosen few, it is likely to become counter-productive in the long run. There will invariably be some in every church who will not attend home groups or seek personal ministry and their fears will only be fed with doubt and suspicion if spiritual gifts remain permanently lodged in secret societies.

I have made many mistakes in trying to create space for God to do whatever he desires in church, and I am very grateful to the supportive and forgiving members of our church. They have not been slow to encourage anything they thought was of God and to forgive whatever has obviously been of me. I am now beginning to realise that if things of the Spirit are carefully explained and taught, fears can be allayed and many more people helped to discern more of God. People are naturally afraid of the unknown and rightly suspicious of new phenomena that leaders claim to be of God. Paul's magnificent homily on love in 1 Corinthians 13 comes right in the middle of his teaching on using spiritual gifts in church and can help us, I believe, to overcome this hurdle. It is, however, a word about love and not about fear, given in the context of *using* gifts in church and not of burying them in the ground.

At one Sunday evening service there were only about thirty or forty present when I felt God saying to me, 'I want you to encourage members of the congregation to receive and give "words" from me.' So when I had finished preaching I shared this and everyone sat in silence while I asked God to speak to us. In our modern Church of England service book there are several places, normally after the reading of God's word or during communion, where it says, 'Silence may be kept.' On this occasion we followed these recommendations from the prayer-book and after a while I asked if anyone had anything to share. Three people shared things: there was a 'word', a picture and a feeling. Someone claimed each one and received ministry after the service.

One of these communications from God was particularly memorable. Julia is married with children and cannot often come to the evening service but about tea-time she felt a strong compunction to come at six o'clock. Sheila also normally comes in the morning, but that day was the anniversary of her mother's death and, having done other things in the morning with her family, she decided to come in the evening. Sheila is a little wary of charismatic gifts, although she has always supported her husband and other members of our church who feel naturally more comfortable with this kind of ministry.

When the Spirit of God moved gently among us Julia received a physical pain in her right shoulder which she sensed might be from God so she shared it at the appropriate moment. Julia was sitting at the front of church and Sheila at the back, but when I gave Julia's 'word from God' Sheila acknowledged it via her husband as a condition she had. She had experienced some discomfort for several days in exactly the same place where Julia received her pain. When people prayed the pain eased, but Sheila recognised immediately this 'word' from God was not just about her shoulder. She felt the love of God through the special 'word' for her on this special day as she received the laying-on of hands from caring brothers and sisters in Christ. I know the whole experience was a very helpful one for Sheila.

On a day of mourning Sheila had come to a Church of England service of Evening Prayer, wanting to thank God for her mother, be still before him and reflect quietly on the past. She was not in a shout-about, jump-up-and-down, clap-hands kind of mood and the quietness of Evening Prayer seemed most appropriate at the time. If anyone had said beforehand that charismatic gifts were going to be exercised at the service she would certainly have gone elsewhere for the evening, but God seemed to know what he was doing. Sheila was affirmed, Julia was affirmed, I was affirmed, the church and charismatic gifts were affirmed – all by the love of God. Some of the fears we have about receiving a 'word' from God in Sunday services may betray our lack of trust in God and his love for us, as well as in our brothers and sisters. I believe attention to 1 Corinthians 13 can help us to make room for God in church worship.

Receiving 'words' in larger gatherings

'When the day of Pentecost came, they were all together in one place' (Acts 2:1) and as a result of what happened 3,000 were converted (v 41). This must have been a very big place. Some scholars have suggested the 'house' referred to in verse two could have been the Temple, which is certainly where we might expect devout Jews (v 14) to be on the day of Pentecost.[8] But whatever the location, there was a large gathering. God's Spirit came upon the believers, who spoke his words to all who were present.

We ran a ten-week healing course during Lent 1988 and as the weeks went by people began to grow in confidence in God, in one another and in themselves. At the eighth meeting I felt God saying to me he wanted people to receive and give 'words' from him for healing. That night God gave us some 'words' before the meeting, but the majority were received and given by people sitting in the congregation as we all came together. On both occasions I asked God the Father through Jesus to send his Holy Spirit on us and give us good gifts, and no one appeared to receive more than one.

Sue Mitchell had never received a direct 'word' from God before, but the word 'neuritis' formed in her mind. She was not sure if it really was a word, but this was confirmed by someone present with medical knowledge. Someone else had 'an electrical accident'; another person saw a picture of a man's signet ring that was cracked; and the strangest of 'words' came from young Roger, who saw in his mind's eye two syringes injecting one another. I myself received a 'word' about a lady with a squint, and many other 'words' were given, from 'trouble with hypnosis' to 'breast cancer'. One of the most moving was an egg-shaped tumour with jaw problems.

Amazingly every 'word' except one seemed to be claimed. A man wearing a signet ring with a crack in it came out to the front needing prayer for his lungs; the lady with the squint looked just as she had in my mind before the meeting, and we could see the egg-shaped tumour on the jaw of a teenage lad who hadn't been given long to live. This was the only night of the ten-week course he was able to attend and nobody knew beforehand he was coming.

A lady was there who was very concerned for her teenage son who had never grown properly and needed injections three times a week. The 'word' about the two needles inject-ing each other encouraged her to seek prayer because he used a device for the injection where two needles fitted into the same barrel. The first needle was used for measuring into the barrel the amount of water needed to give the correct dilution of the drug. The measuring needle was then taken off and replaced by the second needle, which was used to administer the injection.

The 'word' which wasn't claimed was 'neuritis'. When Sue Mitchell had shared it, something strange stirred within me and I believed a person with the condition was in the meeting. Consequently, I repeated it several times to the congregation, but still no one claimed it. I walked down the aisle to the back of the church, encouraging people as I did to share anything they were receiving, as some people are often too embarras-sed to call 'words' out at a large meeting. When I reached the end of the church I turned to make my way back. I can only describe what then followed: walking up the aisle from the rear of the church, about one third of the way along I swivel-led to the right, pointed straight to someone and said without preamble, because I knew her, 'I bet it's you. I bet you've got neuritis.' After many tests eleven years previously Merilyn had been told she had neuritis which was painful at times and incurable. She had not told anyone about it for some time, but confessed to it as I pointed to her and then led her to the front for prayer. I had no idea she suffered from any such virus or even had an illness of any kind. Unfortunately it was not a 'word' which led to any discernible physical healing although Merilyn certainly felt loved by God at a time in her life when she needed to feel this.

There were about 180 at the meeting and most of the 'words' were eventually claimed. It was one of those occasions when the anointing from God's Spirit seemed to flow freely among us creating an easy atmosphere in which to receive and give 'words' from God. Those who claimed a 'word' came forward for ministry, and everyone present received more faith to believe in the God who speaks. The advantage of doing this in a larger meeting, particularly as some 'words' were quite detailed, was the larger number of people who could see, experience and take part in this ministry on one occasion. There were representatives from over fifty different churches present that night.

'No man is an island' but it is possible for individuals who cannot initially find a support group to begin receiving 'words' from God while alone, whether in the quiet time or the busy time. Gifts from God, however, are intended for the building-up of the whole church, the body of Christ, so I always encourage individuals who start hearing God to try and form groups in which they can give away everything which is given to them. It is not always possible to involve the minister in such groups initially, but whenever it can be done this is likely to benefit the whole church more quickly. I am sure that the more people can be encouraged to believe in the God who speaks and learn to receive 'words' from him, the more equipped the saints of God will become for doing his work.

Notes

1. David Pytches, Vicar of St Andrew's, Chorleywood has produced a very helpful video on the subject in the series 'Ministering in the Power of the Holy Spirit', entitled *Spiritual Gifts,* available from The Vicarage, 37 Quickley Lane, Chorleywood, Herts WD3 5AE.

2. Bernard Shaw, *Saint Joan: a Chronicle Play in Six Scenes and an Epilogue* (Constable and Company Ltd: London, 1924), p 60.

3. Stephen Verney, *Into The New Age* (Fontana: London, 1976), p 92.

4. Jessie Penn-Lewis and Evan Roberts, who were both greatly used in the Welsh Revival of 1904, mention the danger of passivity in their book entitled *War on the Saints.* While I accept fully the dangers of surrendering our will to someone else through activities such as hypnosis or drug-taking, it seems to me the book misinterprets some of the phenomena apparent during the brief period of the revival. I suspect people did not receive demons when they opened themselves to the Holy Spirit but rather the Spirit revealed demons which had been present for some time. Maybe if Jessie Penn-Lewis and Evan Roberts had ministered to such people for a sufficient length of time, they would have found this to be the case. Jessie Penn-Lewis, *War on the Saints* (Thos E Lowe Ltd: New York, 1973).

   John and Paula Sandford add further light on this subject in *Healing the Wounded Spirit:*

   > Secular psychiatrists have told Paula and me that after a great revival has come through an area, their offices, more than at any other time, are filled with desperate clients. This is because we neither understand our nature nor the function of the Holy Spirit.
   >
   > Picture it like an old dry well. Sticks and leaves, spiders and insects litter the bottom. Now let a great rain fill that old well with water. All that trash, along with its living inhabitants, rises to the surface of the water. In the same way the water of the Holy Spirit forces to the surface whatever rotten old things have been lying dormant in our natures. (John and Paula Sandford, *Healing the Wounded Spirit* (Victory

House, Inc: Tulsa, OK, 1985), p 330.)

It is not that revival brings problems; revival reveals problems. When Jesus comes, 'he will bring to light what is hidden in darkness' (1 Cor 4:5).

5. Ed: Robert Backhouse, *The Spiritual Exercises of St Ignatius of Loyola* (Hodder & Stoughton: London, 1989).

6. Charles M Sheldon, *In His Steps* (Spire Books: Westwood NJ, 1963).

7. Brother Lawrence, *Practice of the Presence of God* (Hodder & Stoughton: London, 1982).

8. In Luke 11:51 the same word, *oikos* which is used here for the 'place' where they gathered together, is used for 'temple' or 'sanctuary' (A.V.).

9

Testing 'Words' from God

One night I woke up with a jump. I felt afraid and ill at ease, as if I had been experiencing a nightmare. I opened my eyes and knew something was wrong. As I lay there a sense of urgency came over me, accompanied by this thought: 'If you go to the window and look out you will see a light on in the home opposite. There is someone in the room up to no good.'

So I went to the window, drew back the curtain and there, sure enough, was a light on in the house opposite. 'Quick, Carol!' I said, as she was also awake, 'Can you find the binoculars?' A short while later, as I peered out with magnified vision, I saw a man who happened to be West Indian doing something suspicious-looking in the front room. Carol declared authoritatively, 'A white couple with a baby live in that house.'

There had been a lot of break-ins in the Lane recently, including one at our own vicarage, so I phoned the police and gave them the number of the house. They also insisted on knowing my identity. I went back to the window and found the light had gone out and all was in darkness. Very quickly two police cars roared into the Lane, stopped outside the house and while two officers went round the back, two went to the front door.

A West Indian couple in their night clothes opened the upstairs window, exchanged a few words with the police and then smiled. At this point the officer turned round and looked in our direction. I sank down quickly beneath the level of the window in shame. Rising cautiously to peer through the curtain I saw a policeman start over in our direction then change his mind. I was relieved to see them drive away.

In the morning Carol said, 'I made a mistake. The white couple with a baby live in the house next door.' I suspect something demonic was trying to make a monkey out of me and had succeeded. On reflection, the fear I felt when I awoke plus the common sense fact that burglars do not operate in a front room with the curtains open and the lights on, should have told a thinking man this was not God speaking.

I am sure we all desire a phone that rings once when it is ourselves, twice when it is Satan and three times when it is God. To know for certain every time God is on the line would soon transform the arduous journey of faith into a comfortable sight-seeing tour; but this is not what God has promised us in his word.

He has said we live in the last days when the prince of this world is defeated but not dead. Until the day of judgement the wheat and the weeds will be allowed to grow alongside each other, and the sheep and the goats to co-habit. Those of us who are born again by the Spirit of God have a new nature; we have passed from death to life; though we die yet shall we live. But the old nature still follows us around. We have not yet put on immortality. The good we would do, we do not do, and the bad we would not do, that we do. Though we now have eternal life our bodies and our world are groaning in travail and still subject to decay. We live in the tension of the already and the not yet. Already we are the children of God, sons and daughters of the King, inheritors of his kingdom, endowed with power and authority from on high. But not yet do we live in the place appointed for us without sin or suffering where we shall dwell with God. For now we are still at war, a war that is fought as much within as without; though we can all know God, from the least to the greatest, by the Spirit whom Jesus has released upon us, we can see him only through faith and not through sight. For this moment we see in part through a glass darkly, and prophesy in part; only then will we see God face to face.[1]

This is the big problem for ministers and those in authority. This is one of the reasons why so few churches in the West are willing to risk seeking spiritual gifts. There is no certainty. 'As soon as we encourage everyone to believe they can all hear God,' said one clergyman to me, 'all hell will be let loose; in a manner of speaking, of course.' Those in positions of church leadership know exactly what he means.

But even though God allows hell to be let loose for a season, he has not left us comfortless. Ministers who are godly men and well versed in the Scriptures can learn to test 'words' from God even if they are unfamiliar with charismatic gifts themselves. The Bible is our main yardstick, but common sense and the body of Christ can help at least to narrow down possibilities to a manageable and acceptable level. Individual Christians, too, can be encouraged to learn how to test 'words' from God for themselves.

A wildly enthusiastic young Christian man was dramatically converted from a life of sin, and some demons were cast out of him. As soon as this happened he wanted to get out there proclaiming the kingdom, healing the sick and casting out demons himself, but he found it so difficult to take 'no' for an answer. He met with some success. On one occasion he bought two tickets to hear Nicky Cruz in Birmingham Town Hall, which he did because he felt God told him clearly that one was for him and one was for a tramp he would find outside. When he arrived, there was a tramp outside who accepted the ticket, came in and went forward when the appeal was made.

Following this success he prayed powerfully at the prayer meeting for Joan. Although she was over sixty she was due to have her leg amputated on the following Wednesday and had already agreed to it. Joan had been in a wheelchair for some time and there was a lot of medical sense in this decision because she was in considerable pain, but we didn't like the idea. The young man prayed for complete healing, not only for the leg to be saved, but for Joan to be walking into our church unaided within a week. He had a picture in his mind of her walking down the centre aisle and everyone being amazed.

This is the kind of situation many leaders and ministers find very difficult. An enthusiastic young Christian who knows about Jesus healing the sick and faith moving mountains, prays a prayer for which the leader himself either lacks the faith or does not believe to be of God. On this occasion I felt it was a prayer of enthusiasm rather than faith, but what was to be done? If I said he was wrong I could be accused of lacking faith, but I still remembered, when I was a curate, the pain and hurt caused to my crippled friend by well-meaning Christians challenging him to walk away from his wheelchair. I prayed silently for help and, as I did, sensed God telling me to pray for the pain to go and the leg to be saved, and no more. So I asked the young man in the group why he had prayed as he did, and he said he believed God was telling him to pray that way. I said he might be right, and would he and all who believed this to be of God, pray in faith for this to happen. I then shared what I believed God had told me and prayed accordingly.

Surprisingly on the Wednesday the specialist couldn't fit Joan into his schedule and said he'd operate in three weeks when he came back from holiday. During those three weeks the pain went and when he returned the specialist was delighted not to have to amputate. Joan continued to need her wheelchair, until she died over a year later but the excessive pain never returned.

Maybe we did lack the faith to see Joan completely healed, but if so God seemed to know that. At the very least he appeared to show us the true level of our faith and encouraged us to grow more by meeting us at the place we were. I believe we all learned an important lesson on the difference between real faith and enthusiasm, and the 'word' was simply tested by seeing if it came true.[2]

It is far easier to say when a 'word' is not from God or
unlikely to be so than to claim when a 'word' is definitely
from him. Most of the tests we can apply are negative ones,
but viewed together I believe they can give us guidelines for
when the most likely source of a 'word' is God; in many practical and pastoral situations this may often be good enough.
If we mark out a harbour with enough poles to show where it
is not safe for ships to sail, we finish up simultaneously mark-
ing out an area where it is safe. This is what I think the following tests may help us to do with 'words' claimed to be from
God.

The test of Scripture

John the elder warns us against deceivers and gives us this
test: 'Anyone who runs ahead and does not continue in the
teaching of Christ does not have God; whoever continues in
the teaching has both the Father and the Son' (2 Jn 9). The
teaching of Christ, as passed on or approved by those who
knew him, has unique authority and can help us to discern
what is of God and what is not.[3]

I remember reading an article by Doris Stokes in a
woman's magazine my mother left lying around. In it Doris
described several of her meetings in which she claimed spirits
of the dead were giving her information. She then gave
specific words of knowledge about people who had died, followed by words about their relatives who were present in the
room. According to the article all the details were later verified as being correct, and invariably the so-called departed
spirits said what a pleasant place they were in, what peace
they had found, and told their loved ones not to worry any
more about them.

This is a very sinister counterfeit, but one that is easily
exposed by Scripture. The Bible forbids us to contact the
dead or have anything to do with mediums (Lev 19:31; Deut
18:10–12; 1 Chron 10:13; 2 Chron 33:6; Is 8:19; Gal 5:19–
21; 1 Tim 4:1; Acts 13), and will not allow us to believe in

universalism (Rev 21:8). Clearly, if Satan can convince people that everyone who dies will be saved, there is limited value in the gospel of Christ. Because everyone who received a word of knowledge at Doris Stokes' meetings felt greatly assured their loved ones were happy, many people assumed it was good and even of God. This is why Scripture must always supply the rock foundation, and 'words' of knowledge can only ever build on that. The Bible is our major source in discerning whether words in our minds are from God or not.

Our first and perhaps firmest pole is vital. Any 'word' which contradicts the teaching of the Bible is not from God, while any 'word' which is positively supported by Scripture is more likely to be from God.

Trial and error

Deuteronomy 18:22 says, 'If what a prophet proclaims in the name of the Lord does not take place or come true, that is a message the Lord has not spoken. That prophet has spoken presumptuously.' This means any 'word' claimed to be from God must at the very least come true.

I was invited to speak and minister at a joint service in Rowley Regis when I was feeling more comfortable in asking God to send the Holy Spirit on meetings than giving 'words' for healing. There had been a time when I was more at ease giving such 'words', but that hadn't happened for a while, so when I prayed before the meeting I was only looking for guidance on my sermon. As I prayed and waited the thought came, 'Words for people God wants to heal,' and I resisted them. I just didn't feel like taking risks that night, but four 'words' came, so I jotted them down. After a while I felt most uncomfortable and uncertain about one of them so I crossed it out.

This 'word' was for a young man with muscle weakness who couldn't walk very well. I didn't feel very happy in myself that it was God I was hearing: the 'word' seemed rather strange. After further prayer I felt it right to give the other three, but not this one. It was quite a small gathering of people, about forty or fifty, and there was nothing visible to make me change my mind, but as we worshipped I decided I might as well give all four 'words', just in case.

As soon as I gave them out a young man dragged himself to the front, unable to walk very well. The hospital had wondered about bone disease and several other conditions but after extensive tests informed him his condition was 'muscle weakness'; those were the exact words they used.

This had a profound effect upon the rest of the meeting. As the young man promptly claimed the 'word' and testified to its accuracy there was a visible rising of faith among those present. People from several different churches were present, but few of them were used to this style of ministering and some were a little cautious. Those from the young man's own congregation who knew about his condition, and knew I had never been to their church, felt immediately this was authentic, and God speaking. In due course the other three 'words' were also claimed and those present saw the power of God come on them as we prayed publicly for their healing. Two of the four went over in the power of the Spirit and there were signs of God's presence on the faces of the other two. Consequently, when I then asked the Holy Spirit to come on the whole meeting, many responded with faith and trust in God in a way that doesn't often happen so quickly with those unfamiliar with this kind of ministry.

I chose this particular example because the young man himself was not healed that night. Others received healing, but he limped home in the same way he had come. Was this 'word' from God? Most of those who were present believed it was, and the claiming of the 'word' certainly raised faith in the midst of the assembly. I myself doubted the 'word' beforehand, but became convinced as the young man gave his testimony, and his church leader verified his case later. I just wish he had been healed. It seems possible that God wanted to heal him, but our faith was insufficient on the night.

The truth is we cannot be sure if this 'word' was from God or not. If the young man had not been present then the Deuteronomy test would have enabled us to be more certain it was not from God. As it was, we can at least conclude that the 'word' given on the night about a young man with muscle weakness whom God wanted to heal fell on the right side of the trial and error pole: it did not contradict Scripture and it was not found to be untrue. For many practical purposes in local churches a 'word' that does not contradict Scripture and comes true may be considered 'good enough' to be treated as from God.

Testing the counterfeit

'The coming of the lawless one will be in accordance with the work of Satan displayed in all kind of counterfeit miracles, signs and wonders' (2 Thess 2:9).

Unfortunately, there are times when a prophet proclaims something that does come true which is still not of the Lord. Instant confirmation of a 'word' or sign is not of itself sufficient to prove the source is God.

When I was in South Africa in 1988 I heard many tales concerning the Xhosa tribe and their witch-doctors. Aubrey Elliott writes about his father's experience with a witch-doctor named Njajula.[4] His father lost a litter of three well-bred spaniel puppies born on his farm. He travelled in some distress to see the witch-doctor, who had never been to his farm, but described it in detail to all present. He said the puppies had been stabbed to death with a pitchfork and hidden in a disused manger. Aubrey Elliott writes, 'My father got home and found the puppies where Njajula had told him they would be, and all the details of the incident were found to be correct.'

Later in 1988 I visited Malawi to encounter similar phenomena, witch-doctors or 'healers' who gave very accurate and specific details about clients on a first encounter, before prescribing all kinds of weird and gory cures for the particular illness.

My immediate reaction to these stories was to try and out-prophesy the prophets. Just as Aaron's snake devoured Pharaoh's snake (Ex 7:12) and the signs and wonders which God did through him exceeded everything the Egyptian magicians could do (Ex 8:18–19), I expected God to give me far better and more accurate 'words' than the witch doctors; but he didn't. Every time God gave me a 'word' it was just sufficient information to identify one person in a meeting. 'A man who has been ordained over ten years, with pain down his side'; 'a lady married to a priest who has been ordained less than ten years, with stomach trouble'; 'a person with eye trouble sitting in these two rows' and so on. Each time only one person claimed the 'word', and ministry in Jesus' name proved to be a blessing to them.

When I came home a lady who had been involved in many evil things in her life came to me for help. As the Holy Spirit came upon her swear words and blasphemies came from her mouth, and her body was thrown around violently to such an extent that those ministering ended up being kicked, punched, spat upon, bitten and scratched. The lady herself was then very upset and apologised most profusely for what had happened. Despite feeling real oppression in her flat, nightmares, voices and several attempts to commit suicide, she kept coming back to find out more about Jesus. People had done evil to her in Jesus' name, so it was not easy for her to believe in the real Jesus, but gradually through interces-sion, ministry and an incredible amount of love shown by Christians close to her, the violent manifestations began to die down and control came into the situation.

Long before any demons had been cast out of her, but after she had accepted Jesus as her Saviour this lady said to me: 'The power's gone. I can't do it any more. I can't read people's minds like I once could. I used to know what people were going to say before they said it, but now it's all van-ished.'

As I said, 'Praise the Lord' it suddenly dawned on me. Luke

writes this:

> As we were going to the place of prayer, we were met by a slave girl who had a spirit of divination and brought her owners much gain by soothsaying.... Paul was annoyed, and turned and said to the spirit, 'I charge you in the name of Jesus Christ to come out of her.' And it came out that very hour. But when her owners saw that their hope of gain was gone... (Acts 16:16–19, RSV).

Without the spirit of divination the financially profitable power had gone. When demons are bound by the Holy Spirit or cast out, the person loses the power to give accurate and specific details about other people's lives. Satan tempted Eve with knowledge (Gen 3:5), but God calls us to faith and trust even in the darkness. 'Words' from God about other people are invariably just small pieces of information leaked to us for the purpose of encouraging the person to respond in faith to God.

In 1 Samuel 16 the Lord tells Samuel to visit Jesse of Bethlehem as God has chosen one of his sons to be King. It would have been very easy for God to give a prophet of Samuel's stature and experience a few more details than this, but Samuel obeys and has to see all eight sons before he is told to anoint the last one. Even Jesus' 'words' for individuals which encouraged faith in himself were not always very specific (Lk 5:4; 19:5; Jn 1:48). God seems to release enough information for his purposes to be fulfilled, and no more.

If someone started giving accurate detailed 'words' about people's private lives publicly I would be somewhat suspicious. Such 'words' about individuals that accuse rather than convict, convince people of false teaching as described in Scripture, or do not lead eventually to the fruits of the Spirit, are possibly of a demonic source and to be rejected.

I therefore dare to suggest very tentatively that 'words' given which include information surplus to requirements are at the very least to be received with great caution – they may have a demonic source. It is not a pole I would want to put much weight on by itself, but Deuteronomy helps us to stabilise it a little:

> If a prophet, or one who foretells by dreams, appears among you and announces to you a miraculous sign or wonder, and if the sign or wonder of which he has spoken takes place, and he says, 'Let us follow other gods' (gods you have not known) 'and let us worship them,' you must not listen to the words of that prophet or dreamer (Deut 13:1-3).

When someone gives a 'word' surplus to requirements the test of holiness may be applied. Holiness is not righteousness, though holy people are called to be righteous; holiness is being set apart for God. Righteousness is turning from sin; holiness is turning to God.[5] The test of holiness mentioned in Deuteronomy 13:1-3 can therefore help us to check out a 'word' which seems almost too detailed for comfort. Is the person who receives and gives it seeking to worship the Lord, love, serve and honour him, and him alone?

The lady I mentioned earlier lost her demonic power as soon as she began seeking to serve and honour the Lord, even before we began casting out her demons. The extraordinary supernatural power Njajula seemed to be able to use, which enabled him to invade other people's privacy, is simply not available to those who are seeking the Lord and his kingdom. We cannot serve two masters. It therefore seems right to say that if a 'word' is remarkably detailed and accurate but the person giving it is not seeking the Lord Jesus Christ and his kingdom, the 'word' is to be rejected. Both tests are helpful because in many churches the leader will not know every member personally. Therefore, if a 'word' surplus to requirements is given he can take steps, albeit afterwards, to check out the sincerity and holiness of the person.

The test of a change in direction

'The Lord had said to Abram, "Leave your country, your people and your father's household and go to the land I will show you"' (Gen 12:1).

As a general principle, if we are doing everything right and going in God's direction, we don't need a 'word' from him. It is often the thought which cuts across our carefully made plans that proves to be the most authentic and powerful 'word' from God.

'But Moses said to God, "Who am I that I should go to Pharaoh and bring the Israelites out of Egypt?"' (Ex 3:11).

'"But Lord," Gideon asked, "how can I save Israel? My clan is the weakest in Manasseh, and I am the least in my family"' (Judg 6:15).

'And the word of the Lord came to him: "What are you doing here, Elijah?"' (1 Kings 19:9).

When God spoke Naaman responded with rage to a 'word' which led to his healing (2 Kings 5:12); Samuel assumed Eli was calling him (1 Sam 3:6); Isaiah thought his world was coming to an end (Is 6:5); and Jeremiah was certain he was too young to be a prophet (Jer 1:6).

In the New Testament Mary questions how she was to have a child (Lk 1:34) and Zechariah doubted the words of Gabriel (Lk 1:18). When Peter, full of the Spirit, was called to the Gentiles he responded, 'Surely not, Lord!' (Acts 10:14) and Paul, on his way to persecute Christians in Damascus, was stopped in his tracks and turned around by a 'word' from Jesus (Acts 9:4). Even Jesus wanted to go a different way from the route chosen by his Father (Lk 22:42).

Although many of those people of God initially questioned a 'word' from him, in the end they all obeyed. To question and seek to test a 'word' from God while being prepared to obey it is, I believe, a healthy sign. I have never found those who feel 'words' come to them easily from God and assume everything in their head to be from him to be very reliable prophets. Instinctively I listen more readily to those who struggle and sweat and then quietly say, 'I may be wrong but I think God might be saying something like this ....' A true knowledge of self is not easy to find – even for those with a good wife, honest friends and a large mirror. A change in direction cannot provide a firm test but may prove to be a helpful pointer in deciding if a 'word' is likely to be from God or self.

Working in a parish on the edge of the inner city I have always been a little embarrassed about our formal evening service. It is now many years since large sections of the community were familiar with chanting psalms and canticles, and at times I found myself actually discouraging local enquirers from coming to church in the evening. We began a more informal time of praise and ministry at 8 pm, while still maintaining formal evening prayer at 6 pm, and the later service became reasonably popular. Eventually I doubted the future of the service at six and suggested to the church council it be replaced with a said service for the faithful few. This would then encourage the musicians and those more enthusiastic about modern worship songs to put everything into the eight o'clock service. This, I believed, would encourage us to invite more local people to join us.

The church council gave me permission to do what I felt God was telling me to do. I knew what I wanted to do, but realised this might not be the same thing. I therefore invited everyone who was concerned about evening worship to pray with me in church one Sunday evening to seek the mind of the Lord.

The meeting began slowly. Everyone sat still with their eyes closed, waiting on God, but hoping someone else would be called to make the first move. Gradually 'words' of encouragement came from trembling lips. We were encouraged not to be afraid of listening, to speak out, and to believe God could speak through us.

It is difficult now to remember specific 'words', but while some were quite happy with things the way they were, no one prophesied against my new idea. The first 'word' which really caught my attention came from Roger who was then our director of music. 'I believe the Lord may be saying something like this,' he began. 'I will support whatever you do providing you consider each other. Listen to one another and love one another, and I will bless you.' This was a 'word' to be noted because Roger is not a traditionalist and this was quite a conservative message.

Carol remembers me being a little depressed that night because I did not have a recognisable 'yes' or 'no' from the Lord. The next day our church administrator approached me, totally unaware of what had transpired the night before as he hadn't been able to attend the meeting. 'I think the Lord may have given me a "word" for you about the evening service,' he said. 'As I prayed I sensed him saying he does not mind what we do as long as we worship him.'

Our administrator was even less of a traditionalist than Roger and this is why I took particular notice of what they both said. Humanly speaking I would have expected neither to take a conservative, traditional line and this persuaded me to leave the services as they were and concentrate on worshipping God and loving each other. As I write a year later both services are flourishing.

'Words' that do not mirror our own thoughts and feelings are often worth noting. The test of a change in direction may be helpful when all others have failed to give specific guidance or confirmation.

The use of the fleece

'Gideon said to God, "If you will save Israel by my hand as you have promised ... make the fleece dry and the ground covered with dew." That night God did so' (Judg 6:36–40).

When I first believed God was speaking to me there were many times when he gave me a sign to encourage me to give his 'word', just as he did with Gideon.

One Friday morning I felt God gave me ten 'words' for people in our own church for the Sunday morning service. I was not keen. Some other church, yes, but not ours. 'I'll need a sign, Lord,' I said. 'Very well,' said God. 'If there are seven of you from Christ Church at the meeting tonight and one goes over in the Spirit, then give the ten "words" on Sunday.'

That was fine: we were going to Sutton Coldfield to a joint meeting and only three people had agreed to come. With me, that made four. I had also asked Angela from our youth group if she'd like to come and she said she might do, but not to wait. A maximum of five was fine. As long as there were not seven I would not have to give the ten 'words' in our own church on the Sunday.

As we assembled in the car park, with Angela present, some non-Christian members of the Youth Club asked us where we were going. I told them we were on our way to a Christian meeting where exciting things could happen, and four wanted to come: two girls and two boys. We had two cars and nine was fine. It didn't matter if it was five or nine, as long as it wasn't seven.

As the sermon progressed the four non-Christians rose, said they'd been conned, were going home on the bus, and walked out. We were five again and that was still fine. The preacher asked the Holy Spirit to come and nothing much happened initially, but very slowly people were engaged by the Spirit and after a good fifteen minutes Angela gently keeled over on the seat. I went to her and as I did I saw our two non-Christian lads at the back. The two girls had gone home, but the lads had stayed at the back, nipping out for a cigarette from time to time. They smiled and waved. As one of our members went over in the Spirit we were seven, just as God said we would be. I had no choice but to give the ten 'words' on the Sunday; interestingly some of them were clearly wrong, though some were claimed. God was apparently encouraging me to be obedient to what I thought he was saying – even if I was wrong.

It is worth noting that when Gideon asked God for a sign and made a bargain it was after God had taken the initiative. When I asked for a sign about giving 'words' at the Sunday morning service, it was after I felt God had spoken to me with ten 'words' of knowledge. I have sometimes encountered Christians who take the initiative and ask for signs or try to make bargains with God about guidance in their own lives, but Gideon's fleece was simply testing what he thought God had already said, and sometimes this is right to do.[6] I found in my own life there was a time when God said to me, 'No more fleeces. It's time you were trusting me more now.' There is always a next step when we have to move out more into the deep, but God is very merciful and understanding, especially when we start. He may graciously encourage us with a sign or a 'word' to confirm a 'word' when he speaks to us and this can be a very helpful pole in guiding us to safe water.

Applying guidelines and tests to ourselves

Some of the tests we can apply to 'words' from God are only relevant after a 'word' has been given. This makes it difficult deciding beforehand whether to give a 'word' or not. Here are a few questions I ask people as they begin to wrestle with this problem:

(a) Are you a Christian?

(b) Are you sure you are a Christian?

(c) Have you received the Holy Spirit?

(d) Are you sure you have received the Holy Spirit?

(e) What makes you sure you are a Christian and have received the Holy Spirit? It is amazing how many church people are not sure of the simple basics of Christianity and I think it is important to build on firm foundations. Once these truths are confirmed I proceed:

(f) Are you worshipping regularly with other Christians, reading your Bible daily and praying for others to be saved, healed and set free? It must be said that Saul on the road to Damascus was probably not doing any of these things and still heard the voice of Jesus, but that was a 'word' to him. For Christians 'words' from God, especially for others, will normally come to those already seeking to do what Jesus did. After we have asked such 'basic' questions we can then turn to the more specific details of the 'word' itself:

(g) Does the 'word' contradict Scripture?

(h) Does Scripture support this kind of 'word'? Although

this is the most vital test, it is one which new Christians may not be able to apply themselves. I believe it is important for someone to help them because those young in the faith are often more open to the Spirit while not being so well qualified to test that which is of God. The enthusiasm of a newcomer, plus the experience of a mature saint, can often lead to an increase in faith for both.

(i) Is this 'word' necessary or will common sense do? On one occasion I finished a funeral at the crematorium and suddenly realised I was near a maternity hospital where two of my parishioners had just produced offspring. 'Will they be there, Lord, or have they gone home?' I asked. I felt very strongly the Lord saying, 'I will never give you a word of knowledge you can find out another way. You should have phoned before coming out.' I took a chance and found one had gone home and the other was still there, but I remembered the lesson.

I do not believe God ever intends to do our thinking for us. In Christianity the supernatural is frequently added to the natural rather than replacing it.

(j) What damage will be done if the 'word' is wrong? Just occasionally we may receive a 'word' of warning for someone else in our minds which could do a lot of harm if wrong. 'That man over there in the green sweater is committing adultery. Go and challenge him with it.' If a wrong 'word' can do damage like this one, it is probably worth asking for a sign, laying a fleece before God or seeking advice from a more experienced Christian.

(k) Is it a well-worn path or a change in direction? If a 'word' is the sort of thing you often say to others in your own name then be a little cautious. If you have given several 'words' of this type before which have been claimed and proved helpful, then go ahead – Jeremiah said the same thing again and again. If not, or it is your first ever 'word', then it may be worth asking God for confirmation before giving it, as it may be from your own sub-conscious rather than the Spirit of God.[7] Instinctively, most of us feel a 'word' is more

likely to be authentic when it is not the sort of thing a particular person would say, than when it seems to be a projection of that person's own personality.

(l) What good might be done if it is right? As well as asking if this 'word' is likely to advance the kingdom of God, I think we also need to look at how specific it is. I have come across people giving 'words' like 'a pain in the back' to large gatherings. It may be right to ask, 'Have I enough details to identify one person in this meeting?' Obviously we cannot be sure, but as a general guideline it may be helpful. The larger the meeting, the more details we would expect a 'word' from God to contain.

If a 'word' comes into the mind of a Christian who is seeking first the kingdom, does not contradict Scripture, will not do any harm if wrong (except to our own ego), is not from the well-worn path of our own sub-conscious but may greatly help someone else if right, then we grit our teeth and give it.

After we have given the 'word' we can then apply the 'trial and error' test to see if it is claimed or comes true and eventually leads to more fruit of the Spirit.

But there are two further reasons which may prevent us from giving the 'word', apart from the fear factor. We may feel unworthy or suspect our own motives.

(m) Unworthiness. In tackling the problem of unworthiness these biblical truths need to be borne in mind. The gospel of Jesus Christ is based on grace, not works (Jn 1:16–17); Jesus taught us that spiritual power and righteousness do not always go hand in hand (Mt 7:21–23); there is a vast difference between spiritual fruit and spiritual gifts; fruit is grown after much labour and takes time; gifts are received on the spot by holding out our hands; a 'charismatic' is one who has received a free gift of grace without deserving it.

It is right for all Christians to turn from sin and seek after righteousness but God in his mercy does not wait until we arrive before giving good gifts. They come to those who will ask and receive (Lk 11:9–10) in faith (Mt 21:21–22). Through the blood of Jesus Christ faith is reckoned to us as righteousness (Rom 4:23–24) and it is because of his works, not ours, that we may call God our Father and hear his voice (Gal 4:4–6; Jn 10:14–16).

This means when Satan says, 'You cannot give this 'word'; you are not worthy,' we simply reply, 'We can, for worthy is the Lamb who was slain' (Rev 5:12). Righteousness of the vessel is never a reliable test for the quality of what is in it (2 Cor 4:7). Even John the Baptist doubted his own prophecy (Lk 7:20).

(n) Motive. I believe doing what is right takes precedence over thinking what is right. Thinking of killing someone is not good but it is better than doing it. Doing what is right is right, whatever we think. 'To do the right deed for the wrong reason' is not the 'greatest treason' (with apologies to T S Eliot).[8] The 'greatest treason' is to do the wrong deed for the wrong reason.

Supposing God gives me a 'word' for healing in a large meeting. I immediately think, 'Won't I look good if I give it and it's right! All those people will think I'm super-spiritual.' But then I think, 'Oh dear! That's wrong, that's pride. I'd better not give it.' So I don't and Satan is delighted.

Suppose I do give it, feeling proud and boastful. Someone claims it, is healed, and 200 people give the glory to God. Then Satan slinks away defeated. My own sin still needs attention, but the kingdom of God has advanced because doing what was right took precedence over thinking what was right. What we do is a stronger expression of what we believe than what we think, and if we keep doing what is right we often end up thinking what is right. The reverse is rarely true. If we start using our motives as a yardstick for 'words' from God, Satan will have a field day because sowing seeds of doubt in the mind is one thing he does well.

If a 'word' in the mind passes all other guidelines and tests, I believe we should give it, whether we feel unworthy and suspect our motives or not, even if we have good reason for thinking the 'word' may be wrong.

Before a meeting I was due to take in a local church I

thought God gave me six 'words' for healing. One of them went like this: 'There is a man here in full-time employment who is troubled with an arthritic leg. Most people do not know he has this problem as he tries to cover it up when he walks.'

As I came to the moment after my talk when I felt it right to give the 'words', I could see only two men in the congregation in front of me. One was elderly, and I happened to know the other one fairly well. I hesitated before giving it, decided eventually it was God's responsibility, not mine, and said everything I had written down previously on a piece of paper. A brave voice from behind me suddenly claimed it. I had forgotten the elder who introduced me at the start of the meeting and remained seated on the platform behind me. 'Yes,' he said, 'every detail fits me exactly.' After prayer he testified to improved symptoms. Objective tests are more reliable than subjective doubts when it comes to testing a 'word' from God in our own minds.

Applying tests in the body of Christ

From Abraham to Samuel, the leader of God's people was also their prophet. The Spirit of the Lord seemed to come specially upon the one in authority who, if necessary, took on everyone else with God to support him. When God and Moses led the Israelites into the wilderness all the people would have returned to Egypt if government had been by consensus. In those times the leader in authority made the important decisions.

From King Saul to the time of Jesus, the Spirit of the Lord came on a number of 'prophets' apart from the king. They brought 'words' from the Lord to the king and sometimes the people, but it was always the king who made the important decisions.

During the brief years of Jesus' ministry Jesus himself received words from God and made all the important decisions. He has rightly been described as 'prophet, priest and king'.[9]

In the Acts of the Apostles the Holy Spirit is poured out on all believers. Peter is led to take the gospel of Jesus to the Gentiles, and the council of Jerusalem meets to discuss the implications. After much discussion James appears to make the decision (Acts 15:19). It seems likely he was the one in authority, responsible for giving the final judgement (Acts 21:18).

The church in Corinth, despite the presence of many spiritual gifts, experienced disputes and divisions. Paul writes this to them: 'If anybody thinks he is a prophet or spiritually gifted, let him acknowledge that what I am writing to you is the Lord's command. If he ignores this, he himself will be ignored' (1 Cor 14:37–38). Paul is clearly of the opinion that the one in authority must be obeyed.

I believe democracy and consensus are not biblical principles for testing 'words' from God. It is my experience that when spiritual gifts are allowed and encouraged in church meetings, greater not lesser authority is required from the leader. It appears to me biblically correct to say the person in authority over a church should make the final judgement, having listened carefully to what others believe the Lord is saying. It is almost inconceivable to believe James could have been more charismatically gifted than Peter or Paul, but he made the judgement in Acts 15. It therefore seems right to conclude that a godly leader well versed in the Scriptures, is the one who should test a 'word' from God to the church.

Here are some guidelines for the leader:

* The content of the 'word' must be tested against Scripture.
* The character and lifestyle of the person giving the 'word' may be tested against Scripture (1 Jn 4:8).
* A person whose previous 'words from God' have proved right is always worth a hearing (2 Chron 18).
* People whose previous 'words from God' have proved right may be valuable in testing someone else's 'word' (1 Cor 14:32).
* Consensus is worth noting (Acts 15:25).

* A 'word' apparently confirmed by signs and wonders is a powerful 'word' (Acts 11:11–18).

* A 'word' that a person finds difficult to give or goes against what they normally say is to be noted (Acts 10:14).

* A 'word' in harmony with Scripture from a proven prophet of good character with signs and wonders following is as good as we are likely to get on this side of the grave.

I used to belong to the East Birmingham Renewal group which acts as a support and fellowship group for Roger Jones in his Christian Music Ministries. One Thursday night about fifteen of us gathered together in the vicarage to pray before two performances of Roger's Christmas musical, *While Shepherds Watched*, due to be held in the Birmingham Town Hall.[10] It has always been our policy to offer ministry at the end of a performance; over the years there have been some notable decisions for Christ, and other healings and blessings have occurred. These two performances were scheduled for the afternoon and evening on the Saturday before Christmas, and we were praying specifically about the form of ministry to follow up each one.

As God's Spirit came among us I sensed a 'word' forming in my mind and in due course shared it with the group. I felt God saying we should invite all the children in the audience to go with the members of the cast into the bar after the performance. The cast could then sing songs and share something of Jesus with the children while we ministered to the adults as the Lord led us. (I hasten to add that the bar is not open for drinks when we book the Town Hall but provides a large, separate area where the choir often meets for prayer before a production.)

Some practical problems were aired, but there was a general consensus that this was a good idea and might even be a 'God idea'. Unfortunately, Roger was unable to be present that evening so the message was duly conveyed to him on the Friday. Word came back to me that Roger was not very keen on the idea, so I simply left it. Having given what I thought God might be saying, the responsibility was no longer mine.

On the Saturday morning I drove Roger with members of the cast and the costumes in our mini-bus to the Town Hall. On the way Roger told me he was unhappy with my 'word', which others had conveyed to him. Immediately, I responded, 'You must make the decision. It's your musical, you're in authority. You know I've sometimes been right and sometimes been wrong. See what you feel the Lord says to you as the morning goes by.'

I believe authority is given by God for specific situations and roles. I do not feel we have authority over another person except in such definable areas. When I was at St John's College I was under the authority of our principal, Michael Green, while involved in all college activities. All, that is, except cricket: I was the cricket captain. Michael sometimes played for our college cricket team and when we were on the field of play he came under my authority when, I'm delighted to say, he did everything he was told. As the field of activity changed, so did the authority role. When we are in church where I am the vicar, Roger comes under my authority. When he gave the 'word' about evening worship I weighed it and made the decision. In the Town Hall, however, our roles were reversed: he was in authority, I gave a 'word' and Roger was left to weigh it and make the decision. He accepted his responsibility fully and agreed to think and pray about the 'word' I'd given him.

As the large choir prayed before the rehearsal Roger chose to share my 'word' and people made encouraging prophetic noises. Not being a singer, I was then asked to check with the management while the others were rehearsing to see if it was possible to use the bar, and they were very helpful and co-operative. Obviously if they had refused us permission we would have had a negative but definite answer to our prayers.

Shortly before the performance Roger relaxed in his dressing-room and as he did so the Spirit came upon him and seemed to confirm the 'word' in his own mind, so he acted upon it. The children loved it: Joseph and Mary, the shepherds and angels held their hands, took them to a side room, sang songs with them and shared stories about Jesus. Roger asked God to come on the adults and one or two 'words' about sexual and other sins were given. Roger had been able to weigh up the 'word' itself, the one who had given it, the little sign of the management's co-operation, and his own inner conviction, all of which led to a blessing for young and old. In some ways his hesitation and testing made the eventual obedience and blessing so much more sure and helpful.

Learning to test 'words' is vital for anyone seeking to hear the voice of God and even more so for church leaders who bear the responsibility of making the important decisions. For the individual there needs to be a balance between practising the presence of God and not believing that everything which comes into our heads is from God. Living in the world of the 'already and not yet' means there will be times when we hear God's special 'word' to us and inevitably other times when we sadly fail in our struggle to overcome the world, the flesh and the devil, and another voice directs our path. Learning to test 'words' from God will help us to minimise the problem and maximise the blessings God wishes to pour out upon us.

Once we know Scripture, its guidelines and tests, we are free to unfurl the sails, weigh anchor and head for the thrill of the open seas. A harbour is built to help mariners sail, and safety posts are given to encourage them on their way. Such scriptural safety posts, which are vital in helping us to recognise God's voice, also take away our excuses and fears. Testing 'words' from God may sound negative in substance, but in reality this discipline provides the passage and gateway to spiritual life. To be criticised, tested and assessed is to be affirmed and released to enjoy the promises of God.

Notes

1. George Eldon Ladd in his book *Jesus and the Kingdom* further

discusses the 'tension between the Kingdom of God and a sinful world, between the age to come and the present evil age'. His conclusion regarding the 'Second Coming of Christ' is particularly relevant: 'The consummation as Jesus viewed it would not be a "historical" event like other events but would be the inbreaking of God into history.' This means we can expect no relief from the tension of the already and the not yet until that final consummation. History is not moving towards it: when it happens God will break in sovereignly and until then faith rather than sight will be our pathway. (George Eldon Ladd, *Jesus and the Kingdom* (SPCK: London, 1966), pp 334,331.)

2. Romans 12:6 says, 'We have different gifts, according to the grace given us. If a man's gift is prophesying, let him use it in proportion to his faith.' I believe we need to learn to use all gifts God gives us in proportion to our faith, while praying daily for more faith.

3. Although I consider the whole Bible to be the inspired word of God, I find it can sometimes be dangerous to use Old Testament passages on their own to test 'words' from God. The Yorkshire Ripper attempted to kill prostitutes because he claimed God told him to do so. Leviticus 11 could be seen to support this claim until viewed through the eyes of Jesus in John 8:1–11, 'If any one of you is without sin, let him be the first to throw a stone at her.' Jesus fulfilled the Old Testament and therefore I believe the Old Testament should be interpreted through God's revelation to us in Jesus.

4. Aubrey Elliott, *The Magic World of the Xhosa* (Collins: London, 1970), p 123.

5. R A Finlayson in his article on 'Holiness' in *The Illustrated Bible Dictionary* says, 'It is clear that, in Scripture generally, holiness means separation, and the term is used with reference to persons or things that have been separated or set apart for God and his service.' (R A Finlayson, *The Illustrated Bible Dictionary Part 2* (Inter-Varsity Press: Leicester, 1980), p 656.)

6. I think Adrian Plass exposed the weakness of this approach when faced with the decision of watching a James Bond film or going carol-singing: 'Laid a "fleece". If a midget in a Japanese admiral's uniform came to the door at 9.04 precisely, I would know that God wanted me to sing carols.' (Adrian Plass, *The Sacred Diary of Adrian Plass* (Marshall Pickering: Basingstoke,

1987), p 7.)

7. I often think to know self is the beginning of knowing God; to love self is the beginning of knowing self; and the receiving of God's love is the beginning of loving self. We can love ourselves because he first loved us (1 Jn 4:19). We therefore need to be sure we have received God's love and mercy before we can expect to know and hear God. People who hate self can be so lacking in peace and so defensive that they fail to hear and learn objective truth about themselves and, being short of self-awareness, consequently struggle to recognise the voice of God because they cannot recognise their own voice. When helping others to hear God it may be necessary to test their self-awareness and lead them gently to believe what Jesus says about them as sons or daughters of the King, before tackling the specific subject of 'words' from God.

8. T S Eliot, *Murder in the Cathedral* (Faber & Faber: London, 1935).

9. J Newton, 'How sweet the name of Jesus sounds', *Hymns Ancient & Modern Revised* (William Clowes (Publishers) Ltd: London, 1972), verse 4, line 2.

10. Roger Jones, *While Shepherds Watched* (Anfield Music Ltd: Birmingham, 1987), available from Christian Music Ministries, 325 Bromford Road, Birmingham B36 8ET.

10

Giving 'Words' from God

One day a Spirit-filled man received a message in his mind about one of his best friends, which he believed was from God: 'He has committed adultery and murder. Go and confront him.'

It is never easy to recognise, receive or test 'words' from God, but *giving* such 'words' to individuals often causes the greatest pain. How do you proceed with one like this, which may or may not be right? Whether it is true or not, the person will almost certainly deny it. If it is not true, the Spirit-filled man will probably lose a friend and if it is true he may possibly lose his life as someone who has killed once may do it again. There are times when it is safer and more secure to close the ears to any possible message from God.

From humble beginnings in rural parts the man's friend had found work in the city and ascended the social ladder at frightening speed. He was a firm believer in God, normally open to the Holy Spirit and refreshingly sensitive to his own failings and shortcomings. But this was a state in which capital punishment was still practised. This particular 'word' from God carried the costliest of all price tags.

Part of the 'word', at least, seemed possible: the friend had ill-advisedly married the boss' daughter soon after his arrival in the city and subsequently she'd run off with another man. Following the failure of this union he married again, but if he had any weakness, it seemed to be with the ladies. Now that he had entered the world of politics his high pedestal made him an obvious and vulnerable target. There are not many Spirit-filled men who can maintain holiness when power, wealth and sex are so easily available.

Maybe the 'word' *was* true, but even so, who was going to believe the claim it was from God without any evidence to substantiate it? There are times when a word of knowledge from God is of very little use witout a word of wisdom to accompany it, and this was one of those moments. When a man is desperate and throws himself wholeheartedly at the mercy of his Creator, God's voice rarely remains silent. As the Spirit of God came upon him he knew what he had to do.

In total obedience to God he made an appointment to see his friend and kept it. Immediately he told the tale of a rich man who, although possessing everything he wanted, had stolen from a very poor man and killed in order to satisfy his greed. He told it in such a way that the friend believed he was being asked for his help in a real situation. Being normally compassionate, anger grew within him and he promised instantly to use his power and influence to make the man pay for what he had done. 'The man who did this,' he said, 'deserves to die.'

'You,' said Nathan to David, 'are the man!' (2 Sam. 12:7).

It is a mark of great grace and forgiveness that King David was allowed to live and continue as king by the God who initiated the death sentence for adultery and murder. Indeed it is interesting to note how two other most prolific contributors to the Bible, Moses and Paul, were also guilty of murder but never executed. It is because of this merciful nature of God that Nathan received the 'word' from God in the first place.

I suspect difficult 'words' from God for individuals are often given to us for the good of the person concerned, but even so I doubt if David would have repented without the brilliance of the parable which preceded the message. It is a classic example of the importance of knowing how to give a message. When I first began giving 'words' from God I automatically assumed a 'word' would always be well received, no matter how it was given, but I have found to my cost that a genuine 'word' from God carries no guarantee of its successful outcome. Learning to give 'words' is as important as learning to receive them.

At a small meeting of about twelve people I was sharing the importance of confessing sins to one another (Jas 5:16). Immediately, a lady who doesn't normally find it easy to speak even in small meetings objected to what I was saying: 'I thought we could go straight to God through Jesus with our sins,' she commented. 'Do we really have to confess our sins to one another?'

I corrected myself immediately. Of course not. She was theologically accurate. We do not *have* to confess our sins to any other human being. *But* I have found there is sometimes a practical difficulty in letting go of our sins, or believing we are forgiven by going to God only in private. It certainly does not cost much to confess sins to God who knows everything anyway. Satan often says to us, 'If they knew what you are really like ....' The truth is, most Christians wouldn't bat an eyelid if they knew what we are really like because they know what they are like themselves. This is often a lie from Satan which imprisons sin and guilt within us and stops us from experiencing our liberty as children of God. We need to be cautious in whom we confide, but it can be a source of great emotional healing when sin is confessed to another human being and is dealt with in love.

I shared all this with the group while re-emphasising how the biblical truth I was explaining was not a necessity, but something which often proved to be helpful. Turning from our sin and confessing it to God is the indispensable step. Most of those present seemed to understand the point and the meeting closed with prayer.

During the week I prayed for the lady in my own quiet time and as I did I sensed God telling me of a sin she had committed which still worried her. I made a mental note and then prayed for some time for God to show me what to do with the information I believed he had given me. No further illumination came so I left it with the Lord.

The following Sunday I bumped into her in church while alone and sensed a God-given opportunity. I thanked her for the contribution she had made to the meeting the previous week and asked if anything was still troubling her. Something was, she said, but there was no way she could ever tell another human being. Suddenly I knew how to give this 'word' to this person at this moment.

'If I told you what your sin was,' I asked, 'would you confess it to me?'

'If you tell me what it is,' she said nervously, calling my bluff, 'I'll tell you if it is right.'

I did, and it was – an isolated sin of many years ago which still haunted her, attacked her and prevented her from ministering confidently to others. 'You can't do that,' said the accuser. 'Not after what you've done. If they only knew ....' But Satan lost that one. A word of knowledge, plus a word of wisdom from God, released a dear sister in Christ from that particular bondage of the Enemy.

There have been blunt, none-too-polite Christians in the history of the church who have given 'words' from God with direct, challenging certainty and been greatly used by the Lord. This can be acceptable in some instances, providing the person is always right – we can never afford to be both rude and wrong. But I am not convinced the teaching of 1 Corinthians 13 or the example of Jesus ever justifies a lack of love. Insensitivity does not appear to have been Jesus' own style when confronting individuals alone.

In John chapter 4 Jesus begins an encounter with a Samaritan woman which, within the culture of his day, was rather risky and ill-advised. It was an act of love, making himself exceedingly vulnerable and open to misunderstanding. He asked the lady for a drink of water, and in this request she immediately recognised Jesus' acceptance of her: 'You are a Jew and I am a Samaritan woman. How can you ask me for a drink?' (Jn 4:9).

This opened the way for a proclamation by Jesus of himself as the 'living water'. We cannot be sure if Jesus had information about the lady before the conversation began, or whether it was revealed to him as they began to talk, but the way he brings it in is most illuminating: 'He told her, "Go, call your husband and come back"' (Jn 4:16).

Within her culture it would have been natural to assume the lady was married. Jesus appears to know she is not married, but still asks her to call her husband. This is being both wise and loving. If Jesus had asked, 'Are you married?' the correct response could well have been, 'How dare you!' followed by a slap across the face. But Jesus' request observes the etiquette of the day and also gives the Samaritan woman an opportunity to be honest, which she takes. The question and subsequent answer achieved three things:

(a) A loving, correct approach which would not cause the lady to be defensive or aggressive.

(b) The discovery that she was open to truth – I am sure some people in her position would have lied at this point.

(c) The discovery that the suspected 'word' from God or supernatural knowledge was so far correct. Jesus himself may not have needed this confirmation but lesser mortals like me often find such early affirmation to be faith-building.

In this loving example we can learn some principles for giving suspected 'words' from God to individuals. A polite request leads to an open and honest response and a confirmation of the 'word'. This enables Jesus to share the full extent of his knowledge: 'You have had five husbands, and the man you now have is not your husband' (v 18). This accurate 'word' then led many to become believers (v 39). Jesus does not rush in with his 'word', but leads up to it with courtesy, wisdom and a sharing of the gospel which later proves decisive as the 'word' confirms the prophet and his message. If Jesus was as sensitive as this with a 'word' he inevitably found to be right, how much more should we learn to be the same with 'words' which may not prove to be so accurate. I believe that if we learn to be loving in the way we give 'words' from God, we don't always have to be right.

At one meeting when I was sitting in the congregation I sensed God might be saying to me, 'That lady sitting over there is demonised and I want you to minister to her.' This was obviously not going to be easy. I thought it through prayerfully for a while and then proceeded. I found a mature Christian lady, shared the matter with her and asked her to stand by in case I was right. It can be very threatening if two people descend on one innocent victim initially, though obviously I prefer to have a lady with me eventually when ministering to another lady. I cautiously approached the person in question and said, 'Excuse me; forgive me if I'm wrong, but I feel God is saying he would like me to pray with you. Is there anything you would like prayer for at the moment?'

She promptly said she was going into hospital the following week for an operation and would be delighted to have prayer. At this point I invited the other lady to join us and we talked together for a while. The sick lady's marriage relationship had caused some problems and she shared a number of other difficulties. We listened carefully and then asked God to send his Spirit upon her. The other lady placed her hands gently in the area where the operation was to be, and we waited. Blessing upon blessing came upon her, as her face beamed and heat spread deeply into the affected physical problem. There were no signs of distress or demonic activity whatsoever.

Afterwards the lady was overjoyed with the way she felt after the prayer, hugged us all and we exchanged addresses. It seems I was wrong and yet God did what he wanted to do. I am sure he did want us to minister to the lady, but we certainly found no demons. In my experience when God wants to bring demons to the surface and the person relaxes and allows God's Spirit to come upon them, as this lady apparently did, we will normally discern a demonic presence reasonably quickly. I can only conclude I was in error, but being wrong did not matter, as God's work still went ahead.

When we seek to give 'words' with sensitivity, love and humility as Jesus did, it does not always matter if we are mistaken.

I believe we always need sensitivity and love when giving a 'word' from God and sometimes, if it is a difficult 'word' for someone to receive, we may need a word of wisdom. There are also times when in addition to sensitivity, love and wisdom, we may need common sense.

When Jesus sent his disciples to borrow a donkey for his triumphal entry (Lk 19:28–35) and then an Upper Room for the Passover feast (Lk 22:7–13), it looks as though some of the instructions he gave were based on supernatural knowledge:

'Go to the village ahead of you, and as you enter it, you will find a colt tied there, which no-one has ever ridden' (Lk 19:30).

'As you enter the city, a man carrying a jar of water will meet you' (Lk 22:10).[1]

On both occasions Luke takes the trouble to say the disciples found things, 'just as Jesus had told them' (Lk 19:32; 22:13), but it also seems highly likely that Jesus had done some preparation for these two important prophetic incidents. Certainly we can see how Jesus gave some common-sense instructions as well:

'If anyone asks you, "Why are you untying it?" tell him, "The Lord needs it"' (Lk 19:31).

'Say to the owner of the house, "The Teacher asks: Where is the guest room, where I may eat the Passover with my disciples?"' (Lk 22:11).

The 'if' in the donkey story speaks of human planning and common sense directions and the Passover room appears to have been pre-booked at a time when every available room would have been hired out long ago. Jesus himself seems to be relying partly on supernatural knowledge, but he gives the disciples straightforward instructions to cover all contingencies. Both stories come across as a mixture of careful planning, supernatural knowledge and common sense. In learning to give 'words' from God it is my experience all three are often necessary.

One Wednesday evening I was due to take a healing meeting in another church. I had already prepared my talk and decided what I thought God wanted me to do during the time of ministry. Before leaving home I retired to the smallest and quietest room in our vicarage, when a 'word' came into my mind – 'spondylitis'. I had no idea what it meant, but as it had a medical ring about it, I naturally assumed it was for the evening healing meeting.

While I was in there the door bell rang and Carol answered it. As delicately as possible she explained to our cub mistress, Mary, that I would be available shortly and she decided to wait. When I eventually emerged I saw her standing in the hall and greeted her with the words, 'Hello, Mary. Have you any idea what "spondylitis" means?'

'Yes,' she said, a little surprised, 'I've got it myself.'

'Oh great!' I responded. 'Can you describe it to me in detail so that I can impress the people at the healing meeting tonight?'

I noted down everything I was told about the back condition of 'spondylitis', agreed a date for a Scout and Cub service, and made my way to the local Methodist church.

There were about fifty present that night, all very impressed with my knowledge of spondylitis, but no one there had the condition. It was only as I stood at the front, struggling to cope with my embarrassment of giving a wrong 'word', that I began to realise why God had given it to me and for whom it was meant. I offered later to pray with Mary, but she never took up my offer – the moment appeared to have gone. It seems right to say that when God leaks a piece of information to us about someone else he does expect us to use a modicum of common sense about giving it.

In this illustration and the previous one I made mistakes. This is why we need to test 'words' and why I think we should learn to approach someone with humility. When dealing with a 'word' from God as opposed to the word of God I believe there are very few circumstances when it is right to declare authoritatively to another person, 'God says,' or 'God told me.' In most instances nothing is lost by weakening it to, 'I think God may be saying...', and this makes it easier for the person to test our 'word' without feeling they have offended us. I consider this to be much more in keeping with biblical teaching on the need to test the spirits (1 Jn 4:1), and its declaration that we live in the age of the already and the not yet (Rom 8:22–25). I always encourage our folk to be careful what they claim before it has been tested.

In giving 'words' from God to individuals, there may be times in difficult situations when we need to ask for a word of wisdom. At all times, however, I feel we need to learn to approach people with love, sensitivity, common sense and humility so that God's 'word' may be received more easily and his kingdom advanced.

Giving 'words' to small groups

All the same principles for giving 'words' to individuals apply when giving 'words' from God to small groups, with one additional problem – other people are listening. This means more people may believe or receive increased faith as a result of one 'word', but it also means serious thought must be given to the possibility of public embarrassment. With increased potential for good comes increased potential for harm and we need to be fully aware of both when giving 'words' from God to small groups.

On the night before Jesus died he gave four direct supernatural 'words' to the small group of his disciples. All four contained elements of prediction which were given to build up the faith of those present and those who were to come after them. 'I am telling you now before it happens, so that when it does happen you will believe that I am He' (Jn 13:19).

The first one is the betrayal by Judas: 'One of you will betray me' (Mt 26:21).

The second concerns his sacrificial death portrayed

graphically in the bread and wine: 'This is my body given for you... This cup is the new covenant in my blood' (Lk 22:19–20).

The third is the desertion by all the disciples: 'You will all fall away' (Mk 14:27).

The fourth is the denial by Simon Peter: 'I tell you the truth, before the cock crows, you will disown me three times!' (Jn 13:38).

The prophecies concerning Jesus' death and the disciples' desertion were meant for the whole group to hear and whenever this happens we do not normally have to worry about how to give them. Everyone can hear what God wishes to say because the 'word' is for everyone. We may note, however, Jesus' dramatic and visual use of the bread and wine in the context of the Passover feast. Such an event had the unique stamp of God upon it, prophetically highlighting the end of the Old Covenant and the beginning of the New. It explains the theological significance of Christ's death so memorably that Christians in many churches are reminded of its life-changing reality week by week in their services. The use of the bread and the wine adds a powerful visual aid to the piercing 'word' from God. There may be times when God also gives us an important 'word' for a whole group and desires a more interesting presentation of his 'word' than normal.

Two of Jesus' 'words' are for the whole group and the other two concern individuals. The 'word' about Peter is personal but not private. Peter appears to have been with the others on Easter Day (Lk 24:9; Jn 20:19) as though Jesus' public prophecy of his denial enabled the others to minister to him, and he to them. Although Jesus knew Peter was going to deny him he still commissioned him to strengthen the others (Lk 22:32). I suspect Jesus' confrontational 'word' to Peter in front of the group helped to keep them together throughout this desolate weekend. Jesus seems to have known that Peter could cope with this public embarrassment and giving the 'word' in front of the group would be beneficial to them all.

The same is not the case with Judas and I think it is important to grasp the sensitive nature of Jesus in dealing with difficult 'words' in small group situations. Jesus announces to his disciples that one of them is going to betray him (Jn 13:21). After the twin deaths of Judas and Jesus we cannot possibly assess how important having heard this prophecy became for the disciples on Good Friday and Easter Saturday. When their world appeared to fall apart, they must have been comforted by knowing Jesus had said this would happen. But even so, Jesus is still very sensitive to Judas. Maybe this was a last attempt to save him from suicide and bring him to repentance.

Traditionally at the Passover meal the president 'dips the sop' and gives it to the person whom he loves most. Jesus apparently gave it to Judas (Jn 13:26). He also released him early from the festivities without the others knowing the full truth. '"What you are about to do, do quickly," Jesus told him, but no-one at the meal understood why Jesus said this to him' (Jn 13:27–28).

Jesus' sensitivity to Judas in front of the group teaches us an important lesson. Jesus is in possession of supernatural knowledge concerning Judas, but feels it right to give only some of it to the whole group, while indicating to his betrayer he knows more. A 'word' from God, even if it is correct, never exonerates the responsibility of the receiver in the way he gives it.

One evening in a small group meeting we were all taken by surprise when two regular church-goers suddenly manifested demons. Assisted by a member of our healing team, I began trying to help one of them while a few others sought to help the other. As I heard the other group struggling to expel evil spirits I sensed God telling me of a specific sin which was halting the ministry, so I left my person and went to help. 'You'd better find someone to whom you can confess your sin privately,' I said. 'The demons won't go until you do.' In subsequent ministry the person confirmed that the detailed 'word' I had received about the particular sin was correct and I was glad, for once, to have been reasonably discreet. It seemed right to me that those seeking to minister should be told why they had been unable to expulse the demons, while taking care to preserve as much as possible the dignity and privacy of the person receiving ministry.

We have also found that the sensitive nature of God in giving 'words' for people in groups may at times result in a 'word' which needs de-coding. On one occasion, with about ten people present, I felt God was saying he wanted to minister to a person with a twinge in the left knee and someone else with a pain in the left side. Immediately the left knee was claimed and when I pointed to the exact spot in the side, the second 'word' was also claimed. The two people who received these 'words' were married to each other, so it seemed appropriate to send another married couple to minister to them in a separate room.

It soon became apparent to those ministering that the main problem was not the knee or the side but communication within the marriage. Within a few minutes everyone had forgotten about the minor physical ailments as counselling and prayer were concentrated on bringing the two who were claiming the 'words' closer together. The couple felt greatly helped and blessed by the ministry but both said afterwards neither of them would have claimed a 'word' about problems in their marriage (Jn 3:17).

When Jesus gave supernatural 'words' to people in small groups he worked hard at giving them with maximum clarity in a vivid manner and went to some trouble to avoid personal embarrassment. He was not afraid to deliver important 'words' to groups, but his four different and appropriate approaches with four messages to the same group on the same night displays what is likely to have been an accurate discernment of what the Father was doing. I believe we should seek to do what Jesus did and pray for that same discernment when giving 'words' from God to small groups.

Giving 'words' in the local church

In 1 Corinthians 14 Paul advises against the excesses of the church in Corinth and also says some very positive things about worship. Here are some of the ingredients he advocates:

'Some revelation or knowledge or prophecy or word of instruction' (v 6).

'Spiritual gifts ... that build up the church' (v 12).

'A hymn, or a word of instruction, a revelation, a tongue or an interpretation (v 26).

'Two or three prophets should speak' (v 29).

'Be eager to prophesy, and do not forbid speaking in tongues' (v 39).

'Everything should be done in a fitting and orderly way (v 40).

This follows instructions on the Lord's Supper (1 Cor 11:17–34), and if we add Paul's teaching elsewhere about intercessory and petitioning prayer (1 Tim 2:1–4), and the importance of preaching, teaching and the public reading of Scripture (1 Tim 4:13), we can soon gather together the items Paul considers worth having in Sunday services. The majority of Christian churches include most of these items – except spiritual gifts.

If there are people in a church who are used to receiving spiritual gifts I believe those gifts ought to be exercised from time to time in public worship. I think much division can be caused by doing things secretly in a corner or behind closed doors. If there is good leadership, good teaching and an atmosphere of love brought into being through repentance, forgiveness and prayer, then it need not cause the problems many people consider inevitable. Paul certainly did not believe the use of spiritual gifts must automatically cause division.

The advantage of a direct 'word' from God, especially for healing, which bears fruit is that everyone can appreciate its value. Every church prays for the sick and if through God's spoken response a sick person is made well, most Christians will conclude this is a good biblical principle, and of God. I believe we therefore need to learn how to give 'words' from God in church 'in a fitting and orderly way' which glorifies his name.

The most common practice seems to be to give 'words' from God for healing at the end of a service and invite people to come forward for ministry after the closing prayer. This is probably the simplest and neatest method for regular weekly use, but it does have limitations. It automatically reduces such ministry to an appendix – after the service – and we need to ask ourselves what the place is for *private* prayer and ministry in *public* worship. There were times when Jesus saw people privately or took them away from the crowd, but most of the time he ministered publicly. Certainly the testimony of a person who claims a 'word' from God and is healed after everyone else has gone home is somewhat less faith-building than if it occurs in the middle of worship for all to see. I suspect 'after the service' may be the place to start and may need to remain the most common practice, but I would like to encourage more congregations, from time to time, to try public ministry in public worship.

We encourage people to pray together in the side-chapel for fifteen minutes before the service. When we have a special healing service, the healing team will normally meet to pray for an hour before we start. Everything which is received as from God is voiced and the leader of the service has the final say as to what he does with it. Here are some of the ways we believe God has led us from time to time:

1. Giving one or two 'words' for healing and asking the people to come forward for ministry and prayer in front of the congregation. Sometimes it has then appeared to be right to encourage others to ask for prayer and delegate authority to those nearby, or to members of the healing team, to minister to them. Others can be encouraged to pray or sing worshipfully as this is taking place.

2. Inviting everyone to come forward to the altar rail for the laying-on of hands from authorised people, who tell them

what they believe God is saying, or pray accordingly.

3. For the leader of worship, sensing spontaneously the movement of the Spirit, to pause, allowing people to exercise spiritual gifts which God then releases. Sometimes a number of people may sing in tongues; one person may sing or speak in tongues with an interpretation following; two or three may prophesy; a person may share a vision, a dream or a picture as God directs. The leader will need to be in firm control, encouraging interpretations where necessary or allowing specific 'words' or messages to be tested.

4. Twice I have been in meetings when the Spirit of God began falling on people during worship and the leader sensitively stopped the worship and encouraged people to receive what God was doing.

5. To have a time of quiet when everyone is encouraged to listen to God. When it seems appropriate the leader may then invite people to share what God has been saying, with any necessary ministry following. I have found people share more easily if the leader or his assistant wanders through the congregation, notebook in hand, noting the 'words' – rather like a waiter taking orders. Not many British people find it easy to shout out 'words' from the congregation.

6. Just occasionally it has seemed right to incorporate 'words' given before a service into the intercessions. This may happen something like this: 'I sense God may want us to pray tonight for those who have been recently hurt: someone who has been bereaved; someone whose daughter has just left home....' and so on. 'O Lord we pray for....'

There are times when 'words' can be given like this, or during ministry, without asking people to claim them personally, but I am not happy giving too many of these without comeback. Whenever I have felt God asking me to give a number of 'words' like this I have often been encouraged by phone calls, letters or people coming to see me privately for ministry concerning 'words' that fitted their situations. I think we must be careful not to give too many 'words' which we feel may be from God, without allowing them to be tested

(1 Cor 14:29,32).

7. Sometimes the leader may feel led to trust God for direct 'words' to be given at a particular moment in the service. He may feel it is right to stay at the front and give them or to move among a congregation to sense or feel 'words' for people seated in certain areas. I have done both, but tend not to do it in my own church where I know most people quite well.

8. There may be times in a large congregation when people find it easier to break into small groups and listen to God together. God may then give 'words' for others in the group or to be recorded by a leader and brought back to the main meeting. In one meeting of over 150 people we divided into fourteen groups whose leaders eventually presented me with about eighty 'words' to give to the assembly. A good percentage were claimed and ministry followed. It is obviously easier to have your 'word' read out with eighty others than to give it alone to a group of 150 or more.

I have found there to be a number of advantages in receiving 'words' before a meeting. I remember once receiving a 'word' before a service that fitted a person I knew well, but I received it as from God beforehand and gave it because she never usually came to that particular service. That night she felt compelled by God to be at the service and surprised us all with her presence. On another occasion I doubted a 'word' I received beforehand because I knew someone whom it fitted, but that person was not present and someone I did not know came to the service and claimed it.

In a smallish congregation like ours these incidents encouraged us to trust 'words' from God given before services when we could not be sure who would come, rather than during a service when we might inevitably be influenced by seeing who was present.

As Paul says, 'There are different kinds of working, but the same God works all of them in all men' (1 Cor 12:6). I feel certain that if we learn to listen to God and obey him, this variety will be reflected in our worship. If our God is a God who speaks, then I am sure we should make room for him to do so when we come together.

Giving 'words' at large gatherings

As Jesus is on his way to heal Jairus' daughter a woman touches the hem of his garment and is healed. Mark and Luke both record that Jesus asks, 'Who touched me?' (Mk 5:30; Lk 8:45). Jesus spiritually discerns power has gone out of him and stops to find out who has touched him. It is difficult to know how long this took. I am sure Jairus would have become agitated at this point and must have wondered when news arrived of his daughter's death why Jesus delayed to hold such an interrogation just then.

The disciples seemed to think it was pointless asking who touched him in such a large crowd, 'but Jesus kept looking around to see who had done it' until the woman owned up. We do not know exactly why Jesus did this. When he found the lady he praised her for her faith. Maybe it was simply to reassure her she had done a good thing. Maybe if she had gone away feeling guilty the sickness would have returned. Maybe Jesus wanted others to know that God had healed someone, and to give God the glory. Maybe he wanted the crowd to know what could happen to them if they also had faith. Maybe this was the first time Jairus had seen Jesus heal anyone and he needed to hear the testimony to help him believe for his own daughter's healing.

Whatever the reason, Jesus stopped, made a fuss in front of a large crowd, insisted on finding out who the healing was for, and while he did this somebody else died. I believe we need to take note of Jesus' persistence in identifying the person whom the Spirit had told him about through his own body. Anyone who has given 'words' from God at large gatherings knows the problem of encouraging people to claim their 'words' publicly.[2]

In November 1988 I visited Malawi on behalf of SOMA (Sharing Of Ministries Abroad). I had never been inside a church in Malawi nor spoken with an interpreter before. As I prayed on the eve of my debut I felt God saying he wanted to give me three 'words' for healing and, through those who came forward, teach the congregation how to pray for the sick. At such a moment life can be very lonely. Carol and the children were thousands of miles away and I longed to be with them. My American hosts were due to be in another church so I had to go alone to minister in a place where the language and the culture were foreign to me and I knew no one. Why couldn't I just share a few simple blessed thoughts like I used to do in the good old days?

I was in the second poorest country in the world. Most of them would not own books of any kind and many knew precious little about the Bible. I was told to speak for no more than fifteen minutes in the context of Holy Communion. My hosts told me to approach the subject of healing cautiously because a previous travelling evangelist had caused a lot of people to regard healing prayer with antagonism. They also urged me to be careful with 'words of knowledge' because the local witch-doctors were expert at it. Could God really be telling me to give three 'words' and teach people about healing the sick?

When I arrived alone at half past seven in the morning for the eight o'clock service I felt even more alone. It would then have been half past five in the morning in England. 'I haven't even got anyone praying for me at home,' I moaned to God. 'They'll all still be in bed.'

'One is praying for you right now,' said God, 'Sister Mary is already on her knees. And I am with you.' I took some comfort in this and in fact Sister Mary confirmed it later. As the two local priests arrived I asked them if I could talk about healing and pray for a few sick people. They were not at all keen, but at ten to eight the bishop rang to confirm travel arrangements for the rest of the day. When the presiding priest returned he said, 'The bishop has told me you must be allowed to do whatever you want to do.'

There were over 200 present at the service. Later in the

week we ran into a herd of aggressive elephants in the bush, but I think I registered more fear on this Sunday morning in church than I did on encountering the elephants in the game park.

'Is there a young man here,' I asked through the interpreter, 'who is very keen to go to university, but is hindered in his studies by poor eyesight?'

Immediately an old man of about seventy leapt to his feet at the back of the church and hurried forward. The priest saw him coming, emerged out of hiding from behind the altar, pushed past me and went to meet him like the sheriff on his way to a showdown at the saloon.

'I've got bad eyes,' said the old man.

'Yes,' said the priest, 'but you're not going to university. Go back.'

I wasn't very keen on a stand-up fight in the middle of the aisle so I assured the priest it was all right for the man to stay and I would pray for him. I tried again.

'Is there a man here whose first wife has died, has married again, and suffers from pain all down the right side of his back and leg?'

A man from behind me dressed in cassock and surplice approached enthusiastically. 'That's me,' he said confidently.

'Fine,' I said, 'where does it hurt?'

'All over,' he said. 'All over my back.'

I didn't have the courage to ask how many wives he'd had, did have or intended to have – somehow it no longer seemed to be very relevant. Fortunately, my faith was restored a little at this point as another man who fitted the description exactly came to the front.

'Is there a lady here,' I continued, 'who has suffered the death of two children and now has a disease in the spine?'

This time no one came forward at all. I asked the interpreter to repeat the question carefully, but he assured me there was no such person present.

People laid hands on the three men as they stood at the

front of the church and we asked God to send his Holy Spirit on them. There was virtually nothing to see happening. By now the time allocated had long since gone, when suddenly the man in the cassock and surplice began dancing down the aisle claiming he'd been healed. The man with poor eyes said he could see a little better and the other man hobbled back to his seat. At this point I melted gratefully into the background and the holy mysteries continued.

After the service a young man named Macdonald and several of his friends came to see me. In Africa there is great respect for the elders and this youth had not wanted to come forward to embarrass the older man. He was very intelligent, longed to go to university, but had virtually given up studying due to poor eyesight. As soon as I began to pray over him the power of God came upon him, his head was thrown back and an unpleasant-sounding tongue language came from him which I checked was not his native Chichewa. There appeared to be some conflict taking place, but as I broke the power of evil in Jesus' name and commanded the eyes to be healed, so peace came upon him. Eventually he opened his eyes and began to describe objects to me on the horizon which he had been unable to see before. Several weeks later he wrote to me in excellent English, indicating an ability to benefit from a university education, and said: 'I am now the fittest boy at the Secondary School.'

As I sat drinking coffee with the leader of the Mothers' Union she said to me, 'That lady you described was present; she was just too shy to come forward.' I encouraged her to pray with the lady and left somewhat richer in experience though weaker at the knees.

This can be the problem with giving 'words' from God to large gatherings, whatever the culture, but it does seem that Jesus recognised the importance of identifying the woman healed of the haemorrhage before a vast crowd. I believe if God speaks in this way we have a duty and a responsibility to work at giving 'words' to large meetings as skilfully as we can.

Two days after my first meeting in Malawi God gave me
three similar 'words' for healing in a gathering of about thirty
or forty clergy and their wives. I told them the story of the
previous Sunday and they all laughed, including the two
priests who had been present. I emphasised the importance of
listening carefully to the 'words' and responding only if they
felt God was speaking to them. Similarly I encouraged the
ladies not to be shy and made sure I had other ladies ready to
pray. All the 'words', including one for a lady, were accurately claimed.

I think the example Jesus gives teaches us the need for persistence without manipulation. Jesus said, 'Someone
touched me,' and when many people laughed at this he
would not be put off. He stated the facts: 'Someone touched
me; I know that power has gone out from me' (Lk 8:46). He
then continued to wait and looked around until the lady
claimed the 'word' for herself. I believe if I had done this at
my first meeting in Malawi, Macdonald and maybe the lady
would have responded. I am sure God wanted all the people
to see his power coming on the young man rather than just a
few afterwards in a corner.

At the same time it needs to be said that Jesus did not
threaten or manipulate. He did not say, 'I'm not going to
Jairus' home until the person owns up.' He did not say, 'Who
knows what God will do to you if you do not confess him
before people?' Jesus did not beg, plead, make excuses or
threaten. He stated what he believed to be the facts, stood his
ground and waited patiently.

I personally find it helpful when speaking away from home
to 'preach for the ministry', bringing God's word to God's
people to prepare them for what I believe God wants to do. I
spend some time in prayer before the meeting and simply prepare my sermon according to the way I believe God is telling
me to minister after I have preached. This is why I think it is
often preferable for the one who is preaching to lead the time
of ministry. I believe we can learn from people like Billy
Graham who in the context of evangelism are excellent at

bringing people to the moment of decision and getting them out of their seats. What he preaches has the main purpose of winning souls for Jesus: he 'preaches for the ministry'.

Here are some suggestions I have found helpful:

(a) Take time to prepare people. Billy Graham has a very carefully worked-out, ten-minute talk which he gives after his sermon before people are asked to respond.

(b) Teach that Jesus often required people to ask for healing and to declare their faith publicly (Mark 3:1–5).

(c) Share stories where a 'word' given and claimed publicly was a blessing to many.

(d) Teach the need to be honest and bold.

(e) If a 'word' is not claimed immediately, give others and come back to it.

(f) Teach that if some minor details are incorrect, the person may still feel an inner anointing that it is for them (cf my own experience: chapter 1, p 34).

(g) Do not hastily say the person can come afterwards for prayer – unless God tells you to do so.

(h) It may be right to ask the Holy Spirit to come to prepare people's hearts to receive God's 'words' before giving them.

(i) Even though we are petrified and unsure the 'words' are from God, being relaxed, confident, matter-of-fact, loving and sensitive – even at times humorous – is more likely to encourage faith than ranting and raving.

Sometimes I feel it right to give one 'word' and wait. Sometimes it seems more appropriate to give four or five all at once and then ask all the people to come out together. On one occasion I moved among the congregation pointing to groups of eight to twelve people at a time where I thought the person was sitting. This had the effect of speaking face to face with small groups and such intimacy led to a very good response on the night. I did it, of course, only because I felt God was telling me to do it.

Occasionally, God may give us a 'word' about a 'word'. I

was delighted one Pentecost Sunday to be invited to a nearby
Assemblies of God church to speak and minister. After the
sermon I gave out twenty 'words' for healing and asked
people to raise their hands if one fitted them. As I did so,
Brian, their pastor, sat on the front row with his back to the
congregation, eyes firmly shut, head bowed in prayer. About
seventeen hands were raised; it is not easy to be more precise
as some were going up while others were coming down, but
there were definitely no more than seventeen. I didn't count
the hands out loud, so Brian had no way of knowing how
many had been claimed. I was greatly encouraged with
seventeen out of twenty and was about to tell everyone to
begin praying for each other when Brian leapt to his feet and
asked to speak at the microphone. 'The Lord has just told
me,' he said, 'there are three people here who have not
claimed their "words" from him. Where are you?'
Immediately, three sheepish hands were raised and *then* the
ministry began.

As with most spiritual activities, failure may not be due to
doing the wrong thing, but doing the right thing badly. I
think we need to persevere in doing what we believe God is
telling us to do for some time before we conclude we were
doing the wrong thing. Like praying for the sick, giving
'words' in large gatherings is often an acquired art rather
than an instant success.

I have to confess that in the days when I had little experience
of giving 'words' from God I messed up several situations
and relationships through insensitive handling of the information God was giving me. Unfortunately, I cannot tell the
stories publicly because of the sensitive nature of what I
received, and for the sake of the people whose feelings I hurt.
Even though the 'words' were sometimes correct, the church
was not always built up nor the kingdom of God advanced. I
now realise a hot line to God is simply a way of receiving
information from the King which, if used properly, will
enable us to do his work. It is not a guarantee of success in all

we do. It is my most recent experience that learning to recognise, receive, test and give 'words' from God is just like learning any other discipline. There are no easy answers and there is no cheap grace. But just as the concert pianist or tournament golfer reaps the reward of hard work, so an ambassador for Christ will never regret learning how to use spiritual gifts with sensitivity and love. There is no thrill comparable to leading a person to Christ, seeing the sick made whole, or releasing the captive.

Notes

1. It is perhaps worth noting that a *man* carrying a jar of water would have been a rare sight in Jesus' day when it was normally the task of women.
2. Some Christians doubt the validity of giving 'words' for private individuals in public meetings. Nigel Wright asks some searching questions in *Renewal* No 153, February 1989 (*Renewal*: Crowborough), p 12.

Here are a few thoughts to add to the discussion:

Biblical principles

(a) In 1 Corinthians 12–14 Paul talks about receiving and using spiritual gifts in the body of Christ, when the church comes together. Whatever is meant by a 'word of wisdom' or 'knowledge', its use publicly appears to be supported by Paul, as long as it is done 'in a fitting and orderly way' (1 Cor 14:40).

(b) Jesus tries publicly to find a home for the 'word' he received about power going from him for healing, as already stated (Mk 5:24–34; Lk 8:42–48).

(c) Jesus gives a 'word' in front of others about his denier and his betrayer.

(d) In John 5:1–23 Jesus, who 'can do only what he sees his Father doing' (v 19), picks out one man from a crowd publicly and heals him.

(e) Individual 'words' to people like Nathanael (Jn 1:43–51), Zacchaeus (Lk 19:1–10) and the rich man (Lk 18:18–23) are all given in front of others.

We may not be able to draw a straight line from Bible times to the twentieth century, but I believe the principle of giving 'words' from God for individuals publicly is biblical.

Present experience

Michael Harper tells the moving story of a boy healed of emphysema at a Kathryn Kuhlman meeting. She gave out the 'word' publicly that this was happening in a very similar way to Jesus giving the 'word' for the lady who was being healed of the haemorrhaging. When 'words' are given by Christians seeking first the kingdom of God, and a person is saved, healed or delivered, we need to ask why God gives such 'words' if he does not agree with the principle. It is not as if Christians can go out and get 'words' from God; we can only receive what God gives. (Michael Harper, *The Healings of Jesus* (Hodder and Stoughton: London, 1986), p 13.)

Decent and in order

I agree entirely with Nigel Wright when he criticises in his article the 'scattering abroad of large numbers of free floating words of knowledge looking for a home'. This is not very honouring to God. The place for experimentation is, I believe, the small group. If a leader believes God wants to give 'words' for healing in a large meeting then I think he should give them himself or receive them beforehand from known people. To ask a sizeable congregation of largely unknown people to call out 'words', and praise God if one in fifty is claimed, can be seen to be very dishonouring to the Lord. But because something is done badly does not mean it should not be done. I believe if we work at testing 'words' and encouraging prophets to test prophets (1 Cor 14:32), God will help us to give 'words' in large meetings which do bring honour and glory to his name.

11

Going Through the Pain Barrier

I didn't want to go to church. It was August 1983 and being on holiday away from the parish, I felt I'd earned the right to spend Sunday in bed. The day before, I'd finished an exhausting week away with our church teenagers in Mid-Wales, driven them by mini-bus back to Birmingham and then travelled alone to a small village just outside York to join my family who were staying with Carol's parents. I wasn't against God – we'd experienced his presence with us during the previous week in a special way – I just wanted a break from organised religion. I was tired.

I eventually emerged from the bedroom on the Sunday morning feeling like the last marathon runner to finish, and finding the others have gone home. I sought a crumb or two in the kitchen while the rest of the family hustled and bustled in preparation for church. 'I'll look after Amanda,' I said nobly to Carol, 'then you can go with your parents.'

Amanda was two at the time and seemed to relish a rare moment with her daddy, wandering through the sleepy, picturesque Yorkshire village on a summer's morning. In the city animals live in books, but here in the country real live sheep, ducks and cows made conversation with us, enabling my little daughter to test her repertoire of quacks and moos in reply. It was our own version of the versicles and responses taking place elsewhere at the same time.

We arrived at the church a little early and enjoyed our-selves immensely in the graveyard climbing up the headstones and jumping off. I was glad no one saw us. I don't expect many other churches had vicars playing outside among their tombs during the Sunday morning service.

In the afternoon Carol's mum, Anne, invited me to the evening service at St Michael-le-Belfrey. There was no evening service in the village, so they often went there to worship on Sundays at 6.30 pm, having quite recently both become Christians. I searched the wide, empty spaces of my mind for an excuse, and as Anne could see me struggling in arid places, she said, 'David and Anne Watson will be there.'[1] I was persuaded.

We drove into York with the river Ouse on our left, passing the law courts and Kirk Museum on our right. I still wished I was at home in front of the television, but it was good to see the old place where I was born and brought up as a boy. High on a grassy mound stood Clifford's Tower dominating the river valley like a child's toy castle in fairyland – a familiar sight to me, though I could never remember going inside.

When we arrived at St Michael's there was no room left in the main body of the church, but I managed to find two places among the organ pipes where we could at least see what was happening, even if we might not hear too well during the worship. I bowed my head in prayer: partly out of habit, partly out of guilt because I'd rather have been at home, and partly to ask God to guide the worship team to use guitars rather than organ for accompanying the worship.

As my eyes closed, power and heat hit me forcefully and unexpectedly for I was unfamiliar with such phenomena in those days. Even so I still knew it was the presence of God. In my mind I began to see a picture similar to one I had once seen before while praying in John Finney's home[2] for a clergyman with cancer, but this time the details were different.

I found myself standing inside Clifford's Tower or some-where similar on grass, completely surrounded by a high, cir-cular wall with no way of seeing through it. The grass was illuminated with brilliant sunlight so I knew there was no roof on the tower. I was quite happily leaning against a wooden post minding my own business when a voice spoke to me from above: 'If you will join me on the cross you will see as I see.' I looked up and there was Jesus on a very high cross, high enough to see over the wall, while I was leaning against the base of the cross, unable to see anything. I greatly surprised and disappointed myself with the instant answer I gave: 'No, Lord,' I replied. 'I am not ready yet.'

I expected to be reprimanded and told about sins in my life and how to tackle them, but Jesus' quick response soon made me realise *I* was not the important person in this picture. 'No,' he said, 'that is right. But one there is who will join me: my servant David, my chosen in whom I delight. And when he has joined me on the cross you will see as I see.' That was all. The power and presence remained, but the picture faded away. I wrestled within myself to understand the 'word' from God and discover what to do with it. I believed from then on that David Watson was not going to be healed from the cancer he had, but more knowledge and wisdom than this eluded me.

I still sweat and struggle considerably to give any 'words' from God in meetings, or even to pray extemporarily, but I think if opportunity had been given during the service for 'prophecies' I would have given it. Maybe this shows how sensitive Graham Cray, the vicar, was to the Spirit because it certainly would not have been right. The power on me reached its height as Graham and others laid hands on David and Anne, and then it melted away. As David began to preach I relaxed completely and cooled down to normal. I was relieved to think I would not now be asked to give my 'word' from God.

The next day I scribbled down my picture and sent it to Douglas Greenfield who was then the administrator at St Michael's, receiving a courteous response. In the letter I said how I believed the 'word' was meant for Anne, to be filed away in case a moment arrived when it might be of some comfort to her. I said I didn't think David would live much beyond the end of the year which was the medical prognosis for his condition.

I struggled with the meaning and purpose of this 'word' for a long time. The power of it seemed out of proportion to its value. Throughout this time I prayed, along with countless others, for David's healing. As the year progressed I was pleased to hear of David's television, radio, video, cassette and book ministry continuing to develop and of his being used powerfully to spread the gospel.[3] Many Christian preachers tell others not to be afraid of death, but here was an authentic voice illustrating the word of God from his own experience. When *Fear No Evil*[4] was finished I thought maybe this book, together with his other books, tapes and videos might be the fulfilment of God's prophecy. Maybe people would take more note of David's helpful teaching once he was no longer with us. Tears came to my eyes when I heard David had died, which surprised me a little as I'd never met him.

Later in 1984 Geoff, an assistant minister from the local Baptist church, asked me if I was going to the Third Wave conference in London at which John Wimber was speaking.[5] 'John who?' I asked politely, and only a few weeks on when I read *Fear No Evil* did I learn of the kind of ministry God was exercising through John, and of his friendship with David Watson.[6] Unfortunately, I still didn't feel inspired enough to cancel other plans, find the money and leave the family to attend the autumn conference.

On Saturday 3rd November 1984 our new Baptist minister, Peter Radford, was inducted at the local church and Alan Pain from Sutton Coldfield Baptist Church came to preach. He had spent all week at the Third Wave conference in Westminster and though he tried to speak about other things, he totally failed. It had obviously been a life-changing kind of experience for him and nothing he did or said could stop him from communicating this truth. I took note of it. I took note of it because of David Watson and Geoff, and because Alan was already the minister of one of the liveliest and largest charismatic congregations in Birmingham.

Alan arranged a mid-week local follow-up day to the

Westminster Third Wave conference, in his own church, which I attended. I arrived late for lunch due to a funeral, sat on a table with other ministers and full-time workers and could hardly believe what I was hearing. There was a prison worker who had started Bible studies and found through introducing the power of the Spirit that many prisoners were now attending and being saved; a minister who gave out a 'word' at the front of his church for twisted fallopian tubes, which led to a lady being healed; a lady who had visited non-believers in their homes and prayed for all kinds of sickness, pain and ulcers. Each person was so thrilled with the instant healing they experienced that they asked her to pray for the dog which was also sick. We didn't hear if the dog was healed or not, but other reports kept coming.

I'd had lunches with many ministers, before but never one like this. Instead of the dull, cynical moans and groans about baptisms, buildings and bishops, here was articulate enthusiasm about authentic spiritual life. Again I took note of it.

As my own pain and problems increased throughout the year, the refusal to join Jesus on the cross myself seemed a somewhat tame and insipid excuse. I was already beginning to experience hell at grass level; could the suffering really be that much worse on the cross? As I posted my letter of application for the Signs and Wonders conference of 1985 and crossed the threshold of Sheffield Town Hall,[7] it felt like the first pain barrier was being penetrated. At that stage it didn't seem too dificult to die to self, but it still hurt.

While lying in hospital after the Signs and Wonders conference, having had my left testicle removed as a precautionary measure, I read *The Long Road Home* by Wendy Green.[8] It was highly recommended by Anne Watson and rightly so. When I read about the death of Wendy's husband, I suddenly realised I was no longer afraid to die, but perhaps even more important, I was no longer afraid to live.

I wrote to David MacInnes[9] about my picture at St Michael's and my experience at the Sheffield conference and this is what I said:

Maybe the picture I received was for me alone. The way I felt about David Watson dragged me against the odds to John Wimber – where I found healing – new power – and a new life. I am certain had David not died, I would not have gone. In many ways the responsibility of making Jesus' death count was left with those who came after, and in some ways I feel like this about both Jesus and David who, with John Wimber and David Pytches,[10] have helped to set me free. It will now take God himself, or at least a very powerful angel to stop me asking the Spirit to come until the day I'm called home.

I fear the passion has lessened a little with the passing of time, but the sentiment is still true.

When I was at school we had an annual four-mile cross-country competition round the Runnymede playing fields by the River Thames. I only ever remember completing the course walking. I often began with enthusiasm, firm in my belief and conviction I would do well, and determined to finish the race running as smoothly as I had started. But I always forgot about the pain which afflicted me after the first mile, and regularly gave up at this point, convinced that the superstars who completed the course still running were blessed with bodies immune to pain. I later discovered from the victors that this was not so, but rather it was their determination to complete the race which took them through the pain barrier and on to the finishing line.

Going to the Sheffield conference, claiming a 'word' from God, receiving ministry and coming home determined to 'do the stuff' – all within a week – was for me the crossing of my first pain barrier which led to new vision. From that moment I began to see a little more clearly as Jesus sees from a somewhat altered perspective. Many previous conference leaders and speakers had left me feeling what great men and women they were and how mightily God was using them. This one left me feeling that, in the power of the Holy Spirit, I could do it myself, even if I wasn't quite prepared at the time for the further pain which was to come.

Jesus and David Watson went through the cost of early

physical death, and in this way David joined Jesus on the cross. The death, Resurrection and Ascension of Jesus released the power of the Holy Spirit to all believers, and the death of David played its part in opening my eyes and heart to begin receiving that power. In that sense, when David joined Jesus on the cross, I did begin to see as Jesus sees, especially through John Wimber whose God-given ministry I initially received because he had been David's friend. This I now believed to be the beginning of the prophecy's fulfilment for me, but I couldn't forget the first part of the picture I had seen at St Michael-le-Belfrey: 'If you will join me on the cross you will see as I see.' It seemed as if the ministry of John, the death of David and the cross of Christ were simply bringing me back to Jesus' original offer, enabling me this time to respond more positively.[11]

In 1984 Lyn wrote to me, 'If you wish these seeds to bear fruit follow the path of obedience whatever the cost and let the Spirit lead you at all times' (chapter 4, p 102). I knew my own cross was not at this stage to be a physical one, but rather the pain of learning to hear and obey a supernatural God in a secular and hostile world. Jesus said, 'If anyone would come after me, he must deny himself and take up his cross and follow me' (Mt 16:24). It is my experience that seeking to follow Jesus and do what he did is not an easy road.

The pain of evangelism

I came home from hospital in November 1985 and my thoughts turned to Christmas. By then small signs and baby wonders were beginning to pop up from time to time and I was encouraged to try and take slightly larger steps of faith as I believed God directed.

'When is it really going to happen, Lord?' I enquired. 'When are they going to shake, rattle and roll in the aisles like they did at Sheffield?'

I paused and waited for an answer.

'Christmas Eve,' I thought God said, 'at the midnight

communion service.'

Now that was a thought: full church – some real outsiders present – everyone relaxed and happy through inebriation. Our church is not far from the local hostelry and it is amazing who finds their way into our Christmas Eve service after 'chucking out' time. It was an amusing thought, but also a very serious one. 'You will receive power when the Holy Spirit comes on you,' said Jesus, 'and you will be my witnesses' (Acts 1:8). The coming of God's Spirit often accomplishes many things, but evangelism seemed to be the number one priority in the Acts of the Apostles. I began to take the idea on board, wondering if ministry in the Spirit would be more powerful and more welcomed by outsiders than Christians.

'What shall I do, Lord?' I asked.

'Invite twenty people on whom you have seen the Spirit come to meet with you on Christmas Eve at 10 pm. They will be your ministry team. Pray together first and then ask me to come in the service.'

As I racked my brains to think of anyone on whom the Holy Spirit had made the slightest impact, from sixteen to seventy-four-year-olds, I came up with eighteen names. Carol's parents, Gavin and Anne, were coming down for Christmas so that completed the twenty who duly received written invitations.

Nearer the time panic began to set in, followed by rigor mortis. 'Help, Lord!' I pleaded. 'How do I know it's you speaking?'

'What if I were to heal Mary's ears?' offered the other end of the dialogue. Mary suffered from very poor hearing and I had been praying every day for her to be healed ever since she had failed to claim a 'word' for healing given at a meeting because she didn't hear it! 'If you heal Mary's ears, Lord,' I said, 'I'll do anything you say.' The discussion then continued on reasonably amicable lines. In my own mind this is what was agreed: at ten o'clock I would ask the Spirit to come on the gang of twenty, during which time I would speak healing in Jesus' name to Mary's ears. If they were healed I'd ask God to send his Spirit on the whole congregation later, and if not I'd do an ordinary service. This seemed a reasonable bargain and as I relaxed, life flowed back into my weary bones.

On Christmas Eve I spent the whole day at the home of the Nursing Sisters of St John the Divine, fasting, praying, sleeping (unscheduled) and reading the Bible. I felt I needed to throw everything into it and this was my way of taking God as seriously as I could.

While praying God led me to the Exodus story and I read it through with excitement and encouragement. God called Moses, gave him a new ministry of signs and wonders and sent him back to his people. Just like me. When he shared with them his new message God showed the Hebrew slaves some signs and wonders which helped them to believe and support Moses in his new mission. Just like me. (At least I hoped the twenty would turn up.) Moses went to Pharaoh with the promise of God and the backing of his people, and amazing things happened. God said, 'Take your staff and throw it down before Pharaoh and it will become a snake' – and it did (Ex 7:9–10). God said, 'Stretch out your staff and the dust will become gnats' – and it did (Ex 8:16–17). God said, 'Stretch out your hand towards the sky so that darkness will spread over Egypt' – and it did (Ex 10:21–22). 'That's the way to do signs and wonders,' I thought. I was sure I had the principle right. Through a series of miracles the Hebrews were set free and many people believed. God said, 'Lay hands on Mary's ears and they will be healed.'

'May it be so, Lord,' I prayed, 'tonight.'

Encouraged and rested, though rather hungry, I met with most of the twenty at ten o'clock in the side-chapel of the church. I asked the Spirit to come and do what he wanted and at an appropriate moment I laid hands on Mary's ears. 'How do you feel, Mary?' I asked when I'd finished.

'Fine,' she said, 'very relaxed and blessed.'

'How about the ears?' I enquired nonchalantly, not, of course, having dared share my 'bargain' with anyone else.

'About the same,' she said.

Suddenly others started sharing. 'I saw a picture of a curtain,' offered one, 'and someone was pulling the wrong cord.'

'Oh!' I said.

'I feel the Lord is saying you should preach on evangelism,' chipped in a second.

'Yes,' said a third, 'with an altar call.'

'Oh!' I said.

'I've got a real burden for the unsaved,' volunteered a fourth. 'We must tell them about Jesus and give them a chance to respond.'

'Oh!' I said.

By now there were only a few minutes left before the service was due to start and I needed to robe. 'Leave it with me,' I concluded, and began to move. As I did so Stephen, aged sixteen, stopped me and said, 'It's not going to be easy, you know.'

'You can say that again,' I thought. I'd never really made an altar call before and I didn't have an evangelistic sermon prepared.

I did my best. I wasn't very good. As I came to the challenge I asked the ministry team to stand in the side aisles so the people could go to them if they wanted to receive Jesus. I thought this would make it easier for people to respond, but it turned out to be a big mistake. As believers surrounded the visitors on all sides worry and pain registered on the faces of the imprisoned strangers. It had a look of the walls of Jericho about it, with the hosts of saints encamped around. When I asked people to go to the counsellors if they wanted to accept Jesus, not a muscle twitched in the fearful, deep-frozen bodies I saw before me. I harangued them—encouraged them —tried to persuade them with every inch of my powerful personality, but not a soul moved. As verbal diarrhoea began to set in Christine, who was standing at the back prayed, 'Lord, please shut him up.'

I stopped instantly in my tracks and uttered not another word. I wonder how many lay people down the centuries would have loved to receive the gift Christine exercised that night! We then waited in silence with still no response.

Before the meeting I had given the instant ministry team permission to go and speak as led – just for the night. Dramatically, in the middle of the silence, Brian, the man with the deep emotional burden for the lost, burst into the besieged fortress, marched down the centre aisle in full view of the watching world and went up to a church member who was sitting at the front. From a distance of six inches he shouted publicly, 'Have you been saved?' Fortunately, Jim had gone forward at the 1984 Billy Graham rally and was able to say, 'Yes.' Brian then stood in front of the second person and repeated his challenge.

'Yes,' said Edna as firmly as she could.

'Oh no,' I thought, 'he's going to go round the whole congregation one at a time.'

Fortunately at that point he realised enough was enough, or maybe Christine prayed again, and he retired from the scene. As quickly as I could I announced 'Silent Night' as the next carol, which seemed appropriate at the time, and Jericho was relieved.

I cannot find words to express how I felt during the rest of the service. I suspect 'white-hot anger' would be nearest the mark. Carol commented afterwards how the bread I gave her at the communion seemed to burn. 'Why, Lord?' I asked before I began the Eucharistic Prayer.

'Because I love you,' he said, 'like no one else.'

I knew what he meant. No earthly father would have let me make such a fool of myself. I don't know how I managed the services the following morning, but I certainly didn't speak to God for several days after they were all over. Christmas lunch had a different taste that year.

When I did eventually offer a prayer, the conversation in my mind went something like this: 'OK, God. Tell me about it,' I began.

'Read the Exodus story again,' he said, 'properly this time.' So I did.

When Moses went to Pharaoh the first time, he was given

no opportunity to do any signs and wonders. Pharaoh not only sent Moses and Aaron packing, but he ordered the Hebrew slaves to make bricks without straw as a punishment (Ex 5:7). I'd rather glossed over this bit on Christmas Eve.

The Israelite foremen went for Moses and Aaron when they returned, and blamed them for the increased oppression, rather understandably. 'Moses returned to the Lord and said, "O Lord, why have you brought trouble upon this people?"' (Ex 5:22). The only answers I could find were in Exodus 6:2, 'God ... said to Moses, "I am the Lord"', and Exodus 6:6, 'say to the Israelites: "I am the Lord"', and Moses was ordered to go back to Pharaoh.

'Will you still do everything I tell you to do?' God asked me. Pause.

Eventually I said, 'There is no other. No other way, no other hope. I will continue to do whatever I think you are telling me to do. You are the Lord.'

'If you will join me on the cross,' said Jesus, 'you will see as I see.' Though I do not understand everything about Christmas Eve nor about making bricks without straw, the conditional prophecy began to be fulfilled.

The very first 'word' I received after the incident was for George and Alice (chapter 2 pp 50 ff), followed by five for the mid-week group in church (chapter 2, pp 51 ff) and five for St Thomas' Church, Aldridge (chapter 2, pp 56 ff), and all were claimed. Wherever we went for the next six months God gave us 'words' which punctured many hard and unbelieving hearts. Nearly everything we shared during this time found a home and brought a blessing. Surprisingly not a single person left our church as a result of the Christmas Eve service — even though many regular members were present.

The pain of healing

A short while after the Sheffield conference, and despite the Christmas Eve débâcle, we agreed as a church to form a healing team of twelve who would be taught by me and operate under my authority. After prayer, the twelve were invited to Saturday morning training sessions to be held from ten o'clock until one.

For several months I had been praying regularly for a two-year-old boy who had a rare terminal illness. I visited him in hospital and at home, always laying-on hands and praying for healing. His photograph and an account of his sad plight were featured in the *Birmingham Evening Mail*. At eight o'clock on the morning of our first healing session his mother telephoned me to say he had died, and would I come round. I responded immediately and they left me alone in the bedroom with the dead child. I prayed and wept, but to no avail, consoled the family and came home. My youngest daughter Hazel was quite small at the time and all I could do was to pick her up and hold her tightly for several minutes.

Eventually, I pulled myself together and went over to church to prepare for the session when I would teach others about healing. I had only been there for a few seconds when a lady came to the front door of the church looking for the vicar. Her little baby had just died; would I do the funeral? It seemed almost unbelievable.

When I left theological college I could give philosophical answers to the problem of pain without much difficulty. I felt my high church colleagues' reliance on the *Mysterium Tremendum* of God was rather unnecessary. But at moments like these I almost wished I didn't believe in a God who heals. Signs and wonders are no easy option. Once I began preaching a God who still does miracles and loves us, and had seen him heal some people, the pain of healing for some and non-healing for others began to bite. Interestingly, a present and a former church warden both received the gift of tongues in the subsequent session, which led them both to go on and receive more of God's blessings and healing power. I suppose there wasn't much of me left to get in the way of God's Spirit that morning.

After the Christmas Eve trauma we began to receive and

give many 'words' from God for healing which were claimed, but few were healed. The night which caused me the greatest pain was the one I referred to in chapter 8 which occurred on the ten-week healing course we ran from January to March in 1988. Virtually every 'word' which was given was claimed by someone, but as far as I know, nobody who responded to one that night was cured. There were quite a number of 'words' given, so I would expect some of the symptoms to have improved, but of the very specific and serious illnesses which were described and claimed, many people were blessed, but none was healed. I must admit that while most people were basking in the joy of receiving, giving and identifying 'words' from God, I was very angry.

Why were people not healed? This was not a game. Peter was thirteen years old and only came on one occasion to our healing course. He was dying of cancer and that night Nick saw in his mind an egg-shaped tumour and jaw problems when we asked God whom he wanted to heal. As Peter came forward we all saw in real life the tumour which Nick had seen in his mind, but despite much prayer, Peter died a few weeks later. He died a Christian. He died encouraged that God had shown his love for him by picking him out of a large gathering with a specific 'word'. But he died.

I can theologise as well as most people about why God doesn't heal everybody. When you take as many funerals as I do, it becomes of necessity an acquired art. I know Peter is now healed and in the nearer presence of Jesus, but it still hurts and it hurts enough to want to ask questions and learn lessons.

That night, I now believe, we had faith for 'words' from God, but we did not have faith for healing. I think we still have much to learn about the 'prayer of faith'. Most of us expect that if God gives a 'word' for healing and the 'word' is claimed, then God will automatically do it.

Daniel 9:2–3 says this:

I, Daniel, understood from the Scriptures, according to the word of the Lord given to Jeremiah the prophet, that the desolation of Jerusalem would last seventy years. So I turned to the Lord God and pleaded with him in prayer and petition, in fasting, and in sackcloth and ashes.

Many believers would have thought that if God had said it, we might as well relax and play golf, but when Daniel discovered what God had said he went on his knees. He prayed in earnest for God to do what God had said he would do, and God did it. I recognise there is something of a mystery here, but it seems from experience that a 'word' received, a 'word' given, and a 'word' claimed is not necessarily a 'word' fulfilled. If God was going to do something automatically and required no response or faith from us, a direct 'word' from him would be unnecessary and irrelevant. We would discover his will simply by observing what he did. I believe a 'word' from God is meant to be a faith-builder, an assurance that he loves us and is with us, a declaration that he is still a God who heals. It is not a fortune-telling exercise. The word of God is a powerful, two-edged sword if received in faith and used in faith. It is a weapon to be used, not a trophy to be mounted on the wall.

I could never say that Peter would have lived if we had exercised more faith; that would be to play at being God. Neither do I believe we should feel guilty if we have displayed a lack of faith. What we don't have, we cannot use. But I do think we need to look beyond just asking for 'words' and the feeling of vindication when those we have given are claimed. 'Words' from God are a way of opening up to us God's spiritual world, the real world that does not pass away. It is a way of seeing what he sees, that we may do what he does. It is a way of building up faith in God, but it is a way and not an end. It is the path and not the prize. Our prayer must surely be for more 'words' from God, so that we may receive more faith from him and do more of his work for God's sake and glory.

That night in a large gathering God gave specific 'words' for healing to many people, some for the first time, and we praise him that as the 'words' were claimed, people grew in faith and expectancy. I am pleased to say that two weeks later on the same course there were some notable healings; we did seem to learn together in stages, one thing at a time. In the follow-up groups which met after the course one group in particular experienced more than one healing a week for several weeks – while I was away in South Africa. I believe we need to keep going, even when the pain of non-healing and lack of faith regularly stares us in the face.

The pain of deliverance

In March 1987 a friend asked me to help him with a lady who was demonised. I responded positively, full of faith, as we were in the middle of a 'wave of demons', when confidence was high. During that time people seemed to manifest demons whatever we did and wherever we went and each time, when we commanded them to leave in the name of Jesus, they left.

This particular lady was seen on about five occasions by my friend, during which time she became a Christian and demons began to leave. We saw her together for about two-and-a-half hours, but the demon which was causing the trouble would not leave. The lady growled and snarled and the demon spoke when challenged in Jesus' name, but it wouldn't reveal its identity and it wouldn't depart, whatever we did or tried to do. My friend was in the process of changing jobs at the time, so I said we would see the lady in our church and do what we could. I thought it would be good experience for our people.

We tried for several weeks with ministry which lasted a total of thirty hours to remove this one demon, and failed. The lady did not live in Birmingham and every day the demon remained meant another day's hotel bill. The most powerful time came when we broke the blood lines, cutting her off from her ancestors and her own children. After this she and her married daughter experienced violent vibrations of the navel, although her daughter was not with us, and continued to feel soreness in that region for several days, as if the umbilical cord had just been cut. But still the demon would not depart.

During this time the lady confessed every sin she could think of and, by phone, cleared her home of anything doubtful. Twelve plates costing one hundred pounds each were destroyed because they had the Zodiac signs painted on them (cf Acts 19:17-20). We tried worshipping, fasting and regularly commanding the demon to go in Jesus' name. We tried communion, prayer, Bible-reading, total immersion and silence. We asked daily for wisdom and knowledge, regularly ordered the demon to name itself without any success, rang up everyone we knew for help and read all the books about demons we could lay our hands on. When I say we tried everything, I mean we tried everything with persistence and determination, but still it would not go. Finally, I developed a huge migraine, missed our annual church meeting and sent the lady home in the same state in which she came to us. This was one of the lowest moments in my life since I had returned from the Sheffield conference.

We kept in touch and the lady had further ministry from many people from different parts of the country. She joined a good, Bible-based church and worshipped faithfully, but still continued to have demonic trouble.

Suddenly, in December 1988, some twenty months later, not having ministered to her again personally I woke up in the middle of the night thinking I knew the name of the demon and how to get rid of it. The name which came to me was 'Anti Christ'.[12] I hinted in my Christmas card to her that I might now know what to do and she came to see me in the early part of 1989.

When the lady arrived I did not tell her my suspicions, but simply ministered to her. All morning a number of demons kept coming to the surface, giving their names and leaving. It seemed as if the one I was hoping to see no longer wanted to surface until the appropriate time. Some while after lunch a familiar manifestation appeared on the lady's face. Having opposed this demon in failed combat for thirty hours, there seemed to be a mutual recognition. I commanded it to name. It spoke very slowly in a dignified manner, one syllable at a time. 'I ... am ... the ... one,' it said through the lady.

'Oh yes?' I said. 'Which one?'

'The ... one,' it repeated.

'What is your name?' I asked with the authority of Jesus.

'Antichrist.'

The lady still did not know at this point what my suspicions had been.

It was a quiet moment. It felt like the conquest of Masada when the Roman legion X Fretensis, after besieging the fortress for two years, discovered the dead bodies of their enemies. There was no glory in victory, just a job to be done — rather like putting the cat out. I commanded 'Antichrist' to leave in the name of Jesus and after a decent struggle, it left through the mouth with a clear manifestation and the lady felt certain it had gone. Subsequent ministry and an improved lifestyle seemed to confirm this to be so.

Deliverance is a very costly ministry at the best of times, but if we deny ourselves and join Jesus on the cross we do eventually begin to see as he sees, though some of us are slower than others. To God be all the glory!

Down to the lowest level

Quite recently a dark cloud came over me for five days, during which time I tried to give some 'words' from God. At the first meeting of over a hundred people I gave six 'words' and only one was claimed. At the second meeting in our own church only two out of five were claimed. Even so, the three that found a home were not insignificant.

The first was for a man with a benign tumour on his head — an unsightly lump normally hidden beneath the hair. Although the lump remained he was thrilled to receive prayer and quite a blessing at a time when, he confessed, he would not have asked for ministry. He testified to many afterwards of God's love as shown in picking him out of a large meeting for prayer which he was glad to receive. The second was for a young lady with stiff knees who couldn't kneel comfortably. This was in our own church service and as the nineteen-year-old girl fell over in the Spirit and witnessed afterwards to being healed, many who saw it found their faith being lifted. The third was for a lady who was very worried about her daughter and as a result was suffering constant tension headaches. This lady also became wobbly on her legs as the Spirit came, and felt blessed. Later that night her daughter, who had left home, stood on the doorstep asking to come back and was welcomed in with loving arms.

Despite these claimants I was still very unhappy. 'Lord, three years ago I used to get five out of five. I would naturally have expected to improve with experience, not become worse.'

'Come with me,' a thought deep in my innermost self seemed to say, 'and I'll show you what you must learn to do.'

In my mind's eye I saw myself with a figure I took to be Jesus. Beginning at ground level, we started descending some steps. Each set of steps led to a large floor space and there were four levels. This is what I believe Jesus showed me about each level:

Level one – obedience

Level one was a shop floor with workers in boiler suits standing before large machines, working hard and carrying out their bosses' orders.

'So you also, when you have done everything you were told to do, should say, "We are unworthy servants; we have only done our duty"' (Lk 17:10).

'There are times,' said the figure in my mind's eye, 'as you are ministering in the power of the Holy Spirit, when obedience will do. It is often the starting point for many.'

I reflected upon this and realised it to be true. In John 2:7–10 the servants, with no expectation or faith, simply did what Jesus told them to do. They filled the jars with water, then drew some out, and the water became wine. Naaman the

Syrian (2 Kings 5:14) and nine of the ten lepers (Lk 17:11–14) were all healed by obeying orders, with no suggestion of faith being present.

I noted that the predominant part of a human being which is needed in obedience is the mind. There have been many times when I have given a 'word' from my mind to a gathering of people while feeling absolutely lousy or wishing God had chosen someone else, and people have still been healed or helped. With obedience, feelings are irrelevant. A person can do what they think is right, however they feel, as Jesus demonstrated in the Garden of Gethsemane. I suspect all who want to do what Jesus did must start here.

Level two – trust

Coming down to the second level, we came to the bosses' office. There were two desks, but only one man present and he was on the 'phone. 'We are partners,' he was saying. 'We have worked together for many years; if he has said he will do it, he will.'

'I no longer call you servants, because a servant does not know his master's business. Instead, I have called you friends, for everything that I learned from my Father I have made known to you' (Jn 15:15).

'There are times,' commented the Jesus in my picture, 'when obedience is not enough and faith is required.'

I knew this to be true also. Peter obeyed Jesus' command to 'come' to him walking on the water, but when he began to doubt and lost his faith, he started to sink (Mt 14:28–31). I recognised this failing in myself. In obedience I had often given 'words' for healing which were claimed, but as I ministered to the person their condition did not improve and my already tiny faith disappeared rapidly. I was appalled to think how someone like me could have seen so much and still trust so little when things appeared to be going wrong. I sensed the important part of us in trusting is at times the emotions. Those who have been battered, abused or let down by people often need emotional healing before they can begin to trust God, and even though I was brought up in a very loving home I also recognised my own need for growth in this area.[13]

Level three – love

The third level revealed a huge children's playroom and there, by the blazing log fire, was a gentle father with two children on his knee. The children had glowing cheeks from a recent bath and were now clothed in pyjamas and dressing gowns, listening wide-eyed to their father, who was cuddling them and reading a story from the Bible.[14]

'How great is the love the Father has lavished on us, that we should be called children of God!' (1 Jn 3:1).

Here my Jesus figure explained, 'To obey me and to trust me is not the same as to do something in my name. To do that you need to know me as a child knows his father.' I remembered the three times Jesus asked of Peter, 'Do you love me?' (Jn 21:15–17). As well as the anointing of the Spirit on the Day of Pentecost, this close relationship appeared to be necessary for the ministry which was to follow.

'A man crippled from birth was being carried to the temple gate ... Peter said, "... In the name of Jesus Christ of Nazareth, walk"' (Acts 3:2–8).

This loving relationship with God as our Father seemed to me to require the commitment of our very soul. Jesus said, 'Love the Lord your God ... with all your soul' (Mt 22:37).

George Carey has defined the soul as 'the totality of human nature'[15] and Isaac Watts wrote this: 'Love so amazing, so divine, demands my soul, my life, my all.'[16]

Love, I decided, could only mean the giving of one's very self which I knew I had not yet managed, and still there was a fourth level to come.

Level four – oneness

As my companion and I reached the deepest level, a sense of awe came over me. Before us was the unoccupied lavish bridal suite of the most expensive hotel I could imagine.

Hallelujah!
For our Lord God Almighty reigns.
Let us rejoice and be glad
and give him glory!
For the wedding of the Lamb has come,
and his bride has made herself ready' (Rev 19:6–8).

My Jesus made no comment.

I was unsure whether this was a future hope or a present possibility.

In John 10:30 Jesus said, 'I and the Father are one.' It was a oneness which enabled Jesus in the next chapter to raise Lazarus from the dead four days after his body had begun to rot (Jn 11:41–44). I am sure it was a unity which touched far deeper than the mind, emotion or even the soul. I believe it must have been a spiritual unity between the God who is Spirit and the man Jesus who was made in the image of God. But Jesus also prays to the Father that all who believe in him 'may be one as we are one: I in them and you in me' (Jn 17:20–23).[17]

When we are born again of the Spirit (Jn 3:5) it seems as if the Spirit of God brings life to our spirit, enabling us to worship him 'in spirit and in truth' (Jn 4:24).

Maybe when the Christian who seeks to obey the Father, to trust and to love him, learns to worship him in spirit too, then there may be brief moments in this life, when sufficient oneness with God is achieved for power even to raise the dead to be released. True worship is, I am sure, the key and although I believe worship should be a top priority for every church, I suspect it needs to be a relationship of worship rather than just a Sunday activity. When I get to heaven all I have learned about evangelism, healing and deliverance will be of no use to me at all, but all I have learned about worshipping in spirit will last for ever. I understood the need to pray daily: 'Your will be done in me as it is in heaven.' Being one in the Spirit with God was the deepest level.

When my guided tour was finished I couldn't help asking

my guide where he thought I'd reached. 'At your very best,' he said, 'halfway between level one and level two.' I felt this was right. Even if the four-level picture came from my own imagination, I realised it was only an illustration of authentic biblical truth which was now challenging me. I still shouted at God when local people wouldn't turn to Christ, or broken bones wouldn't mend and difficult demons remained in residence. Although there were times when I knew Jesus as my friend and often called God my 'Father' in prayer, I sensed that in ministering in the power of the Holy Spirit I did not always trust him as my friend or speak with the authority of a son of the King. There was certainly no way anyone receiving ministry from me ever felt they'd been with someone who was married to Jesus.

I began to realise how my initial burst of enthusiasm to obey everything which came into my head was only a start, and no more. It had almost become a way of escape, passing the buck on to Jesus. Servants do not have to worry about responsibilities and I discerned Jesus was now wanting to call me his friend and fellow-worker and encourage me to move on. It seemed as if my initial burst of accurate 'words' was God encouraging me by doing things for me, but the next step was to let him do things in me. My emotions, soul and spirit were required as well as my mind if I were to touch the very heart of Jesus. I sensed learning to 'trust' would be next on the list.

'Next Wednesday,' he said, 'I want you to stand in the pulpit in front of 150 people and receive "words" from me on the spot.' So I did. We were then in the middle of our weekly Wednesday night Lent meetings with people attending from many different churches. I told everyone present what I felt God had said and they all watched as I prayed and waited with my eyes open. Falteringly about a dozen 'words' came out and every one was claimed. One was particularly memorable.

'There is someone here with a blockage in the right nostril. It's not a cold or catarrh or the common kind of sinus trouble, but something more serious.'

Sue immediately claimed it. She had a growth at the top of

her right nostril on which the surgeon was planning to operate the following Wednesday. He was intending to bore a hole through the roof of her mouth, hoping not to damage her eye too much on the way, and remove the growth which he thought might be cancerous. Such an operation would obviously have left Sue in some distress afterwards, even if completely successful.

Two people prayed publicly with her and after a while she went over in the Spirit, feeling power and a 'fizzing' like champagne bubbles. When the power began to fade she stood up and sensed her breathing was now a little easier.

The following week the surgeon visited her in hospital and was surprised to be asked if she could be examined again before the operation took place, just to make sure. Eying the Christian books and Bible beside the bed somewhat cynically, he said, 'I suppose it's got something to do with that.'

'Yes,' admitted Sue and confessed to receiving prayer. Sue then had a general anaesthetic, enabling the surgeon to explore the area. Despite his cynicism the surgeon could find no trace of the growth and simply carried out a general clean-up of the nasal passages, removing a few common polyps. She was discharged from hospital the next day without a hole in the roof of her mouth.

Sue was overjoyed: the way in which God chose to act had not only dealt with the diagnosed growth but also her emotional trauma at the prospect of going into hospital and all this implied. Although her faith expectancy of total, instant healing was not realised, God's complete healing package met all instead of part of her needs. The 'word' was as special to us for its timing as for its detail: Sue was able to return the following week and give us all the good news before the course ended.

I'm afraid even on my best days I barely touch level two for more than a fleeting moment and there are still times when I call Jesus 'Lord' and do not do what he says, but at least I know what I must prayerfully seek to do to become more like Christ. I am not sure, however, that I can offer anyone else who wants to begin doing what Jesus did an easier route than mine. There does seem to be a need to join Jesus on the cross if we are to see as he sees. But having emphasised the pain of attempted obedience it seems right to say there is often a pain attached to disobedience as well.

On one occasion I was staying with Carol's parents and went with Anne to a small Bible study in someone's home. It was definitely not a charismatic meeting and I wasn't sure if anyone present had ever encountered a 'word' from God before. During the rather formal prayers a thought came to me – 'There's a lady here with a broken heart. Tell her how much I love her.' The prayers were short and sharp and as I hesitated, unsure of the 'word', my standing and their receptivity, I found we were saying the Grace.

As we opened our eyes I felt the 'word' may have been for a particular lady in the room, but still being afraid to speak it out there and then I asked Anne about her afterwards. She was a visitor, quite young, with children and her clergyman husband had died recently. Imagine how she would have felt if, after travelling many miles to stay with a friend, a stranger had told her, 'God loves you and knows about your broken heart.' It hurt me deeply to have let God down yet again. The pain of failing to give a right 'word' far outweighed the pain I had ever felt in giving a wrong 'word', and with this different pain came a new incentive and determination to obey whatever I felt God was saying to me.

I remember while I was at school, winning the occasional short sprint race by virtue of possessing long legs and natural speed. That, however, was my limit. I never came anywhere in the 400 metres, always struggled to finish the 1500 metres and frequently walked in after others had gone home in the cross country race. In athletics I was not one for staring pain in the face, beating my body into submission, and chasing after a crown of fading glory. I soon discovered that golf was the activity for me.

I think when I first encountered the 'Signs and Wonders' ministry I deceived myself into believing it was a short sprint full of explosive power which wouldn't take long to master.

Seeing people minister in God's power at Sheffield was in some ways like watching the last 100 yards of a marathon. The spectator simply has no idea what has taken place before the athletes reach the stadium.

I now know that the tasks of proclaiming the kingdom, healing the sick and casting out demons are simply part of the full gospel of Jesus Christ. They are released by listening to God and obeying his commands, and they come with the same guarantees and warnings as the rest of the gospel.

Jesus never promised his disciples a pain-free existence if they followed him (Mt 10) but he did promise to be with them in and through their trials if they obeyed his commands (Mt 28:20).

The key to doing or seeing what Jesus does and sees often seems to be going through the pain barrier with him; crucifixion love is still the path to resurrection power. There appears to be no way round joining Jesus on the cross if we are to become like him.

As for the problems I mentioned in chapter one, it wouldn't be right to speak so soon of healing, but Bishop David has thus far proved to be correct. Seeking to do what Jesus did has given me something else to worry about rather than myself, and therein may lie a universal truth which can set us all free. I am not what I should be; I am not what I would like to be; but by the grace of God I am not what I was.

Notes

1. David Watson was curate in charge of St Cuthbert's, York, a church which was threatened with closure until his appointment after which considerable church growth took place. From 1973 he was incumbent at St Michael-le-Belfrey, York until his move to London in 1982, a base from which he then worked as a non-stipendiary clergyman for the wider church, concentrating more on his writing. David died in February 1984.
2. The Reverend Canon John Finney was vicar of St Margaret's Aspley when I was at St John's College and attached to the

parish in 1974 (see chapter 1). He has recently written *Understanding Leadership* (Darton, Longman & Todd Ltd: London, 1989).

3. Catalogues of David Watson's message, video and worship cassettes are available from: Anchor Recordings, 72 The Street, Kennington, Ashford, Kent TN24 9HS (tel Ashford 20958).

4. David Watson, *Fear No Evil* (Hodder & Stoughton: London, 1984), which tells the story of David's personal struggle with cancer.

5. John Wimber was speaking at the conference entitled Third Wave, organised by Manna Ministries and held in Central Hall, Westminster in October 1984.

6. Anne Watson has written the foreword to John Wimber's book *Power Evangelism* and John has written about David in the introduction to *Power Healing,* which is dedicated to David's memory. (John Wimber with Kevin Springer, *Power Evangelism* (Hodder & Stoughton: London, 1985), and John Wimber with Kevin Springer, *Power Healing* (Hodder & Stoughton: London, 1986).)

7. Signs and Wonders Part 1 conference held in October 1985 at Sheffield Town Hall (see chapter 1).

8. Wendy Green, *The Long Road Home* (Lion Publishing: Tring, 1985).

9. Canon David MacInnes is now Rector of St Aldate's, Oxford and was, at the time I wrote to him, Birmingham Diocesan Missioner. He has contributed chapter one, 'A Personal View,' in the book *David Watson – A Portrait By His Friends,* edited by Edward England (Highland Books: Crowborough, 1985).

10. The Right Reverend David Pytches, Vicar of St Andrew's, Chorleywood, who ministered to me at the Signs and Wonders conference in Sheffield (see chapter 1).

11. I must make it clear that I see 'joining Jesus on the cross' as a picture image illustrating the cost of discipleship (Mt 16:24). I in no way wish to imply that any Christian suffering or death is a 'lesser Calvary'. As Michael Green points out in *The Empty Cross of Jesus,* there is only one Calvary and only one death which saves us – that of Jesus Christ. (Michael Green, *The Empty Cross of Jesus* (Hodder & Stoughton: London, 1984), p 14.)

12. For further information on the demon of 'Antichrist', see Bill

Subritzky, *Demons Defeated* (Sovereign World Ltd: Chichester, 1986), p 208, 'Finding the Leader of the Pack'.

13. In his book *The Normal Christian Birth* David Pawson reminds us that faith for salvation 'is based on facts, not feelings'. I endorse this wholeheartedly, but when it comes to faith for signs and wonders, and especially for healing in our own bodies, it is often faith expressed through our feelings together with faith expressed with our minds that provides the best conductor for God's supernatural power. (David Pawson, *The Normal Christian Birth* (Hodder & Stoughton: London, 1989), p 32.)

Joyce Huggett says:

> If we would learn to listen to God more effectively, we evangelicals must learn that listening to God involves much more than cerebral activity. It demands a living response: obedience. And it demands attentiveness to God at many levels: intellectual, emotional, spiritual, volitional. In other words, the challenge to the evangelical may well be to tune into God with his emotions, his will and his spirit as well as with his mind. As Jesus put it, love for God involves a whole-hearted dedication of heart, mind, soul and strength. Until we give this, we miss the very heart of the gospel and tune out much of what God is attempting to say. (Joyce Huggett, *Listening to God* (Hodder and Stoughton: London, 1986), p 219.)

14. When I shared this picture with a group of people, one lady found it difficult to receive because she had suffered incest from her father when a child. I apologise to all whose experience of life has been so darkened by the sin of others that they may not find such imagery helpful. I hope God will reveal other biblical images to you and by his Spirit begin healing your painful memories.

15. George Carey, *I Believe in Man* (Hodder & Stoughton: London, 1977), p 28.

16. Isaac Watts, 'When I Survey the Wondrous Cross' in *Hymns Ancient & Modern (Revised)* (William Clowes & Sons Ltd: London).

17. I recognise that Jesus, the Son of God, was not created, and always existed (Jn 1:1–2), but when he became flesh, born of the Virgin Mary, he became a human being like us. That is why he can pray for us to have the same relationship with his Father as he had when on earth.